BOSTON COOKS

Women's Educational and Industrial Union
Boston, Massachusetts

*Cover:* The Women's Exchange of the WEIU was founded in Boston in 1877. This early illustration bears the caption, "The Women's Educational and Industrial Union provides a marketplace for goods made by women at home, vocational training and guidance, and other services. It is a Red Feather Agency and a soundly progressive civic enterprise."

Art courtesy of Marjory S. Dick.

*Page 1:* This needlepoint design is a Union original, dating back to 1976. The canvas is one of a series of twenty Boston scenes, which when joined together form a rug. For information on ordering the canvases, please call our Needlework Department at 617/536-5651.

Needlepoint pillow courtesy of F. Jean McMurtry.

Since 1877, the Women's Educational and Industrial Union has provided innovative and responsive services to the Greater Boston community. Founded the same year that the now famous Swan Boats made their debut at the Boston Public Garden, our founders selected a swan as our symbol—a natural choice due to the Union's proximity to the Public Garden.

Photos on pages 9, 11 and 12 by Judith Sedwick.

Line art for Chapters and Notes by Paul Leahy.

This cookbook is a collection of our favorite recipes, which are not necessarily original recipes.

Published by Favorite Recipes® Press
P.O. Box 305142
Nashville, Tennessee 37230

ISBN: 0-87197-295-6
Library of Congress Number: 91-6958

Manufactured in the United States of America
First Printing: 1991 7,500 copies

# Contents

**RADCLIFFE COLLEGE**

*Ten Garden Street,*
*Cambridge, Massachusetts 02138 (617) 495-8647*
*The Arthur and Elizabeth Schlesinger Library*
*on the History of Women in America*

# Preface

The Women's Educational and Industrial Union, one of America's oldest and most distinguished service organizations still in existence, was founded in 1877 in order to bring vocational and industrial education to women. Its continuing success as a community organization is a tribute to the members' ability to change with the times, always finding new ways to help women to help themselves.

Now they have produced a cookbook which is a perfect vehicle for showcasing the work of an organization because it can provide insights about the work of the group and the nature of its community. The Union's cookbook is indeed a wonderful reflection of this remarkable organization. It informs us about its history, gives us a sense of its community by introducing us to the contributors of these recipes, and provides us with dishes we will be tempted to try.

Like virtue, the offering of good food is its own reward. And the reward in this case is not only tasty fare, but the awareness that in the company of family and good friends, good food becomes fellowship. This cookbook, then, should become a lasting reminder of how groups of community women like those in the WEIU have a long tradition of improving the quality of American life.

*Barbara Haber*

Barbara Haber
Curator of Books

4

# The History of the WEIU

*L*ate in August of 1926, a self-assured woman with short brown hair and a strong streak of independence came to the Women's Educational and Industrial Union in search of employment. Her qualifications included course work at Harvard University, five years tutoring experience, and aeronautical concerns. The woman was placed as a social worker at a settlement house in Boston, where she taught English to immigrant children. Two years later, this former WEIU client, Amelia Earhart, became the first woman to cross the Atlantic in an airplane.

Amelia Earhart is just one of the thousands of women and men who have turned to the Women's Educational and Industrial Union since it was founded in 1877. While our name sometimes causes confusion, the WEIU is actually a nonprofit social service or-ganization, driven by a loyal membership, that has been addressing the urgent needs of the Boston community for well over a century. Today, the Union assists homeless mothers seeking a fresh start; lends support and advice to job seekers and career changers; provides affordable, quality care and companionship to the elderly and disabled; and enables teenage mothers to surmount the many difficulties they face as young parents. Our vital work in the community is carried out by four main service departments—Horizons Transitional Housing Program, Career Services, Home Health Care Services, and Social Services—which together reach more than 25,000 people in the Greater Boston area each year.

But the Union can not be aptly described as just a social service agency. Many Bostonians know us for our charming retail shops, filled with a

*WEIU Gift Shops. Proceeds from the WEIU's Gift Shops support our many social service programs.*

AMELIA EARHART AWARD

Women's Educational And Industrial Union·Boston

*Former Career Services client, Amelia Earhart*

cornucopia of merchandise from floral telephone book covers to hand-painted needlepoint canvases. Few people realize, however, that proceeds from the Shops directly benefit our community services. Other Bostonians are familiar with the Union's day trips and cultural programs, such as the immensely popular Robert Hale Book Review Series, or take advantage of our various meeting spaces, which are located on Boylston Street and overlook the Boston Public Garden.

Without a doubt, the Union is a multi-faceted organization. With our long, admirable history and vital, current services, we are a Boston institution.

In celebration of the Union's 115th year of serving the Boston community, we decided to serve Boston in a slightly different way—with the delicious creations of our members and friends. *Boston Cooks: Favorite Recipes of Historic Boston* catalogues the treasured recipes of our supporters and our restaurants, and

## The Kirmess Cookbook

*The "kirmess" may charm with its hours of delight,*
*With its radiant young dancers entrancing the sight,*
*But the vision will vanish, 'twill last but a day;*
*The picture so lovely fades surely away.*
*Not so with our "cook-book." This friend, tried and true,*
*Will ever be near you, in "broil" or in "stew,"*
*With its "whips" for your foes, and its "kisses" for friends,*
*So for former bad cooking you now make amends,*
*As you buy for yourself, as you buy it for others,*
*Remembering the help it will be to all mothers,*
*And the "Union," long-waiting, expectant, alert,*
*Shall have its well-merited, well-earned "dessert."*

*Boston Women's Educational and Industrial Union 1887*
*Alfred Mudge & Son, Printers, 24 Franklin St., Boston.*

is seasoned with tidbits of Union history. Because the Union, along with a past filled with social pursuits, has a long and illustrious culinary history, we felt it was natural to publish a cookbook. *Boston Cooks* is the third cookbook published by the Union: *The Kirmess Cookbook* was published in 1887 and was followed by *Polly Put the Kettle On* in 1937. *Boston Cooks* brandishes a treasured family recipe from a member, Old-English tea fare from a trustee, a favorite breakfast from a governor, and a cookie recipe from a first lady. It celebrates our supporters' recipes, recounts our past, and, most importantly, supports programs that benefit those in the community who need us.

## Our Beginnings

In 1877, Boston was experiencing rapid industrial growth and a dramatic surge in immigration. Abuse of women and children, crowded housing, miserable labor conditions, and poor sanitation threatened to tear the city apart and created heavy burdens for city officials. Understandably, many Bostonians were troubled. It was in this time that plans for vocational and industrial education were very much a trend. It was in this time of turmoil that the Union was conceived.

Harriet Clisby, M.D.—one of America's first women physicians —was, indeed, troubled by the economic and social conditions of post-Civil War Boston. For several winters she, along with

Julia Ward Howe (writer of *Battle Hymn of the Republic*), Abby Morton Diaz of Brook Farm, Louisa May Alcott, and several others, held meetings at her home to talk about intellectual pursuits, as well as problems with the rapidly growing population of Boston. In May of 1877, Dr. Clisby invited 42 women to a special meeting to discuss plans for an association for the advancement of women. On June 11, 1877, they approved her plan and established the Women's Educational and Industrial Union.

During our early history, the WEIU immediately established itself as Boston's foremost social service provider and garnered national recognition by initiating programs and services that by nineteenth-century standards seemed revolutionary. Under the motto, "The Union of all for the good of all," our founders established programs that were intended "to become to women however circumstanced, a means of aide, protection, elevation or development, according as each may need." *Union* in the late nineteenth century also meant sisterhood or "the union of souls." Our founders' *Union* sought to strengthen and unite the souls of the women and the poor who were members of the Greater Boston community.

Our founders established seven standing committees: Finance, Social Affairs, Moral and Spiritual Development, Industries and Employment,

*The WEIU's founder and first president, Dr. Harriet Clisby*

Hygiene and Physical Culture, Education, and Protection. Because they wanted the Union to be a membership-driven organization, membership fees were set at a low $1.00 per year for basic membership, $5.00 for honorary membership, and $25.00 for life membership. On the first of November, two meeting rooms were opened at 4 Park Street. In 1880, when the Union was incorporated, it moved to larger quarters at 157 Tremont Street. Since the buying and selling of property by women was nearly unknown and unheard of at that time, these actions appeared revolutionary.

But revolutionary actions were not unfamiliar to our founders. In 1877, they established the Business Agency, one

**Career Services.** *Career Services operates one of the largest resource centers in the state that is open to the public.*

of the first vocational guidance and referral centers for women in the United States. At that time, few jobs were available to women. Those with training might teach; others could serve as domestics or labor more than 12 hours a day in a mill. Although the agency initially placed women in domestic service or teaching positions, it soon changed its mission to promote among women a better understanding of occupational and professional requirements, to advance their interests and their efficiency in vocations, and to secure suitable employment. Within a few years, it was renamed "The Appointment Bureau" and became well known for its vocational training as well as its placement of college-educated women in fields other than teaching. In 1905, The Prince School of Management was

established to train saleswomen in the major department stores of Boston. Filene's was the first supporter of the program, and many trainees were later employed there. This program was so successful, it was taken over by Simmons College in Boston, where it remains today. By 1913, the Union's success was so evident that other "Appointment Bureaus" were established in New York, Philadelphia, and Chicago. This was the first of many times that the Union was used as a prototype for successful programs across the nation.

Also in 1877, the Food Salesroom was opened, which sold baked goods on consignment. This provided many women, who otherwise could not secure employment, with an income. Later, the Handwork Department separated from the Food Department. The Handwork

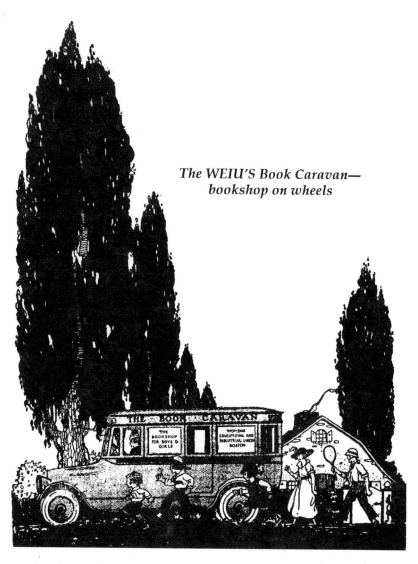

*The WEIU'S Book Caravan—bookshop on wheels*

Department continues today as the five different shops at the Union—including the Needlework Shop, which is the oldest in the country. The Union offered trade classes in hat-making and in salesmanship. Under agreement with the Boston Trade School for Girls, two school shops were opened at the Union, one in millinery and one in clothing. Later, in 1916, Bertha Mahoney Miller founded the Bookshop for Boys and Girls. This important educational bookshop lasted until her retirement in 1935. In 1924, she became the first editor of the *Horn Book Magazine*, which was started to "blow the horn for fine books for boys and girls, their authors, illustrators, and publishers." The Horn book is still in existence today. Ms. Miller

*WEIU Volunteers. Volunteers provide over 3,000 hours of friendly visits to the elderly.*

started a poetry reading series and art exhibits at the Bookshop. Ms. Miller also corresponded with Beatrix Potter—their letters are kept in the Boston Public Library's archives. The Bookshop was one of the first in the country devoted especially to books for children. Today, our shop on Boylston Street houses five separate and unique departments: Gifts, Needlework, Children's, Collectors', and Cards.

In 1878, the Union organized the Protective Committee to provide free legal advice to poor and uninformed workers. Of particular interest to this committee was the status of women and their legal rights—in the late-nineteenth century, husbands could legally beat their wives, the only restriction dealt with the size of the stick that was used. Under the able leadership of Emma Fall Schofield and Jennie Loitman Barron, who later became prominent Boston judges, volunteers collected money that had been wrongfully withheld from workers, gave advice on obtaining divorces, and investigated both installment buying and fraudulent advertising. In 1921, the Protective Committee turned over its cases to the Massachusetts Legal Aid Society with one stipulation—that the society promise to hire a female lawyer.

As different problems arose, the Union continued to establish responsive programs to initiate change. In 1899, the Union addressed the problems of the adult blind. A training program was started to help the blind find employment. The Union's Committee on Ethics provided books in braille for the Boston Public Library. Four years later, the Union initiated a successful state-wide lobbying campaign to establish the Massachusetts Commission for the Blind. Mary Morton Kehew, President of the Union at the time, was responsible for persuading Helen Keller to speak to the Boston

11

*WEIU Parent-Aides.* Mentors work with teen mothers on issues such as self-esteem and parenting.

*Horizons House.* New England's first transitional house for women and children focuses on the needs of the children as well as the mothers.

General Court about the importance of education for the blind.

Sanitary and working conditions continued to create problems for Boston workers. In 1902, the Union developed the Committee on Sanitary and Industrial Conditions. This committee advocated improved health conditions in factories, better ventilation in shops, streetcars and schools, and street cleanliness. The committee made recommendations to the State Board of Health. Also during this time, the Union's Research Bureau was started in response to the need for legislation to protect workers' health and economic rights. This Bureau prepared and published detailed reports on the hours, wages, and living conditions of Boston's working women for the Massachusetts Bureau of Statistics and Labor. This effort produced the first accurate picture of living and working conditions among Boston women. Due to this research, the Union's

*Daily scenes from the School of Housekeeping*

Protective Committee was able to effectively present bills to the Massachusetts legislature regulating installment buying, small loans, the sale of milk, minimum wage, old age pensions, and factory inspection and sanitation. The Union's effects in the areas of working conditions, employment opportunities, and human rights during the early part of the twentieth century is indeed immeasurable.

*Women's Educational and Industrial Union*
*264 Boylston Street*

These are only a few of the many socially responsive programs developed by the Union over the past 115 years. The first credit union was started here early in the century. In the 1960s and 70s, the WEIU sponsored innovative programs dealing with day care training, partnership teaching and job sharing, and psychological and practical support—such as grocery shopping and medical transportation—for elderly and disabled individuals. Also in this time period, the Union sponsored socially conscious programs, such as the lectures given here by Ralph Nader. In 1962, *If You Need a Nursing Home*, a nursing home guide, was published. This is still published by the Union under the title: *The Guide to Nursing and Rest Homes in Massachusetts*, the only publication of its kind in New England. Today, such programs as the Horizons Transitional Housing Program, the Parent-Aide Program for Teenage Mothers, and Companions Unlimited address such problems as homelessness, teenage pregnancy, and the problems and pressures faced by elderly and handicapped individuals. What has made the Union thrive is our ability to sense problems in the community and adapt our programs to fit changing needs. The Union will continue to change over the next century, following the example set by our history.

# But Why a Cookbook?

$A$long with social programs, the Union has had a long and intimate relationship with food. The history of food at the Union dates back as far as the history of the Union itself and is nearly as varied. From the food salesroom to the various restaurants to the school lunch program, the WEIU has always been involved in a number of culinary pursuits.

The Food Salesroom was established in 1877, and, much like the shops today, provided a source of funds for Union activities. The items for sale included jellies, cookies, cakes, candies, and sandwiches. They were sold by the Union on a consignment basis, thus providing an income to many women in the area. A WEIU brochure, first printed in 1917 and entitled *More than Cake*, stated, "Among these producers the Food Shops keeps up its educational work, raising the standard of the products, stimulating experimentation, and teaching businesslike methods..." The Food Salesroom also engaged in shipping goods all over the country and to England. The Candy Kitchen section of the Food Salesroom, opened in 1910, enjoyed such great success that in the year 1917 it sold 13,500 pounds of candy. The Food Salesroom was also famous for its homemade cookies. On December 8, 1966, *The Boston Globe* printed an article on

*New England Kitchen
39-41 Charles Street*

*School Lunch Department
108-112 Pleasant Street*

"Boston's Homemade Cookie House." The article listed poet Ogden Nash, Shirley ("Hazel") Booth, and actor Van Johnson as fans of the Union's cookies.

The Union also had a Members' Lunch Room at 264 Boylston Street, where members and their guests could dine on such fine foods as scalloped potatoes, cold corned beef, salmon croquettes, baked custard, and mince pie. There were also

15

lunchrooms for working men and women located at both the Boylston Street location and at 45 Providence Street. These restaurants began as "an attempt to furnish working people with food at a reasonable price." In addition to these two restaurants, the Union took over the operation of the New England Kitchen in 1907. Originally established in 1890 by Ellen H. Richards, the New England Kitchen experimented in cooking the most inexpensive and nutritious food, using the best methods, and sold this food at moderate prices. Some popular menu items included beef broth, pea soup, corn mush, boiled hominy, spiced beef, and fish chowder.

The Union's food shops and restaurants took active roles in both World Wars. During World War I, the Food Salesroom and the restaurants offered many "Liberty Foods," and pamphlets and blackboards encouraged patrons to purchase these goods, which were made with less wheat and sugar. The New England Kitchen and Food Laboratory conducted experiments to find satisfactory wheatless breads. Breads, cakes, and confectioneries took on a brown color, as white flour, cane sugar, and fats were conserved. Cakes were no longer frosted and

sugar in all recipes was cut down. Use of beef, pork, and veal was reduced by two-thirds and fish and vegetable usage increased. Every Thursday was "corn day" and corn bread and corn dishes were served. One of the cooks at the New England Kitchen made a "Victory Cake" that contained no wheat or sugar. The Union also prepared packages for the troops. During the Second World War, the Union served some No-point lunches to educate the public about the government's "No-point, Low-point" food program. Also during World War II, the Union's Hospitality Committee offered free lunches or dinners to service people.

The WEIU has always been revolutionary in its programs.

One idea developed by the Union, which came into general use across the country, was the School Hot Lunch Program. Ellen H. Richards, founder of the New England Kitchen, first vocalized the need to supply hot, economical, nutritious lunches to children who otherwise would not eat or who would eat candy and pastries. In 1907, when the Union took over the New England Kitchen, it also began making and distributing hot lunches to high school students in Greater Boston. In 1910, the Union catered to sixteen high schools, serving approximately 7,000 lunches daily, and by 1926, twenty-two high schools participated and 18,000 lunches were prepared daily. At first, all cooking and preparation was done in the New England Kitchen, but work was later transferred to a building on Broadway Street. Sixty paid employees, some starting at five o'clock in the morning and working all day, did the necessary work. One hundred and fifty students assisted at school counters and in return received free lunches. The lunches were "a la carte" and included beef barley soup (4 cents), macaroni and tomato (5 cents), coffee jelly with whipped cream (3 cents), vegetable salad (5 cents), lettuce sandwich (3 cents), chopped ham sandwich (3 cents), and cocoa (3 cents). Each day students consumed 100 quarts of soup, 125 quarts of ice cream, 250 quarts of milk, 600 apples and bananas, 1,000 orders of hot food, 15,000 rolls, and 2,500 sandwiches. The School Lunch Program was taken over by the Boston School system in 1938, and served as a model for similar programs across the nation.

The Union also conducted research addressing important issues of nutrition throughout the years. For example, in 1915-1916, WEIU completed a study for the Massachusetts Department of Health on "The Food of Working Women in Boston."

Another study was done comparing the costs of preparing food at home and purchasing ready-made food. Headlines of a local newspaper reporting on the findings of the research stated, "Future House May Have no Kitchen at All." The conclusion of the study reported, "In general, may we conclude that it be possible to do away with all cooking in the house, when the increase in expense is counterbalanced by the saving of time and labor?"

Nearly ninety years have passed since this article was published, and the kitchen is still an important part of many homes. And the Union is still very much an important part of Boston. Largely due to the support of our membership, the proceeds from our gift shop, and the proceeds from this cookbook, the WEIU will continue to provide responsive programs to the Boston community. Looking forward to our next century, we intend to continue to "increase fellowship among women with the purpose of promoting the best practical methods for securing their educational, industrial, and social advancement." Thank you, so much, for supporting us in this endeavor.

# Committee Members

Dawn Adelson
Beth Coolidge
Marie Crocetti
Evelyn Farnum
Lisa Geissenhainer
D'Arcy Goldman, Committee Chairperson
Diane Goldman
Elizabeth Haddad
Mary Heneghan
Meredith Hutter
Terence Janericco
Deborah Katz
Paul Leahy
Kelly A. Leighton
Anita MacKinnon
F. Jean McMurtry
Jamie Rose Therrien

# Special Thanks To

Polly Blanchard
Marie Crocetti
Barbara Haber, The Arthur and Elizabeth
Schlesinger Library on the History
of Women in America
Helen Hodgdon
Paul Leahy
Bob Therrien, Boris Master Color Services

**The Corner Grocery**
*Provisions for daily school lunches were stored at the "Corner Grocery."*

# Boston Cooked
## Memory Recipes from the WEIU

Throughout the history of the Union, the culinary expertise of its members and friends has brought comfort as well as good tastes to the people of Boston.

Whether the quest has been for a satisfying lunch, a mouth-watering sweet, an elegant tea tidbit, or an enlightening lesson in cooking, the Union has sought to satiate the community's palate.

Relive, remember, rejoice, in a few of the memorable recipes from the Union's living history. The following selections are faithfully quoted from *The Kirmess Cookbook*, *Polly Put the Kettle On*, a half-century's worth of newspaper excerpts of Union recipes, and Union cooking classes.

Today, some of these recipes may only satisfy the historically curious, but many have "stood the test of time" and are as delicious today as when they were new. So let us return to the tastes of yesteryear . . . .

# SECRETS OF HORS D'OEUVRES PROBED BY BOSTON HOUSEWIVES

Snowballs are not being used for hors d'oeuvres—yet. But the idea of hors d'oeuvres demonstrations at the Women's Educational and Industrial Union started out as just a little snowball that rolled and rolled.

*from The Christian Science Monitor, March 9, 1940*

## THE UNION'S CHEESE SHORTBREAD FOR COCKTAILS

3 cups flour
1/2 cup confectioners' sugar
1 stick butter
1 teaspoon baking powder
1/2 pound Cheddar cheese
1/4 teaspoon cayenne pepper

Blend all ingredients to make firm dough. Press into large pan, 13 1/2 by 9 1/2 inches. Bake in preheated 325 degree oven about 25 minutes—should be pale. Cut into fingers. Make 44 cuts.

*from The Boston Globe, November 2, 1967*

## TOOTHPICK TREATS

*What was in the little balls that stuck pertly up on the end of toothpicks speared into a head of cabbage?*

* An olive rolled in cream cheese and rolled again in nuts.
* Peanut butter and cream cheese rolled in browned sifted bread crumbs.
* Deviled ham with pickle, mustard, and cream cheese rolled in parsley.
* A sausage stuffed in a long dinner roll which was then sliced into tiny rounds of the meat rimmed with bread.
* A special note of the stunt of hollowing out a dill pickle, stuffing it with cream cheese, then serving it in thin slices.

*from The Christian Science Monitor, March 9, 1940*

# A BIT OF MEAT, A BIT OF SWEET

N ever despair of the old and familiar tea sandwiches
. . . Just give them a brand new dress. Try some of
the following recipes from *Polly Put the Kettle On*, 1937.

## TOASTED CHICKEN SALAD CUBES

**Chicken scraps, 8 ounces**
**Almonds, 1/2 ounce**
**Mayonnaise, 2 tablespoons**
**Season to taste**
**Chopped parsley, 3 tablespoons**

Dice chicken, being careful to remove all skin and tough portions. Add finely chopped almonds and blend lightly with
mayonnaise. Fill toasted cubes until they are slightly rounded
on top and sprinkle with very little bit of chopped parsley.
*Quantity–28 cubes.*

**White bread, 7 1/2 inch slices**

To make cubes: Cut 1½ inch cubes from bread and carefully
hollow out center. Using a brush and melted butter, butter the
cube lightly, inside and out. Wrap in wax paper and let remain
in refrigerator over night. An hour before using set on buttered
cookie sheet and toast in a very hot oven until a golden brown.
Fill as directed above.

## RADISH AND HORSERADISH SANDWICHES

**Radishes, 1 bunch**
**Horseradish, 3 teaspoons**
**Butter, 4 tablespoons**
**Bread, graham, 8 slices**

Combine butter and horseradish and spread bread with mixture. Cover with finely chopped radish. Put on top piece of
bread and cut out in any desired shape.
*Quantity–16 (cutting 4 to a sandwich).*

# BEATEN BISCUIT WITH HAM

Flour, 2 cups
Lard, 5 tablespoons
Salt, 1 teaspoon
Milk and water, equal amounts

Make a very stiff dough of the ingredients. Beat with a rolling pin, folding over continuously, for 30 minutes. Cut with 1½ inch round cutter and prick top with fork for decoration. Put on baking sheet and bake in 400 degree oven for 20 minutes. *Quantity–30 biscuits.*

Ham, sliced, 2 ounces
Butter, 2 tablespoons
Horseradish, 1 teaspoon
Lettuce, 3 leaves

Split biscuits and spread lower halves with horseradish butter. Cover with bit of lettuce and bit of ham, roughly torn. Both should be slightly larger than biscuits so edges will show when cover is replaced.

# EGG SALAD STARS

Eggs, boiled, 2
Lemon, 1
Onion, 1 small
Cayenne and salt to taste
Bread, white, 6 slices
Bread, graham, 6 slices
Butter, 4 tablespoons
Parsley, 12 tiny sprigs

Mash hard boiled eggs very finely and add grated onion. Blend with enough lemon juice to make a soft paste and season. Cut stars from buttered bread and spread half of them with egg mixture. From other half cut a small star out of center by using a garnish cutter. Replace top and insert a tiny sprig of parsley in opening. By making sandwiches so half of them have a dark top and half a white top, a pretty and unusual effect is noted when put on plate. *Quantity–12 sandwiches.*

## NEOPOLITAN SANDWICHES

Pistachio nuts, 3 tablespoons
Maraschino cherries, 3 tablespoons
Bread, white, 3 slices
Butter, 2 tablespoons
Honey, 1 tablespoon

Make ribbon sandwiches using chopped pistachio nuts and butter in one layer and chopped cherries and honey in the other. Let harden in refrigerator and slice wafer thin. Cut in half. *Quantity–20 sandwiches.*

## OTHER NICE VEGETABLE SANDWICH COMBINATIONS

- Bacon and watercress
- Chopped chutney and celery
- Tomato slices on ginger butter
- Grated carrot, peanut butter and onion
- Chopped radish and chive in cream cheese
- Crisp lettuce and mayonnaise with onion salt
- Chopped watercress flavored with lemon juice and mayonnaise
- Individual asparagus rolls (marinate asparagus in french dressing or spread bread with mayonnaise)

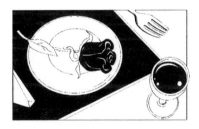

# PLATE DECORATIONS

The attractiveness of tea plates depends on the success with which you combine a variety of shapes, colors, and garnishes. With these as gentle reminders we hope you'll again be stirred to real creative effort.

- One sandwich which has height—such as tiny crustades, bouchees, biscuits, or cream puff shells—makes for more interesting plate arrangements with less difficulty.
- The tear drop sandwich (or oval with pointed end) is a shape which lends itself to many designs.
- Stars and crescents are attractive and good in plate arrangements—but are usually hard to eat.

- Fluted edges on cutters will give added interest to an otherwise prosaic shape.
- Don't despair if you have not cutters—it is surprising what unusual effects you can get with just a knife. Don't forget that jar tops often come in handy, too.
- Finger sandwiches and individual rolls are pretty—if guests are very young or very frivolous, they will love it if you tie them singly or in bundles of three, with colored satin baby ribbon.
- Cornucopias are not familiar to many people, and are so simple to make. You may use rounds of bread or squares. They give a totally different looking sandwich, both are equally interesting. Grand for those who like lots of filling and little bread.
- Remember the pinwheels, how intricate they look and what fun they are to make. Try a double pin wheel, for it is even better.
- It is well not to use different shapes with the same filling for the guests are confused in the event that they do not care for a particular filling. If you do vary shapes, keep all of one flavor on separate plate.
- Ribbon sandwiches and checkerboard sandwiches are especially adapted to using for contrasts in color of bread. You know it is now possible to buy bread in rainbow hues, do you not?
- A slice of white and a slice of dark is a nice way to make your sandwiches.
- The plate garnish which repeats in some way the sandwich filling is always good.
- On a plate of egg salad sandwiches use a tulip-cut stuffed egg in a nest of parsley.
- Lobster claws will tell your guests what sandwiches are on the plate.
- Strawberries are delightfully luscious looking when put in a bed of watercress and accompanying strawberry whirls or hearts.

- A few tendrils of chickory or watercress looks nice on most any plate.
- When you try the toasted carrot rolls garnish your plate with three sections of carrots of varying lengths. Top each one with a tiny cream cheese ball and surround with parsley.
- Don't always put your garnish in the middle of the plate. Let it be near the edge and have your sandwiches radiate from it.

*from **Polly Put the Kettle On**, 1937*

## SELECTING A TEA

Tea is of three types—green, oolong or black. The type is determined by the degree of fermentation which is allowed to occur. Green tea is unfermented, oolong tea is semi-fermented, and black tea is fully fermented and "fired."

Most tea is named according to the size leaf from which it is produced. The tea plant has usually four leaves, and the names applied to the various size leaves differ with the country in which the plant is grown. In China, the top leaf and tip of the plant are known as gunpowder tea, the second leaf is known as young hyson, the third as hyson, and the fourth as imperial tea. Tea from India, Ceylon, Java and Sumatra have the British nomenclature and are known as flowery orange pekoe (tip and first leaf), orange pekoe (second leaf), pekoe (third leaf), and souchong.

Certain very fine teas, as Darjeeling and Assam, which are teas from India, are so named because of the province from which they come. Any tea, so named, is very likely to be a fine tea.

Teas which we have enjoyed are Darjeeling, Jasmine, Young Hyson, Czarina, English Breakfast, Orange Pekoe, and Oolong.

*from **Polly Put the Kettle On**, 1937*

# FINE ART OF PICNIC MENUS DISPLAYED

Winds may be chilly today, but spring and picnics are just around the corner...There's no trick to it and only one serious "don't." Don't spice picnic food too highly. It makes everyone thirsty, and frequently the water supply is limited...

Salads such as tomato stuffed with vegetables or tuna fish are easy to carry in substantial paper containers now available on the market...French rolls, sliced and hollowed out a bit, filled with such mixtures as chopped ham or chicken can come in handy on these outdoor eat-with-your-fingers occasions.

There was a sigh of relief from WEIU cooking class participants that no serious etiquette applies to crusts. They may be left on or trimmed off. Men usually prefer them "with."

How to make moist sandwiches that will not become soggy was another wrinkle jotted down for future reference. Bread well buttered, and drained crisp lettuce was revealed as the secret.

*from **The Christian Science Monitor**, April 24, 1930*

If picnics seem a little far off these cool April days you can use some of these ideas for tea sandwiches as well.

The French rolls with chopped ham filling could be hearty affairs for a picnic or finger-roll size for a tea. The filling is made with a cup of chopped ham, a third of a cup of chopped sweet pickle, two hard boiled eggs rubbed through a sieve, two tablespoons of chopped olives and mayonnaise. Slice off the top of the roll, dig out part of the inside of the roll and stuff with ham filling. Two layer sandwiches—one layer of the ham mixture and one of egg—are attractive.

## SPRING SANDWICH

**2 ounces tomato, just the pulp, no juice or seeds**
**2 ounces cream cheese or cottage cheese**
**1 ounce chopped lettuce**
**1 tablespoon chopped chives**
**Mayonnaise to bind, about 1 tablespoon**

Combine tomato, cream cheese, lettuce, chives, and mayonnaise and stuff frankfurt or finger rolls.

## CREOLE SANDWICHES

**4 tablespoons mayonnaise**
**1/2 teaspoon finely minced onion**
**1/2 cup finely flaked, canned shrimp**
**1 teaspoon lemon juice**
**1/2 teaspoon prepared mustard with horseradish**
**2 tablespoons finely chopped olives**

Cream together well. Should make about 3/4 cup of filling. Spread between slices of buttered bread.
*Makes four whole sandwiches.*

*from The Boston Globe, April 11, 1941*

# PUTTING UP SCHOOL LUNCHEONS

The Women's Educational and Industrial Union pioneered the School Hot Lunch Program, serving hot, economical, nutritious lunches to Boston's school children.

## NUT SANDWICH BREAD

Mix one cupful of warm wheat mush (left from breakfast), one fourth cupful of brown sugar, one half teaspoonful of salt, and one tablespoonful of butter. When the mixture is lukewarm, add one fourth of a yeast cake, broken in pieces and dissolved in one fourth cupful of lukewarm water and bread flour, once sifted, to knead. Cover, and let rise overnight. In the morning cut down, and toss on a slightly floured board; then knead, during the process incorporating two thirds cupful each of English walnut meats, cut in small pieces, and dates stoned and cut in pieces. Shape in a loaf, put in a buttered breadpan, cover, and again let rise. Bake in a moderate oven 50 minutes.

## SARDINE BISCUIT

Mix and sift two cupfuls of flour, four teaspoonfuls of baking powder, and one teaspoonful of salt. Work in three tablespoon-fuls of lard and two tablespoonfuls of butter, using the tips of the fingers; then add three fourths cupful of milk. Toss on a slightly floured board, and pat and roll to one third inch in thickness. Shape with a very small round cutter, first dipped in flour, put close together in a buttered pan, and bake 10 minutes in a hot oven. Split while hot, and put between the layers of sardines freed from skin and bone, separated into flakes, seasoned with salt and moistened with sardine oil.

## SPONGE CAKE WITH FEW EGGS

Put four tablespoonfuls of hot water in a bowl, add the yolks of two eggs, and beat until thick, using an egg beater; then add gradually, while beating constantly, three fourths cupful of fine granulated sugar and one fourth teaspoonful of lemon extract. Beat the whites of two eggs until stiff, and add to first mixture; then cut, and fold in one cupful of flour mixed and sifted with one and one fourth teaspoonfuls of baking powder. Turn into a buttered and floured narrow, deep cake pan, and bake in a moderate oven 35 minutes.

# INGENUITY FLAVORS BROTH

> **E**very good cook should use her own ingenuity in making dishes tasty . . .Seasoning is something one has to learn. It can't be found in books.
>
> *from **The Christian Science Monitor**, February 14, 1950*

## FRESH MUSHROOM BOUILLON

Remove stems from **1 pound mushrooms**; chop fine.
Add:
**1 medium size onion, chopped**
**1 tablespoon caraway seeds**

Simmer together in 2 quarts chicken stock.
Reduce liquid to 1 quart; drain (reserve liquid) and discard stems, etc. Wipe mushroom caps with wet cloth to remove sand; chop caps in chopping bowl until quite fine. Add: 1 teaspoon of any meat base; add mushrooms to liquid and bring to boil; add basil, marjoram, black pepper, salt to taste.
*Yield: 6 cups.*

*from **Christian Science Monitor**, February 6, 1964*

# SALADS

## FRUIT SALAD

**Fresh sections of Orange**
**Fresh sections of Grapefruit**
**Wedges of peeled Tomatoes**
**Wedges of Avocado**

Arrange ingredients on chilled lettuce leaves. Serve with Herb Dressing.

## HERB DRESSING

6 tablespoons of Tarragon Vinegar
1¹/₄ cup salad oil
1 teaspoon sugar
basil-borage-salt-cayenne pepper

In a small saucepan bring vinegar and herbs to a boil. Cool. Add other ingredients. Whip together in your blender or use your hand whip. *Yield: 1¹/₂ cups.*

*from the WEIU's program Boston Buffet, April 24, 1975*

## RAW RELISH BOWL

1 small cauliflower
1¹/₂ cups cubed white turnips
1¹/₂ cups coarsely chopped celery
¹/₂ cup French dressing
¹/₂ cup pimentos (4-ounce can)
2 green peppers

Separate cauliflower into flowerets; mix with turnips and celery. Add French dressing; chill half an hour. Drain. Place vegetables in serving dish. Cut pimentos in triangular-shaped pieces; cut peppers in smaller triangular-shaped pieces. Chop one tablespoon each remaining green pepper and pimento; sprinkle on vegetables. Outline edge of vegetable dish with pimento and pepper triangles. *Serves six.*

*from The Boston Herald, November 30, 1940*

# MAIN DISH

## CODFISH CAKES

1 pound dried cod (best kind comes in a wooden box)
8 large potatoes, peeled and quartered
2 eggs, beaten
Pepper, freshly ground
2 small onions, chopped and sautéed

Freshen cod by soaking in plenty of cold water for at least one hour. Pour off water. Cut cod into pieces with knife, cover with more water and simmer. Repeat this process twice more: make sure to change the pot *and* the water each time.

Add potatoes and cook until tender. Drain, remove skin or bones from fish. Add sautéed onion and mix everything together well. Stir in beaten eggs, plenty of pepper, 1 teaspoon nutmeg and butter. Mix well again. This fish-potato mixture may be somewhat moist. To correct this, add 1/3 to 1/2 cup instant potato granules and whip until tired.

To cook: take one spoonful, drop gently into hot (about 350 degrees) Wesson oil about 1½ inches deep (cakes will float) and cook until golden brown, turning once. Drain on paper towels on a rack. Don't overcrowd pan. Could also just brown in frying pan with a little butter.
*Yield: 10-12 for dinner; 25 for cocktails*

*from "Autumn Delight" WEIU Cooking Class, October 8, 1981*

# VEGETABLE AND SIDE DISHES

## BROCCOLI-CHEESE CASSEROLE

Make sauce as follows:

4 tablespoons margarine
4 tablespoons flour
1 pint milk
1 teaspoon chili sauce
1/8 teaspoon nutmeg
1/8 teaspoon dry mustard
1/4 teaspoon celery salt
Salt and pepper to taste

Sauté:          2/3 cup minced onions
                1/2 cup chopped mushrooms

Add to sauce.   1/4 cup margarine

Place in buttered casserole 2 cups thinly sliced cooked potatoes. Top with one bunch cooked broccoli spears. Pour sauce over broccoli and potatoes, and sprinkle with:

1/4 cup bread crumbs
1/2 cup grated sharp cheese
1/2 cup chopped raw bacon

Bake in 350 degree oven 30 to 40 minutes.
*Yield: 4 to 6 servings.*

*from* **Christian Science Monitor,** *February 6, 1964*

## MASHED TURNIPS WITH CARROT AND POTATO

1 medium turnip
4 carrots
2 potatoes

Wash turnips, cut off tops and peel (thinly). Cut in 2 inch pieces. Peel the carrots and quarter. Peel the potatoes and quarter them. Bring 1 cup water to a boil, add 1/2 teaspoon salt along with the above vegetables. Cook until turnips are tender—about 25 minutes. Drain and mash well. Add 2 tablespoons cream, 2 tablespoons butter and a dash of nutmeg.

*from* **A WEIU Thanksgiving Dinner,** *October 29, 1981*

## BREAD STUFFING WITH APPLES, CELERY AND ONIONS

31/2 to 4 cups soft bread crumbs
1 cup chopped celery
Salt to taste
2 cups water
Several pinches of Bell Seasoning
3/4 cup butter
1 small apple, cored and sliced
1 small onion

Mix above ingredients together. Pour half the dressing into the cavity of the turkey. Then fill it lightly with the remaining dressing and sew up the bird. *(For a 12-14 pound turkey)*

*from* **A WEIU Thanksgiving Dinner,** *October 29, 1981*

## VEGETABLE SOUFFLÉ

6-cup soufflé mold
1 tablespoon butter
1 tablespoon Parmesan cheese
2 tablespoons of green onion
3 tablespoons of butter
2½-quart saucepan
3 tablespoons flour
1 cup boiling liquid (vegetable water and milk ½ and ½)
½ teaspoon salt
⅛ teaspoon pepper
5 egg yolks
1 cup shredded cooked vegetables
½ cup shredded Swiss cheese
5 egg whites
A pinch of salt

Preheat oven to 400 degrees. Butter and sprinkle mold with cheese. Cook the onion in butter for a minute in the saucepan. Add the flour and cook 2 minutes. Remove from heat, and add seasonings and 1 cup liquid. Bring to a boil for one minute.

Remove from heat, beat in egg yolks. Then beat in vegetables and add all but one tablespoon of Swiss cheese.

Beat the egg whites and salt until stiff. Stir in ¼ of whites. Then fold in the rest. Turn into prepared soufflé mold. Sprinkle with remaining Swiss cheese. Set in middle level of preheated oven. Turn oven to 375 degrees and bake for about 30 minutes.

*from WEIU Cooking Class, October 10, 1985*

# BREADS

## BROWN BREAD

Two cups of graham meal, one cup of Indian meal, one cup of rye meal, one cup of molasses, 2 cups of sour milk, one tea-spoonful of saleratus, one teaspoonful of salt. Steam 5 hours.

*Mrs. De. L. Sheplie*
*from The Kirmess Cookbook, 1887*

## GRAHAM MUFFINS

One half cup of sugar, one egg, one half teaspoonful of salt, one pint of milk, three full teaspoons baking powder, equal parts of graham and wheat flour. Make a stiff batter.

*Mrs. G. T. Perkins*
*The Kirmess Cookbook, 1887*

# DESSERTS

## CREAM PUFF SWANS

½ cup butter or margarine
1 cup water
1 cup sifted flour
¼ teaspoon salt
4 eggs
1 quart ice cream

Make a pattern for swan neck and head in a 4-inch S shape with elongated end for bill. Trace 8 patterns onto foil-lined baking sheet. Bring butter and water to a boil in medium heavy saucepan. Add flour and salt all at once. Stir vigorously with wooden spoon until batter forms a ball that follows spoon around pan; remove from heat. Add eggs 1 at a time, beating until batter is shiny and smooth after each addition. Spoon into pastry bag fitted with plain tip. Pipe onto patterns on foil, starting at bills. Bake at 400 degrees for 20 minutes. Remove to wire rack to cool. Spoon remaining cream puff batter into 8 mounds on ungreased baking sheet for bodies. Bake at 400 degrees for 45 minutes. Remove to wire rack to cool. Cut thin circle from tops of swan bodies; cut circles into halves for wings. Scoop soft dough from insides of bodies to form shells. Place shells on serving plates. Spoon just enough ice cream into shells to anchor neck pieces. Set heads in place. Fill shells with ice cream. Arrange wings at angle. May serve with sauce if desired.

*served at many WEIU receptions*

# BAKED BANANAS, HOTEL STYLE

3 bananas
1-3 cup heavy cream
2 macaroons
Lemon juice

Cut the bananas lengthwise and dip in lemon juice. Roll in macaroon crumbs and arrange in shallow baking dish. Pour cream over and bake in moderate oven.

*from The Boston Herald, May 9, 1941*

# CANNOLIS

For filling: Combine and beat until smooth (10 minutes, electric beater on medium-high speed)

3 cups (about 1½ pounds) ricotta cheese
1¼ cups sugar
2 teaspoons vanilla extract

Stir in mixing thoroughly:

½ cup finely chopped candied citron
¼ cup semisweet chocolate pieces

Place mixture in refrigerator to chill.

For shells: Sift together into a bowl:

3 cups all purpose flour
¼ cup sugar
1 teaspoon cinnamon
¼ teaspoon salt

Cut in with pastry blender until pieces are size of small peas

3 tablespoons shortening

Stir in:         2 eggs well beaten

Blend in tablespoon at a time

2 tablespoons white vinegar
2 tablespoons cold water

Turn dough onto a lightly floured surface and knead. Wrap in wax paper and chill in refrigerator for 30 minutes. Set out deep saucepan or automatic deep fryer and heat fat 360 degrees. From cardboard cut out an oval pattern 6x4½ inches. Roll chilled dough ⅛ inch thick on floured surface. With cardboard pattern and pastry cutter, cut ovals from dough. Wrap dough loosely around tubes just lapping over opposite edges. Seal edges by brushing with egg white, slightly beaten. Press edges together to seal. Fry shells one layer deep in fat for 8 minutes, turning occasionally. Cool slightly before removing tubes. When ready to serve, fill with filling, dust shells with sifted confectioners' sugar. *Yield: 16 to 18 cannolis.*

## CHANTILLY CREAM

⅔ cup heavy cream
1 teaspoon vanilla extract
1 teaspoon brandy
1 teaspoon Grand Marnier
¼ cup sugar
2 tablespoons dairy sour cream

Refrigerate a medium-size bowl and beaters until very cold. Combine cream, vanilla, brandy and Grand Marnier in the bowl and beat with electric mixer on medium speed 1 minute. Add the sugar and sour cream and beat on Medium just until soft peaks form, about 3 minutes. Do not overbeat. (Overbeating will make the cream grainy, which is the first step leading to butter. Once grainy, there is no turning back so use on toast!) *Makes about 2 cups.*

*from WEIU Cooking Class, October 17, 1985*

## TINY CREAM PUFFS

Lard, 2 tablespoons
Butter, 2 tablespoons
Flour, ½ cup
Eggs, 1½
Cream, whipped, ½ cup
Sugar, ½ cup

Add flour to shortening and stir in one cup of boiling water. Cook five minutes and cool. Add eggs one at a time. Beat well and drop tiny bits from spoon onto buttered tins. Cook 30 minutes in moderate oven without opening door. Fill from bottom with sweetened whipped cream. Sweeten cream by adding to it ½ cup of sugar which has been carmelized and pounded to a powder.

*from Polly Put the Kettle On, 1937*

# CAKES

## BROWN SUGAR NUT CAKE

1 cup brown sugar
½ cup butter
½ cup sour milk
½ teaspoon soda
1 teaspoon cream of tartar
2 eggs, beaten
1 and ¾ cups cake flour
½ teaspoon each of cinnamon and clove
½ teaspoon salt
¾ cup chopped nuts
1 teaspoon vanilla

Cream the butter with the brown sugar thoroughly, then add the beaten eggs. Sift the soda, cream of tartar, spices, and salt with the flour and add alternately with the sour milk. Then add the vanilla and nuts. Bake in a loaf tin about 50 minutes in a 350 degree oven.

*from The Boston Herald, November 30, 1940*

## "CAKE-PAN" CAKE

*An award-winning WEIU recipe—new inexpensive cake wins high praise. We cut big squares of dark, rich, moist chocolate cake . . . and marveled that here was a cake costing about 25 cents . . . unfrosted . . . so simple to make a 10-year-old could do it, and a cake that called for no eggs, no milk, no greasing of the pan . . . We frankly didn't believe it until we ate Cake Pan Cake.*

*from The Boston Herald, September 25, 1953*

1½ cups King Arthur Flour
1 cup sugar
3 tablespoons cocoa
1 teaspoon soda
½ teaspoon salt
6 tablespoons cooking oil (or melted shortening)
1 tablespoon vinegar
1 teaspoon vanilla
1 cup cold water

Put dry ingredients into sifter. Sift directly into ungreased cake pan (8 inches square). Make 3 holes in dry mixture. Pour cooking oil in first hole. Pour vinegar in second hole. Pour vanilla in third hole. Pour cold water over all. Stir with fork until evenly blended. Bake 35 to 40 minutes in 350 degree oven. Invert to cool and remove from pan; or frost right in the pan.

*from The Boston Post, September 20, 1953*

# COOKIES MADE THE UNION FAMOUS

B oston's homemade Cookie House (the bakery in the WEIU's food shop) . . . 65 delicious kinds in glass cases. Grandmothers with tots in tow recall their first invitation to "choose a cookie" from the trays of sugary golden cookies.

*from The Banner, December 8, 1966*

## SOFT MOLASSES COOKIES

1/2 teaspoon salt
1/2 cup warm water
1 cup soft shortening
1 cup brown sugar
1 egg
1/2 teaspoon salt
1/2 cup molasses
1/2 cup warm water
1 teaspoon ground cinnamon
1/2 teaspoon each ground ginger, cloves
2 1/2 cups flour

Place in big bowl soft shortening, brown sugar, egg, salt and molasses; mix with electric beater until fluffy. Stir soda into warm water. Sift together flour and spices; add alternately with soda and water to cookie dough. Beat at high speed toward end. Dough will be of consistency to drop by teaspoonfuls or tablespoonfuls onto greased cookie sheets. Bake in preheated 350 degree oven about 8 minutes for small, 10 minutes for big cookies. Cool on racks. Store in tight containers, or freeze on cookie sheets then store in plastic bags. *3 dozen large cookies.*

*from The Boston Globe, November 2, 1967*

# BROWNIES

Eggs, 2
Sugar, brown, 1¹/₄ cups
Flour, ¹/₂ cup
Vanilla, ¹/₂ teaspoon
Chocolate, 2 squares
Walnut meats, ¹/₂ cup

Beat eggs slightly and add remaining ingredients. Spread evenly in buttered 7-inch pan and bake 20 minutes in slow oven–325 degrees. Cut into fingers. *Quantity–16 finger slices.*

*from Polly Put the Kettle On, 1937*


# CHOCOLATE COCONUT KISSES

Coconut, 1¹/₃ cups
Chocolate, 1 square
Egg white, 1
Sweetened condensed milk, ¹/₃ cup

Put coconut in mixing bowl. Stir in beaten egg white and condensed milk. Add melted chocolate. Dip up in heaping teaspoonfuls and push off onto well buttered baking sheet. Bake in slow oven 325 degrees to 375 degrees. Remove from sheet while hot. *Quantity–15 cookies.*

*from Polly Put the Kettle On, 1937*


# CHRISTMAS COOKIES

Butter, sweet, ¹/₂ pound
Sugar, ¹/₂ cup
Egg yolks, 2
Flour, 2¹/₂ cups

Mix ingredients. Squeeze through pastry bag onto ungreased cookie sheet. Decorate with bits of citron and glazed cherry. Brush with egg white if desired. Bake in moderate oven.

*from Polly Put the Kettle On, 1937*

# SUGAR COOKIES

Cream together:
### ¾ cup butter (no substitute)
### 1 cup sugar

Add:
### 1 egg well beaten
### 1½ cups all-purpose flour
### 1 teaspoon vanilla
### 1 teaspoon grated lemon rind
### ¼ teaspoon salt

Chill in refrigerator thoroughly. Roll out dough on board lightly floured and sprinkled with granulated sugar. Cut into desired shapes.

Beat well one egg; brush top of each cookie with beaten egg. Sprinkle generously with granulated sugar and bake in 375 degree oven 12 to 15 minutes. *Yield: 4 dozen.*

*from Christian Science Monitor, February 6, 1964*

# VIENNESE CRESCENTS

*(sometimes shaped as fingers)*

### ¼ vanilla bean
### 1 cup sifted confectioners' sugar
### 1 cup chopped pecans
### 2 sticks butter, at room temperature
### ¾ cup granulated sugar
### 2½ cups sifted all-purpose flour

Chop vanilla bean. Pulverize in blender with about one tablespoon of the sugar. Mix with remaining confectioners' sugar. Cover and let stand overnight. Reserve while cookies are baking. Preheat oven to 350 degrees. Chop pecans in blender. With wooden spoon or fingers blend pecans, butter, granulated sugar and flour to smooth dough. Shape dough, about 1 teaspoon at a time, into small crescents, or fingers. Bake on ungreased cookie sheet until lightly browned, about 15 minutes. Cool one minute. While still warm roll the cookies in prepared vanilla sugar. *Makes 6 dozen crescents.*

*from The Banner, December 8, 1966*

## PEANUT COOKIES

2 tablespoonfuls of butter
1/4 cup sugar
1 egg
1 teaspoonful of baking powder
1/4 teaspoonful of salt
1/2 cup of flour
2 teaspoonfuls of milk
1/2 tablespoonful of lemon juice
1/2 cup of fine chopped peanuts

These drop cookies should be baked in a moderate oven.

# PIES AND TARTS

## SWEET POTATO PECAN PIE

Dough:
3 tablespoons unsalted butter, softened
2 tablespoons sugar
1/4 teaspoon salt
1/2 of whole egg, vigorously beaten
until frothy (reserve 1/2 for filling)
2 tablespoons cold milk
1 cup all-purpose flour

Sweet Potato Filling:

2 to 3 sweet potatoes (or enough to yield 1 cup
cooked pulp), baked
1/4 cup packed light brown sugar
2 tablespoons sugar
1/2 egg, vigorously beaten (reserved above)
1 tablespoon heavy cream
1 tablespoon unsalted butter, softened
1 tablespoon vanilla extract
1/4 teaspoon salt
1/4 teaspoon ground cinnamon
1/8 teaspoon ground all-spice
1/8 teaspoon ground nutmeg

Pecan Pie Syrup:
3/4 cup sugar
3/4 cup dark corn syrup
2 small eggs
1 1/2 teaspoons unsalted butter, melted
2 teaspoons vanilla extract

Pinch of salt
Pinch of ground cinnamon
3/4 cup pecan pieces or halves

For the dough: Place the softened butter, sugar, and salt in the bowl of electric mixer; beat on high speed until mixture is creamy. Add 1/2 egg and beat 30 seconds. Add milk and beat on high 2 minutes. Add flour and beat on medium 5 seconds, then on high until blended. (Overmixing will produce tough dough.) Shape dough into 5 in patty about 1/2 inch thick. Dust with flour and wrap in plastic wrap, refrigerate at least 1 hour, preferably overnight. (The dough will last up until 1 week refrigerated.) Roll dough to a thickness of 1/8 to 1/4 inch. Fold dough into quarters. Carefully place in a greased and floured 8-inch round cake pan (1 1/2-inch deep) so that corner of folded dough is centered in the pan. Unfold the dough and arrange it to fit the sides and bottom; press firmly in place. Trim edges. Refrigerate 15 minutes.

For Filling: Combine all ingredients and beat on medium speed until smooth about 2 to 3 minutes. Do not overbeat. Set aside.

For Pecan Pie Syrup: Combine ingredients except pecans. Mix thoroughly on slow speed until syrup is opaque, (1 minute) stir in pecans, set aside.

To Assemble: Spoon filling into dough-lined pan. Pour pecan syrup on top. Bake 325 until knife inserted comes out clean, about 1 1/2 hours. Cool and serve with Chantilly Cream. Store pie at room temperature for first 24 hours, then refrigerate.

*from WEIU Cooking Class, October 24, 1985*

# WALNUT TARTS

3 eggs
1 cup brown sugar, packed
1 cup light corn syrup
1 cup chopped nuts
1/8 teaspoon salt
1 teaspoon vanilla
8 unbaked tart shells

Beat eggs, sugar and corn syrup together. Mix in the nuts, salt and vanilla. Pour into unbaked pastry shells and bake in hot oven—425 degrees—about 20 minutes. Serve warm or cold with or without whipped or ice cream.

*from The Boston Globe, May 7, 1964*

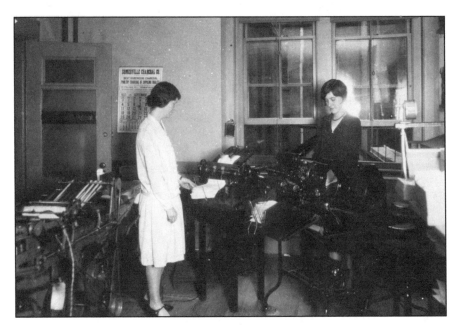

**The Purchasing Agent's Office**
*WEIU employees print notices about upcoming program in 1927.*

**The WEIU's Original Members' Lounge**
*In 1880, women were cordially invited to join the WEIU for $1.00.*

# Appetizers and Beverages

## SANDWICH DECORATIONS

On top of an open sandwich put a bit of colorful jelly or a tiny bit of pimento, carefully cut with a garnish cutter.

A slit cut in the upper piece of bread is just the thing to hold a tiny sprig of watercress and add interest to your sandwich.

Individual celery rolls can be garnished with a bit of celery leaf which is allowed to stick out one end.

Put a whole stuffed olive in the center of a well-piled up cheese filling.

A hole in the top of a sandwich will nest a ring of sliced olive with little difficulty. Easy to do and pretty.

*from **Polly Put the Kettle On**, 1938*

## COLD ASPARAGUS APPETIZER

32 fresh asparagus spears
1 head red leaf lettuce
2 lemons

Sea salt or other coarse salt to
  taste

Snap off tough ends of asparagus spears. Place in boiling water in large saucepan. Boil for 2 minutes; drain and chill. Rinse several perfect leaves of lettuce; pat dry. Arrange on serving platter. Slice lemons crosswise into halves; cut 1 slice from each half. Cut each slice 3/4 through from outer edge. Twist cut edges in opposite directions to form lemon twists; reserve for garnish. Squeeze juice of remaining lemons over asparagus spears; roll in salt. Use twice as much salt as deemed necessary. Arrange asparagus on lettuce-lined platter. Garnish with lemon twists. Serve with dry white wine such as Chablis or Soave. Yield: 4 servings.

**Approx Per Serving:** Cal 44; Prot 5 g; Carbo 8 g; Fiber 3 g;
  T Fat <1 g; Chol 0 mg; Sod 7 mg.

*Clement Cizewsky, WEIU Friend*

## CAVIAR PIE

4 hard-boiled eggs, finely
  chopped
1 medium onion, finely chopped

1/2 cup melted butter
1 cup sour cream
2 ounces caviar

Combine eggs, onion and melted butter in bowl; mix well. Pat over bottom and side of pie plate as for crust. Chill until firm. Spread sour cream evenly in prepared pie plate. Chill, tightly covered with plastic wrap, until serving time. Remove plastic wrap. Spread caviar evenly over sour cream layer. Serve with toast rounds. Yield: 8 servings.

**Approx Per Serving:** Cal 227; Prot 6 g; Carbo 3 g; Fiber <1 g;
  T Fat 22 g; Chol 191 mg; Sod 253 mg.

*Lansdale Gardiner, Former WEIU Trustee*

## EGGPLANT AND CAVIAR APPETIZER

1 eggplant
1/4 cup (about) olive oil

1/2 cup sour cream
2 ounces caviar

Cut eggplant into 1/4-inch slices. Cook eggplant in a small amount of hot olive oil in skillet for 3 to 4 minutes on each side; do not overcook or use more olive oil than necessary. Place 2 slices eggplant on each plate. Add dollop of sour cream. Top with a bit of caviar. Serve with chilled Aquavit. Use oriental eggplant if available. Yield: 8 servings.

**Approx Per Serving:** Cal 119; Prot 3 g; Carbo 3 g; Fiber 1 g;
  T Fat 11 g; Chol 48 mg; Sod 116 mg.

*Margot Kittredge, WEIU Member*

## CHEDDAR CHEESE PUFFS

2 cups shredded Cheddar cheese
1/2 cup butter, softened
1 cup flour, sifted
1/2 teaspoon salt
1/2 teaspoon paprika
48 small pimento-stuffed olives

Combine cheese and butter in bowl; mix well. Add flour, salt and paprika; mix well. Shape 1 teaspoon cheese mixture around each olive, covering completely; place on baking sheet. Bake at 400 degrees for 15 minutes. Serve hot. May refrigerate or freeze before baking for up to 10 days. Yield: 48 servings.

**Approx Per Serving:** Cal 50; Prot 2 g; Carbo 2 g; Fiber <1 g;
T Fat 4 g; Chol 10 mg; Sod 161 mg.

*Jack Hutter, WEIU Friend*

## AUTHENTIC BUFFALO WINGS

4 pounds chicken wings
Salt and freshly ground pepper
  to taste
4 cups oil for deep frying
1/4 cup butter
2 to 5 tablespoons Tabasco sauce
1 tablespoon white vinegar

Remove and discard wing tips. Cut each wing into 2 pieces. Rinse wings; pat dry. Sprinkle with salt and pepper. Heat oil in deep fryer. Add about half the wings. Deep-fry for 10 minutes or until golden brown, stirring occasionally; drain well and place on warm platter. Repeat with remaining wings. Melt butter in saucepan. Add Tabasco sauce and vinegar; mix well. Drizzle over wings. Serve with chilled celery sticks and bleu cheese salad dressing. In Buffalo, my hometown, we like our wings hot and spicy when it's cold and snowy outside! Yield: 6 servings.

**Approx Per Serving:** Cal 207; Prot 34 g; Carbo <1 g; Fiber 0 g;
T Fat 9 g; Chol 109 mg; Sod 242 mg.
Nutritional information does not include oil for deep frying.

*Judy Blackburn, WEIU Employee*

**1854** *Boston Public Library opens as the country's first tax-supported free library.*

# CRUSTLESS CRAB MEAT QUICHE

16 ounces small curd cottage cheese
6 eggs, at room temperature
6 tablespoons flour
10 ounces shredded zucchini
1 cup sliced mushrooms

1 cup shredded imitation crab meat
2 cups shredded Cheddar cheese
2 tablespoons chopped chives
Salt and pepper to taste
1/2 cup melted margarine

Beat cottage cheese in mixer bowl until smooth. Add eggs 1 at a time, beating well after each addition. Add flour; mix well. Add zucchini, mushrooms, crab meat, Cheddar cheese, chives, salt, pepper and margarine; mix well. Spoon into 2 buttered pie plates; spread evenly. Bake at 350 degrees for 45 to 55 minutes or until golden brown. Cut into small pieces to serve as appetizers or into wedges to serve as lunch or supper entrée. May freeze before or after baking and reheat. May substitute chopped spinach for zucchini or omit crab meat or mushrooms. Yield: 40 servings.

**Approx Per Serving:** Cal 75; Prot 4 g; Carbo 2 g; Fiber <1 g;
T Fat 6 g; Chol 40 mg; Sod 142 mg.

*Alice S. Cornish, WEIU Trustee, Former WEIU President*

# HOT LOBSTER CANAPÉS

1 cup minced cooked lobster
1 tablespoon horseradish
2 tablespoons minced black olives

Salt to taste
1/4 cup (about) mayonnaise
36 bread rounds
1/4 cup Parmesan cheese

Combine lobster, horseradish, olives, salt and enough mayonnaise to bind in bowl; mix well. Spread lobster mixture on bread rounds; place on baking sheet. Sprinkle with Parmesan cheese. Bake at 375 degrees for 10 minutes or until bread is light golden around edges. Serve hot. May wrap lobster mixture in phyllo if preferred. Yield: 36 servings.

**Approx Per Serving:** Cal 73; Prot 3 g; Carbo 10 g; Fiber <1 g;
T Fat 2 g; Chol 4 mg; Sod 138 mg.

*Terence Janericco, WEIU Lecturer*

1857 *Legislature votes to fill in stagnant tidal swamps in Back Bay and create a beautiful new neighborhood.*

## MUSHROOM HORS D'OEUVRE TURNOVERS

8 ounces cream cheese, softened
1 cup butter, softened
2¼ cups flour
1 teaspoon salt
1 onion, finely chopped
3 tablespoons butter
8 ounces fresh mushrooms,
 finely chopped

¼ teaspoon thyme
½ teaspoon salt
Freshly ground pepper to taste
2 tablespoons flour
½ cup sour cream
1 egg, beaten

Combine cream cheese and butter in bowl; blend well. Add 2¼ cups flour and 1 teaspoon salt; mix well. Shape into ball; wrap in waxed paper. Chill for 4 hours. Sauté onion in butter in skillet until tender. Add mushrooms. Sauté for 3 minutes. Add thyme, ½ teaspoon salt, pepper and 2 tablespoons flour; mix well. Add sour cream. Cook until thickened, stirring constantly. Cool. Roll cream cheese dough ⅛ inch thick on lightly floured surface; cut with 2½-inch cutter. Place 1 teaspoon mushroom filling on each; moisten edge with water, fold over and press with fork to seal. Make small hole in top of each; place on baking sheet. Freeze until firm. Store in plastic bags. Place frozen turnovers on baking sheet. Brush with beaten egg. Bake at 325 degrees until golden brown.
Yield: 36 servings.

**Approx Per Serving:** Cal 90; Prot 1 g; Carbo 1 g; Fiber <1 g;
 T Fat 9 g; Chol 31 mg; Sod 163 mg.

*Marianne Pedulla, WEIU Friend*

## PEANUT BUTTER STICKS

1  24-ounce loaf sliced white
 bread
½ cup oil

1  28-ounce jar creamy peanut
 butter

Cut crusts from bread and set aside. Cut bread into ¾-inch strips. Place bread and crusts on baking sheet. Bake at 300 degrees for 30 minutes or until lightly toasted. Let stand until cool. Crush toasted crusts into crumbs. Combine oil and peanut butter in double boiler over hot water. Heat until well blended, stirring frequently. Dip toasted strips into peanut butter mixture; roll in crumbs to coat. Place on wire rack. Let stand until firm and dry. Store, tightly wrapped, in refrigerator for up to 2 weeks. Place on baking sheet and bake at low temperature to reheat before serving. Yield: 100 servings.

**Approx Per Serving:** Cal 75; Prot 3 g; Carbo 5 g; Fiber 1 g;
 T Fat 5 g; Chol 0 mg; Sod 67 mg.

*Margaret C. Howland, WEIU Trustee*

# PEPPERONI SQUARES

| | |
|---|---|
| 2 eggs | Oregano to taste |
| 2 cups milk | 8 ounces pepperoni, sliced |
| 2 cups flour | 1 pound Muenster cheese |

Beat eggs in large bowl. Add milk, flour and oregano; beat until smooth. Stir in pepperoni. Cut cheese into small cubes; stir into pepperoni mixture. Pour into greased 9x13-inch baking pan. Bake at 350 degrees for 30 minutes. Cut into squares. May top with additional pepperoni slices before baking if desired. Yield: 60 servings.

**Approx Per Serving:** Cal 60; Prot 3 g; Carbo 4 g; Fiber <1 g;
 T Fat 4 g; Chol 16 mg; Sod 91 mg.

*Michele Norton, WEIU Friend*

## SALTY DOLLARS

| | |
|---|---|
| 1 8-ounce can sauerkraut | 1/2 teaspoon pepper |
| 1 tablespoon caraway seed | 1/4 cup water |
| 1 11-ounce package pie crust | 1 egg yolk |
| mix | 2 teaspoons water |

Pour sauerkraut into strainer; press out liquid. Dry between paper towels. Chop sauerkraut finely. Combine with caraway seed, pie crust mix, pepper and 1/4 cup water in bowl; mix well. Shape into ball. Chill, tightly covered, in refrigerator. Roll 1/2 at a time to 1/8-inch thickness on lightly floured surface; cut with 2 1/2-inch cutter. Place 1/2 inch apart on lightly greased baking sheet. Brush with egg yolk beaten with 2 teaspoons water. Bake at 425 degrees for 12 minutes or until light brown. Serve hot or cold. Yield: 24 servings.

**Approx Per Serving:** Cal 79; Prot 1 g; Carbo 7 g; Fiber <1 g;
 T Fat 5 g; Chol 9 mg; Sod 155 mg.

*Michele Fallon, WEIU Friend*

1870  *Museum of Fine Arts opens.*

## GRILLED BLUE MESA SHRIMP

24 peeled deveined shrimp with
  tails
1 bunch cilantro
1 tablespoon chopped jalapeño
  peppers

½ cup chopped fresh garlic
½ teaspoon salt
½ teaspoon coarsely ground
  pepper
2 cups olive oil

Chill shrimp while preparing marinade. Mince cilantro including stems. Combine with jalapeño peppers, garlic, salt, pepper and olive oil in bowl; mix well. Pour over shrimp in shallow dish; toss until coated. Marinate in refrigerator for several hours. Drain and discard marinade. Place shrimp on hot grill. Grill for 3 minutes. Serve cold or at room temperature with cilantro mayonnaise or other favorite dip.
Yield: 6 servings.

**Approx Per Serving:** Cal 790; Prot 22 g; Carbo 13 g; Fiber 1 g;
  T Fat 73 g; Chol 184 mg; Sod 421 mg.
  Nutritional information includes entire amount of marinade.

*Siobhan Murphy, Cottonwood Cafe*

## MARINATED MEXICAN SHRIMP

2 pounds large shrimp, peeled,
  deveined
1 cup (about) white wine
2 cups (about) water
½ carrot
2 bay leaves
½ medium onion
Salt and pepper to taste

2 red bell peppers
5 scallions
½ cup white wine
1 chili pepper, minced
Juice and rind of 3 limes
Juice and rind of 2 lemons
¼ cup oil

Poach shrimp lightly in 1 cup white wine, 2 cups water, carrot, bay leaves, onion, salt and pepper; add additional liquid if necessary in ratio of 1 part wine to 2 parts water. Drain shrimp well. Cut red bell peppers into julienne strips. Cut scallions into ¼-inch diagonal slices. Combine peppers, scallions, ½ cup white wine, chili pepper, limes, lemons and oil in large bowl. Add shrimp; mix until coated. Marinate in refrigerator overnight. May also prepare this adaptation of Mexican spices to New England food with swordfish, scallops or tuna. Yield: 10 servings.

**Approx Per Serving:** Cal 160; Prot 16 g; Carbo 4 g; Fiber 1 g;
  T Fat 6 g; Chol 142 mg; Sod 167 mg.

*John F. Milan, Different Tastes, Inc.*

## Snails with Hazelnut Pesto

8 ounces (about) frozen puff
  pastry
Egg wash
¼ cup chopped hazelnuts
1 cup fresh basil leaves
2 cloves of garlic
3 tablespoons Parmesan cheese
¼ cup olive oil

2 tablespoons hazelnut oil
5 tablespoons olive oil
60 canned snails
1¼ cups white wine
2½ cups heavy cream
10 fresh basil leaves
30 toasted hazelnuts

Cut puff pastry into ten 2x3-inch diamonds; place on baking sheet. Score each diamond ¼ inch from edge with paring knife. Brush with egg wash. Bake at 475 degrees for 10 to 12 minutes or until golden brown. Let stand until cool. Cut out inner diamond of each pastry shell with knife; set shells and smaller diamonds aside. Toast chopped hazelnuts in 350-degree oven for 5 minutes. Cool. Process in food processor until finely chopped; remove to medium bowl. Add 1 cup basil leaves, garlic and Parmesan cheese to food processor; process until well mixed. Add ¼ cup olive oil and 2 tablespoons hazelnut oil gradually, processing until smooth. Add to finely chopped hazelnuts; mix well. Prepare 1 serving snails at a time in the following manner: Add 1½ teaspoons olive oil to preheated small skillet. Add 6 snails. Sauté briefly. Add 2 tablespoons white wine, stirring to deglaze skillet. Cook for 30 seconds. Add 2 heaping tablespoons hazelnut pesto and ¼ cup cream. Cook until sauce is reduced and thickened. Spoon large circle of sauce into center of serving plate; spoon three smaller circles below large circle. Place pastry shell in center of large circle; arrange 3 snails in shell. Place small pastry diamond across upper corner of shell, partially covering one snail. Place snail in each of small sauce circles. Arrange 3 whole hazelnuts and 1 basil leaf to upper left of pastry shell. Yield: 10 servings.

**Approx Per Serving:** Cal 707; Prot 14 g; Carbo 31 g; Fiber 4 g;
  T Fat 59 g; Chol 114 mg; Sod 424 mg.

*David S. Smith, Bay Tower Room Restaurant*

**1874** *America's first Christmas card is printed in Boston.*

## STUFFED SNOW PEAS

8 ounces fresh Chinese pea pods
1   2¹/₂-ounce package thinly
    sliced spiced beef
1 teaspoon horseradish

1 cup sour cream
¹/₂ teaspoon mustard
¹/₈ teaspoon pepper

Trim ends from pea pods. Bring 3 cups lightly salted water to a boil in medium saucepan. Add pea pods. Cook for 1 minute; drain. Place pea pods in cold water; drain. Chill for 30 minutes. Chop spiced beef very fine. Combine with horseradish, sour cream, mustard and pepper in bowl; mix well. Slit pea pods open on one side with sharp knife. Spoon beef mixture into pea pods. Arrange stuffed side up on serving plate with sides touching to hold upright. Yield: 60 servings.

**Approx Per Serving:** Cal 12; Prot 1 g; Carbo 1 g; Fiber <1 g;
    T Fat 1 g; Chol 2 mg; Sod 20 mg.

*Annette O'Connor, WEIU Friend*

## SPINACH TARTS

3 ounces cream cheese, softened
¹/₂ cup butter, softened
1¹/₂ cups flour
1   10-ounce package frozen
    chopped spinach, thawed
¹/₄ teaspoon salt

¹/₈ teaspoon pepper
2 tablespoons chopped onion
¹/₄ cup melted butter
1 egg, beaten
1 cup crumbled feta cheese

Blend cream cheese and softened butter in bowl. Mix in flour. Chill for 1 hour. Divide into 30 portions. Press over bottoms and sides of small tart pans or miniature muffin cups. Drain spinach well. Combine with salt, pepper, onion, melted butter, egg and feta cheese in bowl; mix well. Spoon into pastry-lined tart shells. Bake at 350 degrees for 30 to 35 minutes or until light brown. May substitute Parmesan cheese for feta cheese. Yield: 30 servings.

**Approx Per Serving:** Cal 89; Prot 2 g; Carbo 6 g; Fiber <1 g;
    T Fat 7 g; Chol 26 mg; Sod 117 mg.

*Dorothea J. Mahoney, WEIU Friend*

1877   *The Women's Educational and Industrial Union was established.*

# SPICED ALMONDS

1 egg white
1 cup whole almonds
1/4 cup sugar

1/8 teaspoon cloves
1/8 teaspoon nutmeg
1 tablespoon cinnamon

Combine egg white and almonds in bowl; mix until coated. Toss almonds in mixture of sugar, cloves, nutmeg and cinnamon. Spread in single layer on buttered baking sheet. Bake at 300 degrees for 30 minutes, stirring after 15 minutes. Let stand until cool. Stir to separate. Yield: 8 servings.

**Approx Per Serving:** Cal 132; Prot 4 g; Carbo 10 g; Fiber 2 g;
T Fat 10 g; Chol 0 mg; Sod 8 mg.

*Tina Therrien, WEIU Friend*

# HOT SPICY PECANS

4 cups pecan halves
1/4 cup melted unsalted butter
1 teaspoon cayenne pepper
1/2 teaspoon crushed red pepper
flakes

1 teaspoon coriander
1/2 teaspoon allspice
Salt and pepper to taste

Spread pecans in single layer on 10x15-inch baking sheet. Drizzle butter over pecans. Sprinkle with seasonings; turn pecans over with spatula to coat with butter and seasonings. Bake at 350 degrees for 18 to 20 minutes or until crisp, turning frequently. Let stand until cool. Mound in serving bowl. Serve as accompaniment to cooling summer drinks. These pecans may be packaged in pretty containers and given as holiday gifts. *The Union's Career Services has been such a wonderful support system for job seekers and career changers. I began my business career after meeting some wonderful women at the Union in 1980.* Yield: 16 servings.

**Approx Per Serving:** Cal 205; Prot 2 g; Carbo 5 g; Fiber 2 g;
T Fat 21 g; Chol 8 mg; Sod 1 mg.

*Donna M. Buonopane-Pinto, WEIU Member*

# BENEDICTINE

1 cucumber
1/2 small onion
8 ounces cream cheese, softened

3 to 4 tablespoons mayonnaise
Salt to taste
1 or 2 drops green food coloring

Grind cucumber and onion very fine; place in strainer or cheesecloth. Press out and reserve juices. Combine cream cheese, mayonnaise, cucumber, onion and salt in bowl; mix well. Add enough reserved juices to make of soft spreading consistency. Tint with 1 or 2 drops of green food coloring. Chill overnight. Make sandwiches of thin-sliced bread; cut into shapes. May serve as cocktail spread. Yield: 10 servings.

**Approx Per Serving:** Cal 125; Prot 2 g; Carbo 2 g; Fiber <1 g;
T Fat 12 g; Chol 28 mg; Sod 99 mg.

*Persis Blanchard, WEIU Employee*

## Broccoli Sandwiches

| | |
|---|---|
| 1 bunch broccoli | 6 tablespoons (about) butter, |
| 6 to 7 tablespoons mayonnaise | softened |
| 20 slices thin-sliced white bread | Salt to taste |

Rinse broccoli; drain well. Trim flowerets from broccoli; mince very fine. Combine minced flowerets and enough mayonnaise to make thick paste in bowl; mix well. Spread bread slices lightly on 1 side with butter; trim off crusts. Spread thin layer of broccoli mixture on half the slices; sprinkle with salt. Top with remaining slices. Cut each sandwich into 4 triangles. Arrange on serving plate. Garnish with watercress. Yield: 40 servings.

**Approx Per Serving:** Cal 62; Prot 1 g; Carbo 6 g; Fiber <1 g;
T Fat 4 g; Chol 6 mg; Sod 82 mg.

*Paul Leahy, WEIU Trustee*

## Montauk Sandwiches

| | |
|---|---|
| 8 ounces sharp Cheddar cheese, | 1/2 teaspoon Worcestershire |
| shredded | sauce |
| 1/2 small onion, grated | 6 slices bread |
| 1 egg | 3 slices bacon, partially cooked |
| Tabasco sauce to taste | |

Combine cheese, onion, egg, Tabasco sauce and Worcestershire sauce in bowl; mix well. Spread on bread slices. Cut bacon slices into halves; place on cheese mixture. Place on rack in broiler pan. Broil until cheese and bacon are brown and bubbling. Cut into triangles. Serve hot. *This recipe is a favorite lunch or supper dish my mother picked up during her years as an army wife. Two of her appliquéd quilts were featured in its window displays when the Union opened in its present location. She was so pleased to have played a part in the Union program.* Yield: 24 servings.

**Approx Per Serving:** Cal 66; Prot 3 g; Carbo 4 g; Fiber <1 g;
T Fat 4 g; Chol 20 mg; Sod 111 mg.

*Mrs. Parker L. Monroe, WEIU Member*

1877 *Swan boats are introduced as a Public Garden attraction.*

## TOASTED MUSHROOM SANDWICHES

8 ounces fresh mushrooms
2 tablespoons butter
2 tablespoons flour
1/4 cup cream

1 tablespoon sherry
Salt and pepper to taste
12 slices thin-sliced bread
1/4 cup (about) butter

Wipe mushrooms with damp cloth. Chop mushrooms very fine. Sauté in 2 tablespoons butter in skillet for 7 minutes. Sprinkle with flour; mix well. Stir in cream and sherry. Cook over low heat until mixture forms thick paste. Season with salt and pepper. Let stand until cool. Spread on half the bread slices; top with remaining bread. Trim off crusts. Brown sandwiches on both sides in a small amount of butter in skillet. Cut into fourths. Serve immediately. The sandwiches can also be served for lunch. *This extremely popular recipe was used for catering parties for weddings and receptions.* Yield: 24 servings.

**Approx Per Serving:** Cal 67; Prot 1 g; Carbo 6 g; Fiber <1 g;
    T Fat 4 g; Chol 11 mg; Sod 77 mg.

*Helen H. Hodgdon, Former WEIU Food Shop Director*

## FRESH STRAWBERRY SANDWICHES

1/2 cup butter, softened
1 1/2 cups confectioners' sugar
1/8 teaspoon salt
1/8 teaspoon nutmeg

1 tablespoon rum
24 slices thin-sliced white bread
1 quart fresh strawberries

Cream butter in bowl. Add confectioners' sugar gradually, beating well after each addition. Add salt, nutmeg and rum; beat until light and fluffy. Cut rounds from bread with cookie cutter. Spread rounds with rum mixture. Chill until serving time. Remove stems from strawberries and cut strawberries into thin slices. Arrange overlapping strawberry slices on sandwiches; arrange sandwiches on serving plates. Garnish with fresh mint and whole strawberries. *This sandwich was used by the Union on outside catering parties for tea parties and receptions. Men were especially fascinated with this sandwich.* Yield: 24 servings.

**Approx Per Serving:** Cal 127; Prot 2 g; Carbo 19 g; Fiber 1 g;
    T Fat 5 g; Chol 10 mg; Sod 147 mg.

*Helen H. Hodgdon, Former WEIU Food Shop Director*

1877   *In the two meeting rooms opened at 4 Park Street, lectures were held on Goethe, astronomy, and Italian art. German, French, and Italian were also taught.*

## CHEDDAR CHEESE BALL

4 cups shredded Cheddar cheese
1 bunch scallions, finely
  chopped
½ cup slivered almonds

½ cup mayonnaise
12 slices crisp-fried bacon,
  crumbled

Let cheese stand at room temperature until softened. Combine cheese, scallions, almonds, mayonnaise and bacon in bowl; mix well. Shape into 2 large or 3 medium balls; wrap in foil. Store in refrigerator. Serve with assorted crackers. Yield: 64 servings.

**Approx Per Serving:** Cal 54; Prot 2 g; Carbo <1 g; Fiber <1 g;
  T Fat 5 g; Chol 9 mg; Sod 73 mg.

*Jan Frank, WEIU Friend*

## PISTACHIO CHEESE BALL

3 cups shredded sharp Cheddar
  cheese
8 ounces cream cheese
2 tablespoons dry sherry

1 teaspoon Dijon mustard
3 drops of hot pepper sauce
¼ cup chopped pistachios

Let cheeses stand at room temperature until softened. Combine Cheddar cheese, cream cheese, sherry, mustard and hot pepper sauce in bowl; mix well. Chill for 30 minutes. Shape into ball. Roll in pistachios to coat. Yield: 64 servings.

**Approx Per Serving:** Cal 37; Prot 2 g; Carbo <1 g; Fiber <1 g;
  T Fat 3 g; Chol 9 mg; Sod 45 mg.

*Willona H. Sinclair, WEIU Friend*

## CREAMY ARTICHOKE DIP

½ cup drained canned
  artichokes
½ cup mayonnaise

½ cup freshly grated Parmesan
  cheese

Combine artichokes, mayonnaise and cheese in blender; process until smooth. Pour into ramekins. Bake at 350 degrees for 15 minutes or until golden. Serve with Melba toast. Yield: 24 servings.

**Approx Per Serving:** Cal 42; Prot 1 g; Carbo 1 g; Fiber 0 g;
  T Fat 4 g; Chol 48 mg; Sod 60 mg.

*Martha Heigham, WEIU Friend*

# HOT ARTICHOKE DIP

1  12-ounce can artichoke hearts      1½ cups grated Parmesan cheese
1½ cups mayonnaise

Drain artichoke hearts; cut into bite-sized pieces. Combine with mayonnaise and cheese in bowl; mix well. Spoon into 3-inch deep by 5-inch diameter casserole. Bake at 375 degrees for 15 to 20 minutes or until top is brown and dip is bubbly. Serve hot with chips, water crackers or other favorites to spread or dip. Yield: 40 servings.

**Approx Per Serving:** Cal 77; Prot 2 g; Carbo 1 g; Fiber 0 g;
      T Fat 7 g; Chol 7 mg; Sod 109 mg.

*Susan Hamer, WEIU Friend*

# CRAB MEAT CASSEROLE

1 pound crab meat                    1 cup mayonnaise
1 cup chopped onion                  1 cup shredded Swiss cheese

Flake crab meat in bowl. Add onion, mayonnaise and cheese; mix well. Spoon into 1½-quart casserole. Bake at 350 degrees until heated through. Serve warm with Ritz crackers. May substitute imitation crab meat. Yield: 40 servings.

**Approx Per Serving:** Cal 59; Prot 3 g; Carbo 1 g; Fiber <1 g;
      T Fat 5 g; Chol 12 mg; Sod 66 mg.

*Annette Athanas, WEIU Friend*

# HUMUS BEECHMONT

2  16-ounce cans chick peas,         2 teaspoons kosher salt
   drained                           1 teaspoon pepper
2 cloves of garlic                   3 tablespoons dried parsley
1 cup olive oil

Combine chick peas, garlic, olive oil, salt, pepper and parsley in food processor; pulse until mixture is smooth. Spoon into bowl. Chill until serving time. Mix humus lightly. Garnish with capers and fresh parsley sprigs. Yield: 40 servings.

**Approx Per Serving:** Cal 85; Prot 2 g; Carbo 6 g; Fiber 1 g;
      T Fat 6 g; Chol 0 mg; Sod 321 mg.

*Charlotte T. Clapp Sammarco, WEIU Friend*

# MEXICAN PARTY DIP

3 medium avocados
2 tablespoons mayonnaise
Fresh lemon juice to taste
2 cups shredded Monterey Jack
   cheese
1 cup sour cream

3 tablespoons mayonnaise
1/2 envelope taco seasoning mix
2 cups shredded Cheddar cheese
1 medium tomato, chopped
1/2 cup chopped scallions

Mash avocados in bowl. Add 2 tablespoons mayonnaise and lemon juice; mix well. Add Monterey Jack cheese; mix well. Spread evenly in 10-inch pie plate. Blend sour cream, 3 tablespoons mayonnaise and taco seasoning mix in bowl. Spread over avocado layer. Add layers of Cheddar cheese, tomato and scallions. Chill, tightly covered, for 1 hour. Serve with tortilla chips. Yield: 30 servings.

**Approx Per Serving:** Cal 128; Prot 5 g; Carbo 3 g; Fiber 2 g;
    T Fat 11 g; Chol 20 mg; Sod 165 mg.

*Mary Delaney, WEIU Friend*

# HOT MUSHROOM DIP

1 pound fresh mushrooms,
   sliced
1/4 cup butter
2 cups sour cream

1 envelope mushroom-onion
   soup mix
1 cup shredded Cheddar cheese

Sauté mushrooms in butter in skillet. Mix sour cream and soup mix in bowl. Add to mushrooms; mix well. Pour into 10-inch pie plate. Sprinkle cheese over top. Bake at 350 degrees for 15 minutes. Serve with wheat thins or other favorite crackers. Yield: 40 servings.

**Approx Per Serving:** Cal 59; Prot 1 g; Carbo 2 g; Fiber <1 g;
    T Fat 5 g; Chol 11 mg; Sod 133 mg.

*Adelaide Tingley, WEIU Employee*

**1880** *The Union is incorporated.*

# LORI GAGNE'S SALSA

1 cup chopped onion
2 cloves of garlic, crushed
½ teaspoon salt
2 tablespoons olive oil
2 teaspoons cumin
½ teaspoon coriander
½ to 1 teaspoon cayenne pepper

Freshly ground pepper to taste
1 teaspoon chili powder
3 cups chopped tomatoes
1 cup water
2 tablespoons tomato paste
2 teaspoons dry red wine
½ teaspoon salt

Sauté onion and garlic with ½ teaspoon salt in olive oil in large heavy saucepan. Add cumin, coriander, cayenne pepper, pepper, chili powder, tomatoes, water, tomato paste, wine and ½ teaspoon salt; mix well. Simmer, covered, for 1 hour or longer; the longer it simmers, the spicier it gets. Serve with corn chips. Salsa may be puréed or served chunky to be more authentic. Yield: 20 servings.

**Approx Per Serving:** Cal 22; Prot <1 g; Carbo 2 g; Fiber 1 g;
T Fat 1 g; Chol 0 mg; Sod 110 mg.

*Beth Andrews, Former WEIU Employee*

# CHICKEN LIVER MOUSSE WITH APPLES

1 pound chicken livers
2 medium apples, peeled, sliced
1 large onion, sliced
5 tablespoons butter
4 cloves of garlic

¼ cup Calvados or apple jack
4 cloves of garlic, chopped
1 cup butter, softened
½ cup cream
Salt and pepper to taste

Remove and discard all membranes from livers. Sauté apples and onion in 5 tablespoons butter in skillet over medium-low heat until tender. Increase heat slightly. Add livers and garlic. Sauté for 5 minutes or until livers are barely pink in center. Remove livers, apples and onion from skillet. Add Calvados to skillet, stirring to deglaze. Combine liver mixture and Calvados in food processor; process until smooth. Remove cover from processor. Let mixture stand until cooled to room temperature. Add butter, cream, salt and pepper to processor; process until smooth. Chill until serving time. May let stand at room temperature for 30 minutes or longer before serving and pipe through pastry bag into decorative servings. Yield: 50 servings.

**Approx Per Serving:** Cal 60; Prot 1 g; Carbo 1 g; Fiber <1 g;
T Fat 6 g; Chol 43 mg; Sod 44 mg.

*Marjorie Alonso Jackson, WEIU Friend*

## SAUTERNE HAM SPREAD

| | |
|---|---|
| 1  12-ounce can chopped ham | 8 ounces cream cheese, softened |
| 1 envelope unflavored gelatin | 1/4 cup mayonnaise |
| 1/4 cup cold water | 1 teaspoon prepared mustard |
| 2/3 cup Sauterne | 1/2 teaspoon onion powder |
| 1 cup cottage cheese | Hot pepper sauce to taste |

Put ham through food chopper using medium blade; set aside. Soften gelatin in cold water. Heat wine just to the simmering point in saucepan. Add softened gelatin; stir until dissolved. Let stand until cooled to room temperature. Combine with cottage cheese in blender; process until smooth. Blend with cream cheese in bowl. Add mayonnaise, mustard, onion powder and hot pepper sauce; mix well. Add ham; mix well. Spoon into 4½-cup mold. Chill until firm. Unmold onto serving plate. This spread is out of this world served with Champagne. Yield: 20 servings.

**Approx Per Serving:** Cal 100; Prot 5 g; Carbo 1 g; Fiber <1 g;
T Fat 8 g; Chol 22 mg; Sod 312 mg.

*Dorothea J. Mahoney, WEIU Friend*

## SPECIAL PÂTÉ

| | |
|---|---|
| 1 envelope unflavored gelatin | 8 ounces cream cheese, softened |
| 1  14-ounce can beef bouillon | 2  3/4-ounce cans goose liver |
| without gelatin | pâté with truffles |

Soften gelatin in half the bouillon in bowl. Heat remaining bouillon in saucepan. Add to gelatin mixture; stir until gelatin dissolves. Let stand until cool. Pour half the gelatin mixture into lightly oiled 2-cup mold. Chill until firm. Mix cream cheese with goose liver pâté in bowl, using wooden spoon. Add remaining gelatin mixture to cream cheese mixture; mix well. Spread over congealed layer in mold. Chill overnight. Unmold onto serving plate. Serve with plain crackers or thinly sliced French bread. Yield: 10 servings.

**Approx Per Serving:** Cal 95; Prot 3 g; Carbo 1 g; Fiber 0 g;
T Fat 9 g; Chol 31 mg; Sod 226 mg.

*Carlotta Ames, WEIU Friend*

1881  *Boston Symphony holds its first concert.*

## SALMON APPETIZER IN-A-MOLD

8 ounces cream cheese, softened
1 10-ounce can cream of
mushroom soup
2 envelopes unflavored gelatin
¼ cup cold water
½ cup finely chopped celery

1 7-ounce can salmon, drained,
flaked
½ cup finely chopped green
bell pepper
1 cup mayonnaise
½ teaspoon curry powder

Combine cream cheese and soup in double boiler over hot water. Heat until well mixed, stirring frequently. Soften gelatin in cold water. Add to soup mixture; stir until dissolved. Add celery, salmon, green pepper, mayonnaise and curry powder; mix well. Pour into 5-cup fish-shaped mold. Chill until firm. Unmold onto serving plate. Decorate with cucumber slices for scales, sliced green olives for eyes, pimentos for eyebrows, mouth and on tail. Serve with crackers. Yield: 30 servings.

**Approx Per Serving:** Cal 100; Prot 2 g; Carbo 1 g; Fiber <1 g;
T Fat 10 g; Chol 15 mg; Sod 173 mg.

*Mrs. Winthrop G. Minot, WEIU Friend*

## SALMON MOUSSE

1 7-ounce can salmon, drained,
flaked
8 ounces cream cheese, softened

4 or 5 scallions, chopped
3 tablespoons lemon juice
Pepper to taste

Combine salmon, cream cheese, scallions, lemon juice and pepper in bowl; mix well. Chill, covered, for several hours to overnight. Garnish with additional chopped scallions. Yield: 15 servings.

**Approx Per Serving:** Cal 70; Prot 4 g; Carbo 1 g; Fiber <1 g;
T Fat 6 g; Chol 21 mg; Sod 109 mg.

*Amy Mazur, WEIU Employee*

1885  *Dickens' Carnival, in Mechanics Hall, raised $6,130.01 for the Union.*

# TUNA MOUSSE

1 envelope unflavored gelatin
2 tablespoons cold water
1/2 cup boiling water
1 small onion, chopped
2  6-ounce cans white tuna,
   drained

1/2 cup mayonnaise
1 tablespoon horseradish
1/2 teaspoon paprika
1 cup whipping cream

Soften gelatin in cold water. Combine with boiling water and onion in blender container; process until gelatin dissolves. Add tuna, mayonnaise, horseradish and paprika; process until smooth. Add cream 1/3 at a time, processing after each addition. Pour into 4-cup mold. Chill for several hours to overnight. Unmold onto serving plate. Serve with rye crackers. Yield: 16 servings.

**Approx Per Serving:** Cal 131; Prot 7 g; Carbo 1 g; Fiber <1 g;
    T Fat 11 g; Chol 36 mg; Sod 121 mg.

*Evie Rose, WEIU Friend*

# CHAMPAGNE PUNCH

5 kiwifruit
5 limes
10 to 12 large strawberries
1  750-milliliter bottle of
   Sauterne

4 cups apricot brandy
2 quarts ginger ale
6  750-milliliter bottles of
   Champagne

Peel kiwifruit; cut lengthwise into halves and cut into thin slices. Cut limes into halves and cut into thin slices. Cut strawberries into halves. Arrange strawberries in bottom of 4-cup ring mold. Arrange kiwifruit and lime slices over strawberries and up side of mold. Fill mold with ice water carefully. Freeze for several hours to overnight. Chill Sauterne, brandy, ginger ale and Champagne in ice for several hours. Blend brandy and Sauterne in large punch bowl. Stir in ginger ale and Champagne gently. Unmold ice ring. Place carefully in punch bowl. Garnish punch bowl with fresh mint leaves. Yield: 50 servings.

**Approx Per Serving:** Cal 141; Prot <1 g; Carbo 14 g; Fiber <1 g;
    T Fat <1 g; Chol 0 mg; Sod 10 mg.

*Mary Maynard, WEIU Member*

## EASY CHAMPAGNE PUNCH

Juice of 2 oranges
2 dashes of bitters
Splash of Cointreau

Sugar to taste
1 750-milliliter bottle of
Champagne

Combine orange juice, bitters, Cointreau and sugar in large pitcher; mix well. Add Champagne. Pour into glasses filled with crushed ice; stir vigorously. Serve immediately. This recipe originated in Guadeloupe where it is known as "Lavie-Boom Boom" and served on New Year's Day. It is meant to bring good fortune (and I expect a large head) to the lucky participant. Yield: 8 servings.

**Approx Per Serving:** Cal 421; Prot 1 g; Carbo 14 g; Fiber <1 g; T Fat <1 g; Chol 0 mg; Sod 33 mg.

*Mrs. Charles Inches, WEIU Friend*

## CRANBERRY-APPLE PUNCH

4 cups cranberry juice cocktail
3 cups apple juice
1 8-ounce can juice-pack
  pineapple cubes
1/2 cup fresh lemon juice

1 ice mold with cherries
1 quart ginger ale
1 750-milliliter bottle of white
  wine

Combine cranberry juice, apple juice, undrained pineapple and lemon juice in pitcher. Chill until serving time. Place ice mold in punch bowl. Pour juice mixture over mold. Add ginger ale and white wine. Ladle into punch cups. Yield: 20 servings.

**Approx Per Serving:** Cal 95; Prot <1 g; Carbo 18 g; Fiber <1 g; T Fat <1 g; Chol 0 mg; Sod 7 mg.

*Mary Maynard, WEIU Member*

## KAHLUA

1 1/2 cups packed brown sugar
1 1/2 cups sugar
2 cups water

1/3 cup instant coffee crystals
2 teaspoons vanilla extract
1 fifth of vodka

Combine brown sugar, sugar and water in large microwave-safe bowl. Microwave on High for 15 minutes or until sugars dissolve, stirring twice. Add coffee, vanilla and vodka; mix well. Let stand until cool. Pour into 2-quart container. Store, tightly covered, for 2 weeks before serving. Yield: 64 servings.

**Approx Per Serving:** Cal 64; Prot <1 g; Carbo 10 g; Fiber <1 g; T Fat <1 g; Chol 0 mg; Sod 3 mg.

*Liza MacKinnon, WEIU Member*

## OLD BEACON HILL HOLIDAY EGGNOG

12 large brown-shelled eggs,
  separated
1  1-pound package
  confectioners' sugar
4 cups milk

4 cups whipping cream
4 cups bourbon
2 cups light rum
2 cups brandy
Nutmeg to taste

Beat egg yolks with confectioners' sugar in large bowl. Beat in milk. Add cream; blend well. Stir in bourbon, rum and brandy. Pour into punch bowl. Beat egg whites until stiff peaks form. Slip egg whites onto top of eggnog in punch bowl. Sprinkle lightly with nutmeg. May spoon dollop of stiffly beaten egg white onto each filled punch cup if preferred. May substitute half and half for whipping cream or alter proportions of the liquors to taste but this is the historically tried and true recipe. Yield: 80 servings.

**Approx Per Serving:** Cal 138; Prot 2 g; Carbo 10 g; Fiber 0 g;
  T Fat 6 g; Chol 50 mg; Sod 20 mg.

*Nichols House Museum, Inc., WEIU Friend*

## PEACH DAIQUIRI

1 cup water
1 cup sugar
1  2x4½-inch piece lemon rind
2 tablespoons lime juice
2 peaches

2 cups crushed ice
½ cup light rum
¼ cup peach schnapps
½ cup club soda

Combine water, sugar and lemon rind in saucepan. Bring to a boil, stirring until sugar dissolves; strain. Add lime juice. Pour ½ cup citrus syrup into blender. Peel and slice peaches. Add peaches, ice, rum, schnapps and club soda. Process for several seconds. Dip rims of glasses into sugar. Pour in peach mixture. Garnish with lime slice. Yield: 4 servings.

**Approx Per Serving:** Cal 335; Prot <1 g; Carbo 63 g; Fiber 1 g;
  T Fat <1 g; Chol 0 mg; Sod 9 mg.

*Meredith Hutter, WEIU Employee*

1886  *The Befriending Committee was partly responsible for a bill that passed the Legislature providing for the employment of police matrons in all large cities in Massachusetts.*

### The School Hot Lunch Program
*The WEIU prepared hot, economical, nutritious lunches for Boston's School Children.*

### Distributing Hot Lunches
*The WEIU prepared and delivered up to 18,000 school lunches a day from 1907 through 1944.*

# Salads and Soups

## SAVORY TOMATO SALAD

**100  2-ounce portions**

| | |
|---|---|
| Lemon Jello | 3 lbs. |
| Tomatoes (#10) | 4 qts.—(1⅓ cans) |
| Cucumbers (diced) | 2½ qts. |
| Green pepper (chopped) | ½ cup |
| Onion (chopped) | ½ cup |
| Vinegar | ½ cup |
| Salt | 2½ oz. |
| Mayonnaise | 2½ qts. |

Dissolve gelatin in heated tomatoes. Add the cucumber, green peppers, onion, vinegar, and salt. Chill. When slightly thickened fold in the mayonnaise. Turn into individual molds and chill until firm. Unmold on crisp lettuce and serve with additional mayonnaise.

*from handwritten cookbook used in Union restaurant, 1940s*

# GOLDEN SALAD

| | |
|---|---|
| 1  3-ounce package lemon gelatin | 1 orange, peeled |
| | 2 medium carrots |
| 1 cup pineapple juice, heated | 1 cup crushed pineapple |

Combine gelatin and hot pineapple juice in blender; process until gelatin dissolves. Cut orange into quarters; add to blender. Process at high speed for 20 seconds. Scrub and coarsely chop carrots. Add carrots and pineapple to blender. Process for 30 seconds or until carrots are finely chopped. Pour into oiled 8-inch gelatin mold. Chill until firm. Unmold onto lettuce-lined serving plate. This three-generation recipe is a great summer salad with chicken. Yield: 8 servings.

**Approx Per Serving:** Cal 97; Prot 2 g; Carbo 24 g; Fiber 1 g;
 T Fat <1 g; Chol 0 mg; Sod 41 mg.

*Mrs. Edwin E. Bastoni, WEIU Employee*

# CHINESE CHICKEN SALAD

| | |
|---|---|
| 1/2 cup rice vinegar | 4 cups shredded iceberg lettuce |
| 1 tablespoon cider vinegar | 2 cups shredded cooked chicken |
| 4 teaspoons sugar | 2 cups shredded carrots |
| 2 teaspoons Chinese sesame oil | 1/4 cup chopped chives |
| 1/2 teaspoon grated fresh gingerroot | 1 1/2 cups chow mein noodles |
| | 1/2 cup sliced unsalted almonds |

Combine rice vinegar, cider vinegar, sugar, sesame oil and gingerroot in bowl; stir until sugar dissolves. Combine lettuce, carrots, chives, and chicken in salad bowl. Add dressing; toss until mixed. Add chow mein noodles and almonds just before serving. Yield: 4 servings.

**Approx Per Serving:** Cal 368; Prot 25 g; Carbo 25 g; Fiber 5 g;
 T Fat 20 g; Chol 60 mg; Sod 243 mg.

*Helen Chen, Joyce Chen Products*

1893  *The Union sent a stained glass window for display in the*
*Women's Pavilion at the Chicago World's Fair. This window*
*is now in the shops at 356 Boylston Street.*

# SOUTH SEAS SALAD

| | |
|---|---|
| 1/4 cup lemon juice | 1 papaya |
| 1 tablespoon minced garlic | 1 mango |
| 1 tablespoon minced fresh | 1/2 cantaloupe |
| gingerroot | 1/2 red bell pepper |
| 1/4 cup oil | 1/2 yellow bell pepper |
| Tabasco sauce and Chinese chili | 1/2 orange bell pepper |
| powder to taste | 1 large carrot |
| 1 pound scallops | |

Combine lemon juice, garlic and gingerroot in bowl. Beat in oil. Season with Tabasco sauce and Chinese chili. Microwave scallops in covered bowl on High for 3 minutes or just until firm; do not overcook. Cut fruits and bell peppers into bite-sized pieces. Cut carrot into julienne strips. Arrange scallops, fruits and vegetables in salad bowl or serving platter. Drizzle dressing over top. May substitute firm fish such as swordfish or monkfish, lobster or shrimp for scallops or use in any combination. Yield: 4 servings.

**Approx Per Serving:** Cal 310; Prot 17 g; Carbo 30 g; Fiber 5 g;
T Fat 15 g; Chol 30 mg; Sod 163 mg.

*Clare and Helen Cotton, WEIU Members*

# LOBSTER AND WILD RICE SALAD

| | |
|---|---|
| 1 tablespoon imported mustard | 2 cups bite-sized pieces cooked |
| 2 1/2 tablespoons red wine | lobster |
| vinegar | 2 medium avocados |
| 1/2 cup corn oil | 1 tablespoon lemon juice |
| 1/2 teaspoon minced garlic | 1/2 cup coarsely chopped red |
| Salt and freshly ground pepper | onion |
| to taste | 2 tablespoons finely chopped |
| Sugar to taste | parsley |
| 4 cups cooked wild rice | |

Combine mustard and vinegar in small bowl; whisk until blended. Add oil gradually, whisking constantly. Add garlic, salt, pepper and sugar; mix well. Combine wild rice and lobster in bowl. Peel and slice avocados; sprinkle with lemon juice. Add avocados and onion to rice mixture. Add dressing just before serving; toss lightly. Sprinkle with parsley. May serve at room temperature or chilled. Yield: 8 servings.

**Approx Per Serving:** Cal 327; Prot 11 g; Carbo 24 g; Fiber 8 g;
T Fat 22 g; Chol 20 mg; Sod 140 mg.

*Mrs. Ezra Merrill, WEIU Member*

# PASTA VINAIGRETTE

1 7-ounce package tortelini
3/4 cup oil and vinegar Italian
 salad dressing
1 cup broccoli flowerets
1 cup cherry tomato halves
1/2 cup green bell pepper strips

1/2 cup radish wedges
1/2 cup black olive halves
4 green onions, sliced
2 tablespoons grated Parmesan
 cheese

Cook tortelini using package directions; drain. Rinse with cold water; drain well. Combine with salad dressing in large bowl. Add broccoli, tomatoes, green peppers, radishes, olives, green onions and Parmesan cheese; toss to mix. Chill, covered, for 2 hours or until serving time. Spoon into shallow lettuce-lined salad bowl. Garnish with Genoa salami curls. May substitute 6 ounces elbow macaroni for tortelini. Yield: 12 servings.

**Approx Per Serving:** Cal 158; Prot 3 g; Carbo 16 g; Fiber 2 g;
 T Fat 12 g; Chol 1 mg; Sod 165 mg.

*Wendy Rose, WEIU Friend*

# RICE SALAD WITH YOGURT AND CAPERS

3 cups cooked rice
1/2 to 1 cup peas
4 scallions, chopped
2 cups plain yogurt

2 tablespoons capers
1 teaspoon juice from capers
1 tablespoon red wine vinegar
Salt and white pepper to taste

Combine rice, peas and scallions in salad bowl. Combine yogurt, capers and juice, vinegar, salt and white pepper in small bowl; mix well. Add to rice mixture; mix lightly. Chill until serving time. Yield: 8 servings.

**Approx Per Serving:** Cal 138; Prot 6 g; Carbo 26 g; Fiber 1 g;
 T Fat 1 g; Chol 4 mg; Sod 41 mg.

*Marjorie Alonso Jackson, WEIU Friend*

1895  *An average of 1500 people entered the Union building. They came "for business, for pleasure, for rest, to meet friends, to read or consult books, to obtain information, to tell sad tales of bitter experiences and to seek sympathy . . ."*

# WEDDING RICE SALAD

1 cup sliced dried apricots
½ cup golden raisins
½ cup currants
¼ cup lemon juice
1 tablespoon finely chopped
    garlic
1 tablespoon finely chopped
    fresh gingerroot

1 teaspoon coriander
1 teaspoon cumin
½ cup oil
2 cups uncooked long grain rice
3 cups water
1 cup chopped onion
½ cup slivered almonds, toasted

Plump apricots, raisins and currants in hot water in bowl for several minutes to overnight; drain. Combine garlic, gingerroot, coriander and cumin in bowl. Whisk in oil gradually. Cook rice in 3 cups water in saucepan for 12 minutes or just until tender; spread rice on large shallow platter. Mix in onion. Add dressing a small amount at a time, stirring and turning as dressing is absorbed and rice cools; do not allow to be become oily. Mix in fruit. Add almonds just before serving. May plump fruit in sherry if preferred. We prepared this for niece Betsy's wedding supper for 80 people and have made it for several smaller occasions since. Yield: 10 servings.

**Approx Per Serving:** Cal 268; Prot 4 g; Carbo 33 g; Fiber 3 g;
    T Fat 15 g; Chol 0 mg; Sod 216 mg.

*Clare and Helen Cotton, WEIU Members*

# DELICIOUS VEGETABLE SALAD MOLD

1 tablespoon unflavored gelatin
½ cup cold water
4 cups boiling consommé

1   16-ounce can cut asparagus
1   5-ounce bottle of pearl onions
5 tomatoes

Soften gelatin in cold water. Dissolve in boiling consommé in bowl. Drain asparagus and onions well. Peel tomatoes and cut into quarters. Arrange vegetables in greased 2-quart ring mold. Add gelatin mixture. Chill until firm. Unmold onto serving plate lined with lettuce or watercress. Serve with mayonnaise. Yield: 8 servings.

**Approx Per Serving:** Cal 46; Prot 5 g; Carbo 6 g; Fiber 3 g;
    T Fat 1 g; Chol <1 mg; Sod 596 mg.

*Maybury V. Tingley, WEIU Friend*

## DYNAMIC CAESAR SALAD

2 heads romaine
1  2-ounce can anchovies
Juice of 1 lemon
4 medium cloves of garlic,
   pressed
6 drops of Worcestershire sauce

1 egg
¼ cup mixed grated Parmesan
   and Romano cheeses
⅓ cup seasoned croutons
Freshly ground pepper to taste

Discard damaged outer leaves of romaine. Rinse romaine; drain, leaving leaves moist but not wet. Tear leaves carefully; avoid hard green outer edges but use lighter green and slightly yellow portions. Chill until serving time. Drain anchovies, reserving oil. Mash anchovies with fork; place in small bowl. Add half the lemon juice, garlic, 3 tablespoons reserved anchovy oil and Worcestershire sauce; mix well. Drain romaine well; place in salad bowl. Pour anchovy mixture over romaine; toss 3 times. Add raw egg and cheeses; toss to mix. Add croutons. Adjust each serving with lemon juice and anchovy paste to taste; add generous grind of fresh pepper. *More than 20 years ago, I discovered Caesar Salad and found that it varied greatly from salad maker to salad maker. I learned how to make it from a man who learned from Caesar himself. What a find!* Yield: 6 servings.

**Approx Per Serving:** Cal 68; Prot 3 g; Carbo 3 g; Fiber 1 g;
   T Fat 3 g; Chol 39 mg; Sod 405 mg.

*Dana Vannasse, WEIU Lecturer*

## CHUNKY CUCUMBER SALAD

1 cup mayonnaise
1½ tablespoons lemon juice
1 tablespoon cider vinegar
1 teaspoon chili powder
½ teaspoon seasoned salt

1 large cucumber
1 large stalk celery, chopped
5 pimento-stuffed green olives,
   chopped

Combine mayonnaise, lemon juice, vinegar, chili powder and seasoned salt in blender; process at low speed until smooth. Peel, seed and chop cucumber. Add cucumber, celery and olives to blender container. Process for 5 seconds. Pour into bowl. Chill, covered, in refrigerator. Yield: 8 servings.

**Approx Per Serving:** Cal 206; Prot 1 g; Carbo 2 g; Fiber 1 g;
   T Fat 22 g; Chol 16 mg; Sod 353 mg.

*Jack Hutter, WEIU Friend*

# DO-AHEAD SALAD

1 head lettuce, shredded
1 cup chopped celery
1 cup chopped green bell pepper
1 10-ounce package frozen peas
1 medium onion, sliced
1 cup mayonnaise

1 cup sour cream
1 tablespoon sugar
2 cups shredded Cheddar cheese
1/3 cup crumbled crisp-fried
   bacon

Layer lettuce, celery, green pepper, uncooked peas and onion in glass salad bowl. Blend mayonnaise, sour cream and sugar in bowl. Spread over salad, sealing to edge. Sprinkle cheese over top. Chill, covered with plastic wrap, for 12 hours. Sprinkle bacon over top just before serving. Yield: 12 servings.

**Approx Per Serving:** Cal 291; Prot 8 g; Carbo 8 g; Fiber 2 g;
   T Fat 26 g; Chol 41 mg; Sod 288 mg.

*Jane Murphy, WEIU Friend*

# SOUTHWESTERN SALAD

3 large seedless oranges
1 medium red onion
1 2-ounce can sliced black
   olives, drained
1 head red or green leaf lettuce
1/4 cup red wine vinegar

1/3 cup oil
1 tablespoon catsup
1 tablespoon sugar
1/2 teaspoon garlic powder
1/4 teaspoon chili powder

Peel and thinly slice oranges and onion. Rinse and drain lettuce; tear into bite-sized pieces. Add orange slices and onion slices. Combine vinegar, oil, catsup, sugar, garlic powder and chili powder in bowl; mix well. Pour over salad just before serving; toss gently. Yield: 8 servings.

**Approx Per Serving:** Cal 187; Prot 1 g; Carbo 11 g; Fiber 2 g;
   T Fat 16 g; Chol 0 mg; Sod 25 mg.

*Judy Blackburn, WEIU Employee*

**1897** *The Handwork Department separated from the Food Department.*

# POTATO SALAD

5 pounds potatoes
4 small red onions
1 green bell pepper
4 hard-boiled eggs
1/2 cucumber
1 1/3 cups mayonnaise

1 1/2 tablespoons vinegar
1 1/2 tablespoons prepared
  mustard
Salt and pepper to taste
Minced parsley to taste

Cook potatoes in boiling water to cover in saucepan until tender; drain. Peel and chop potatoes. Chop onions, green pepper, eggs and cucumber. Combine potatoes, onions, green pepper, eggs and cucumber in large bowl; toss to mix. Combine mayonnaise, vinegar, mustard, salt, pepper and parsley in bowl; mix well. Pour over potato mixture; toss to mix. Chill until serving time. *I have been a long-time volunteer in the Companions Unlimited program of the Union. This delicious potato salad was served at every picnic; the staff gave me the recipe. It seems to be an old Union recipe.* Yield: 20 servings.

**Approx Per Serving:** Cal 253; Prot 4 g; Carbo 31 g; Fiber 3 g;
  T Fat 13 g; Chol 51 mg; Sod 121 mg.

*Enid Lubarsky, WEIU Volunteer*

# SWEET AND SOUR SALAD

1/2 cup slivered almonds
3 tablespoons sugar
1/4 cup vinegar
1/4 cup sugar
1/2 teaspoon salt
1 tablespoon chopped parsley
1/2 cup oil

1 head romaine, torn
1 cup chopped celery
1 small red onion, chopped
1  11-ounce can mandarin
  oranges, drained
1 large avocado, sliced
1 cup sliced mushrooms

Combine almonds and 3 tablespoons sugar in small nonstick skillet. Cook over medium heat until sugar melts and coats almonds, stirring constantly. Let stand until cool. Combine vinegar, 1/4 cup sugar, salt, parsley and oil in jar; shake vigorously. Combine romaine, celery, onion, mandarin oranges, avocado and mushrooms in salad bowl. Add dressing; toss to mix. Add almonds just before serving. May substitute red leaf lettuce for all or a portion of the romaine. Yield: 10 servings.

**Approx Per Serving:** Cal 234; Prot 3 g; Carbo 19 g; Fiber 4 g;
  T Fat 18 g; Chol 0 mg; Sod 125 mg.

*Kathy Roberts, WEIU Employee*

# TOMATO ASPIC

1 cup tomato juice
1  3-ounce package lemon
   gelatin

1 cup tomato juice

Bring 1 cup tomato juice to a boil in saucepan; remove from heat. Add gelatin; stir until dissolved. Stir in remaining 1 cup tomato juice. Pour into 3-cup mold. Chill until firm. Unmold onto lettuce-lined serving plate. Serve with ranch salad dressing or your favorite salad dressing. Flavor improves overnight. May add your choice of additional ingredients such as chopped chives, celery or cucumber. Yield: 6 servings.

**Approx Per Serving:** Cal 66; Prot 2 g; Carbo 16 g; Fiber 1 g;
    T Fat <1 g; Chol 0 mg; Sod 339 mg.

*Markie Phillips, WEIU Trustee*

# ETHEL'S TARRAGON SALAD DRESSING

1/2 cup sour cream
1/2 cup mayonnaise
1 1/2 teaspoons tarragon

Worcestershire sauce to taste
Lemon juice to taste
Pepper to taste

Combine sour cream, mayonnaise, tarragon, Worcestershire sauce, lemon juice and pepper in bowl; mix well. Chill for several hours. Serve on salad of Bibb or Boston lettuce with your choice of cucumbers, tomatoes or other vegetables. Yield: 8 servings.

**Approx Per Serving:** Cal 129; Prot 1 g; Carbo 1 g; Fiber 0 g;
    T Fat 14 g; Chol 15 mg; Sod 86 mg.

*Lydia L. Hale, WEIU Friend*

1903  *The Committee on Sanitary and Industrial Conditions was organized to strive for better conditions for women and children who work in shops and factories making products such as rubber, twine, and cordage. This committee, which grew out of the Hygiene Committee, made recommendations to the State Board of Health.*

# BROCCOLI AND CHEESE SOUP

1 onion, chopped
2 tablespoons oil
3 cups water
3 chicken bouillon cubes
2 ounces uncooked fine egg
  noodles

1  10-ounce package frozen
   chopped broccoli
1/2 teaspoon salt
3 cups milk
1 pound Velveeta cheese, cubed
Garlic powder to taste

Sauté onion in oil in soup pot until tender. Add water and bouillon cubes. Bring to a boil. Add noodles, broccoli and salt. Cook until broccoli is tender. Add milk and cheese gradually, stirring until cheese melts. Cook over low heat until thickened. Add garlic powder to taste. This favorite recipe of the coeds at Plattsburgh may be doubled to feed a crowd. With a salad and bread it makes a hearty meal. Yield: 8 servings.

**Approx Per Serving:** Cal 345; Prot 18 g; Carbo 14 g; Fiber 1 g;
    T Fat 25 g; Chol 66 mg; Sod 1424 mg.

*Liane L. Pfetsch, WEIU Friend*

# CARROT SOUP

6 medium carrots, scraped,
  chopped
1 small onion, chopped
1 bay leaf
2 tablespoons butter

3 cups chicken broth
2 teaspoons sugar
Salt and pepper to taste
1 tablespoon grated lemon rind
1 tablespoon chopped parsley

Combine carrots, onion, bay leaf and butter in heavy saucepan. Cook, covered, over very low heat for 8 minutes or until carrots are tender. Let stand until slightly cooled. Discard bay leaf. Stir in 1 cup broth. Pour into blender or food processor container. Process at low speed for several seconds. Process at high speed for 1 minute. Return mixture to saucepan. Add remaining 2 cups broth, sugar, salt and pepper. Heat to serving temperature. Ladle into soup cups. Sprinkle with lemon rind and parsley. The soup is essentially a vegetable frappé. The method can be applied to a number of other vegetables such as potato and watercress, potato and spinach or potato and cucumber. *This creamy soup without a speck of cream was invented by the English cookbook writer Maurice Moore-Betty.* Yield: 6 servings.

**Approx Per Serving:** Cal 97; Prot 4 g; Carbo 11 g; Fiber 3 g;
    T Fat 5 g; Chol 11 mg; Sod 446 mg.

*Margo Miller, **The Boston Globe***

# CARROT SOUP WITH GINGER

2 cups finely chopped onions
1 clove of garlic, finely chopped
3 tablespoons corn oil
4 cups chicken stock
1 pound carrots, peeled, finely
　chopped

1 tablespoon minced
　crystallized ginger
1 chicken bouillon cube
1 teaspoon minced crystallized
　ginger
Chopped parsley to taste

Sauté onions and garlic in corn oil in soup pot over medium heat for 4 to 5 minutes or until tender; do not brown. Add chicken stock, carrots, 1 tablespoon ginger and bouillon cube. Cook for 30 minutes. Pour into blender or food processor container. Process until smooth. Add 1 teaspoon ginger and parsley. Process for several seconds. Serve immediately or store in refrigerator until serving time. Yield: 6 servings.

**Approx Per Serving:** Cal 139; Prot 5 g; Carbo 13 g; Fiber 3 g;
　　T Fat 8 g; Chol 1 mg; Sod 737 mg.

*F. Christopher Heyl, WEIU Friend*

# CARROT AND RED BELL PEPPER SOUP

1 large onion, chopped
2 medium red bell peppers,
　chopped
3 tablespoons butter
2 pounds carrots, chopped

4 cups chicken stock
1/4 to 1/2 cup low-fat milk
1/4 teaspoon nutmeg
Salt and white pepper to taste

Sauté onion and red peppers in butter in medium saucepan for 5 minutes or until tender. Add carrots and chicken stock. Simmer for 20 minutes or until carrots are very tender. Process in blender until smooth. Add enough milk to make of desired consistency. Return to saucepan. Add nutmeg, salt and pepper. Heat to serving temperature. Ladle into soup bowls. Garnish with seasoned croutons or dollop of sour cream. Yield: 8 servings.

**Approx Per Serving:** Cal 125; Prot 5 g; Carbo 15 g; Fiber 4 g;
　　T Fat 6 g; Chol 14 mg; Sod 472 mg.

*Jack B. Dailey, Jr., The College Club Restaurant*

1904-05　*Old Age Insurance was studied along with systems in*
　　　　　*European countries in the hopes of working out a plan*
　　　　　*for Massachusetts.*

## CHINESE CHICKEN SOUP

1  3-pound chicken, cut up
1  12-ounce bottle of beer

1  4-ounce can pickled
   cucumber

Rinse chicken. Combine chicken, beer and pickled cucumber in 6-quart stockpot. Add enough water to cover chicken. Simmer, covered, for 1½ hours. Remove and discard bones. Pickled cucumber is available at all Asian food stores. Yield: 6 servings.

Approx Per Serving: Cal 240; Prot 33 g; Carbo 3 g; Fiber 1 g;
   T Fat 8 g; Chol 101 mg; Sod 316 mg.

*Nancy C. Jacobson, WEIU Friend*

## CHICKEN VEGETABLE SOUP

4 chicken breast filets
2  14-ounce cans chicken broth
7 stalks celery
7 carrots, finely chopped
1 medium onion, finely chopped
Garlic salt and pepper to taste

2  10-ounce cans chicken with
   rice soup
½ cup uncooked orzo
2 cups uncooked medium egg
   noodles

Rinse chicken; place in 6-quart soup pot. Add water to fill pot ⅔ full. Bring to a boil; skim. Cut celery into ½-inch pieces. Add celery, carrots and onion to stockpot. Simmer for 45 minutes. Remove and chop chicken; return to stockpot. Add canned soup. Bring to a boil. Add orzo and noodles. Simmer for 25 minutes, stirring frequently. May add additional broth or canned soup if needed for desired consistency. Yield: 10 servings.

Approx Per Serving: Cal 141; Prot 13 g; Carbo 17 g; Fiber 3 g;
   T Fat 2 g; Chol 20 mg; Sod 694 mg.

*Dorothy Almeida, WEIU Friend*

1905  *An emergency loan department was established for students and others where they could borrow money for mortgage payments and other ventures. The first Community Credit Union was also opened.*

## THE REVEREND HALL'S CLAM CHOWDER

2 cups chopped potatoes
1 quart clams
1 cup cold water
1  2-inch cube salt pork,
    chopped
2 large onions, chopped

¼ cup butter
8 cups milk, scalded
3 tablespoons flour
1 tablespoon salt
½ teaspoon pepper
Worcestershire sauce to taste

Parboil potatoes; drain and set aside. Drain clams, reserving liquor. Add 1 cup cold water to reserved clam liquor; strain. Bring to a boil in saucepan; set aside. Cook salt pork with onions and butter in 6-quart soup pot over low heat for 5 minutes stirring constantly. Sprinkle with flour, salt and pepper. Stir in hot milk gradually. Add potatoes, clams and hot clam liquor, taking care that clam liquor is not hot enough to curdle the milk. Cook until chowder is consistency of heavy cream. Add Worcestershire sauce. *This recipe evolved from the relationship between the Reverend Hall and an old sea captain from Marblehead. It is a satisfying chowder that has fed the souls of many generations of Halls at Bible meetings and fish fries.* Yield: 6 servings.

**Approx Per Serving:** Cal 441; Prot 24 g; Carbo 41 g; Fiber 3 g;
    T Fat 21 g; Chol 92 mg; Sod 1349 mg.

*Gordon Hall III, WEIU Trustee*

## SOUTH DUXBURY CLAM CHOWDER

6 large potatoes
4 cups water
8 to 10 slices bacon
1 large onion

1 quart quahog meat
4 cups milk
2 tablespoons butter
Freshly ground pepper to taste

Peel and thinly slice potatoes. Cook in water in 4-quart saucepan for 10 minutes. Put bacon and onion through food chopper. Sauté bacon and onion in skillet until bacon is brown. Add to potatoes and cooking liquid. Chop clams finely, reserving all clam juice. Add clams and juice to potato mixture. Cook over medium-low heat for 1 hour. Add milk, butter and pepper. Heat to serving temperature. Garnish with finely chopped parsley. Flavor improves if made day before and reheated. You may substitute sea clams or chicken clams for quahogs but they must be finely ground. *This is the recipe of my grandmother, Cora Hazel Browne. We would walk through the mud in front of our house searching for quahogs with our toes.* Yield: 10 servings.

**Approx Per Serving:** Cal 321; Prot 20 g; Carbo 39 g; Fiber 3 g;
    T Fat 10 g; Chol 56 mg; Sod 222 mg.

*Susan R. Playfair, WEIU Friend*

# CORN CHOWDER

1 cup chopped celery
½ cup chopped green bell
  pepper
½ cup chopped red bell pepper
1 cup chopped ham

¼ cup butter
6  10-ounce cans corn niblets
4 medium potatoes, cubed
2 cups half and half

Sauté celery, green pepper, red pepper and ham in butter in stockpot until tender. Add corn and potatoes. Simmer for 20 minutes or until potatoes are tender. Stir in half and half. Heat to serving temperature. Ladle into bowls. Garnish with a dollop of butter and crumbled crisp-fried bacon, watercress, parsley or paprika. Yield: 8 servings.

**Approx Per Serving:** Cal 375; Prot 12 g; Carbo 53 g; Fiber 5 g;
   T Fat 15 g; Chol 47 mg; Sod 622 mg.

*Conger Metcalf, WEIU Friend*

# CAPE COD FISH CHOWDER

2 pounds fresh haddock
2 cups water
2 ounces salt pork, chopped
2 medium onions, sliced
1 cup chopped celery
4 large potatoes, chopped

1 bay leaf, crumbled
4 cups milk
2 tablespoons butter
1 teaspoon salt
Freshly ground pepper to taste

Simmer haddock in 2 cups water in saucepan for 15 minutes; drain, reserving fish broth. Remove skin and bones from fish. Sauté salt pork in large stockpot until crisp; discard salt pork, reserving pan drippings. Sauté onions in pan drippings until golden brown. Add fish, celery, potatoes and bay leaf. Add enough boiling water to fish broth to measure 3 cups. Add to soup pot. Simmer for 30 minutes, stirring occasionally. Add milk and butter. Simmer for 5 minutes longer or until of serving temperature. Add salt and pepper; mix well. Ladle into bowls. *This recipe has been a favorite in the Kennedy family for years.* Yield: 8 servings.

**Approx Per Serving:** Cal 343; Prot 32 g; Carbo 35 g; Fiber 3 g;
   T Fat 9 g; Chol 93 mg; Sod 477 mg.

*U. S. Senator Edward M. Kennedy, WEIU Friend*

**1906** *The Inter-Municipal Research Committee (with local committees in New York and Philadelphia) studied the conditions which attend household work. It gave a fellowship to a student at Tufts College who studied the lodging house conditions in the West End of Boston.*

## LENTIL AND BROWN RICE SOUP

5 cups (or more) chicken broth
3 cups (or more) water
1½ cups dried lentils, rinsed
1 cup uncooked long grain
  brown rice
1  35-ounce can tomatoes,
  chopped
3 carrots, chopped into ¼-inch
  pieces
1 large onion, chopped

½ cup chopped celery
3 cloves of garlic, minced
½ teaspoon basil
½ teaspoon oregano
½ teaspoon thyme
1 bay leaf
½ cup finely chopped parsley
Salt and freshly ground pepper
  to taste

Combine chicken broth, water, lentils, rice, undrained tomatoes, carrots, onion, celery, garlic, basil, oregano, thyme and bay leaf in stockpot. Simmer for 45 to 55 minutes or until lentils and rice are tender, stirring occasionally. Discard bay leaf. Stir in parsley, salt and pepper. May add additional broth or water for desired consistency. Ladle into bowls. Garnish with grated Romano cheese and serve with fresh crusty bread. Yield: 10 servings.

**Approx Per Serving:** Cal 178; Prot 13 g; Carbo 30 g; Fiber 6 g;
    T Fat 1 g; Chol 1 mg; Sod 671 mg.

*Mary Ellen Pedulla, WEIU Friend*

## BASE FOR LOBSTER BISQUE

25 pounds lobster bodies and
  heads
2 pounds onions
1 pound carrots
1 pound celery
¾ cup whole black peppercorns
20 bay leaves
1 pound of butter

2 bottles of brandy
20 gallons fresh lobster stock
2½ ounces Worcestershire sauce
½ ounce Tabasco sauce
3 pounds butter   •
3 pounds margarine
1½ pounds Hungarian paprika
3 cups flour

Sauté lobster bodies, lobster heads, onions, carrots, celery, peppercorns and bay leaves in 1 pound butter in large skillet. Flame with 1 bottle of brandy. Purée lobster meat and vegetables in food processor. Add to lobster stock in stockpot. Add Worcestershire sauce and Tabasco sauce. Bring to a boil. Melt 3 pounds butter and margarine in saucepan. Stir in flour and paprika. Cook until light brown, stirring constantly. Add to soup pot. Add remaining brandy. Simmer for 1 hour. Press through strainer. Cool lobster bisque base. To make bisque, reheat base in small amounts with enough light cream to make of desired consistency, approximately 2 parts base to 1½ parts cream. Yield: 15 gallons base.

Nutritional analysis for this recipe is not available.

*Anthony Athanas, Anthony's Pier 4 Restaurant*

## MEXICAN OATMEAL SOUP

1¹/₃ cups oats
¹/₂ cup butter
1 large onion, chopped
3 cloves of garlic, minced

6 cups chicken broth
1 teaspoon salt
2 large tomatoes, chopped

Toast oats in large heavy skillet over medium heat, stirring constantly. Remove to bowl. Melt butter in skillet. Add onion, garlic, chicken broth, salt, tomatoes and toasted oats. Simmer over medium heat for 6 minutes, stirring frequently. Serve hot. Yield: 8 servings.

**Approx Per Serving:** Cal 197; Prot 7 g; Carbo 13 g; Fiber 2 g;
   T Fat 14 g; Chol 32 mg; Sod 949 mg.

*Tracy and Brett Dubin, WEIU Friends*

## MINESTRONE

1 pound sweet Italian sausage
2 tablespoons olive oil
1 cup chopped onion
1 clove of garlic, minced
1 cup chopped carrots
1 teaspoon basil
1   16-ounce can Italian
   tomatoes, chopped

2 zucchini, sliced
2   10-ounce cans bouillon
2 cups shredded cabbage
Salt and pepper to taste
1   16-ounce can white kidney
   beans
¹/₂ cup red wine
¹/₂ cup uncooked rice

Cut sausage into slices. Brown sausage in olive oil in skillet, stirring frequently. Add onion, garlic, carrots and basil. Cook for 5 minutes, stirring frequently. Add tomatoes, zucchini, bouillon, cabbage, salt and pepper. Simmer, covered, for 1 hour, stirring occasionally. Add kidney beans, red wine and rice; mix well. Simmer for 20 minutes. Store in refrigerator. Reheat for 20 minutes to serve. Ladle into bowls; garnish with grated cheese. Yield: 8 servings.

**Approx Per Serving:** Cal 346; Prot 18 g; Carbo 32 g; Fiber 6 g;
   T Fat 16 g; Chol 36 mg; Sod 660 mg.

*Bruce Schwoegler, WBZ-TV/WBMX Radio*

1907 *The School Gardens Committee worked with the Boston
School Committee to create twelve school gardens.*

## BILINGUAL ONION SOUP

4 whole cloves
2 cloves of garlic
2 tablespoons unsalted butter
6 large white onions, sliced into
 1/4-inch rings
6 cups concentrated beef
 bouillon
2 cups chicken consommé
Freshly ground pepper

1 teaspoon liquid Maggi
 seasoning
Salt to taste
1/4 cup dry sherry
4 eggs, at room temperature
8 slices French baguette bread,
 toasted
1/4 cup grated Parmesan cheese

Place 2 cloves in each garlic clove. Heat butter in large skillet until it begins to brown. Add garlic and onions. Cook slowly until golden brown, stirring constantly. Add beef bouillon, consommé, pepper, Maggi seasoning and salt. Simmer until reduced by 1/3 and soup is a rich brown color, stirring occasionally. Discard garlic. Add sherry; mix well. Heat to serving temperature. Ladle into 4 bowls. Drop 1 egg into each bowl; top with French bread. Sprinkle with Parmesan cheese. This soup is a combination of 2 favorite soups: Spanish Garlic Soup and French Onion Soup. It is a meal in itself served with a salad and wine or dark ale. Yield: 4 servings.

**Approx Per Serving:** Cal 497; Prot 24 g; Carbo 55 g; Fiber 5 g;
 T Fat 18 g; Chol 234 mg; Sod 2137 mg.

*Lotte Mendelsohn, **The Boston Tab***

## EASY FRENCH ONION SOUP

2 large onions, sliced into rings
2 tablespoons butter
2  10-ounce cans beef consommé

1 consommé can water
Dash of Master Gravy

Sauté onions in butter in skillet until transparent. Combine consommé, water and Master Gravy in 4-quart soup pot; mix well. Add onions. Simmer for 1 hour, stirring occasionally. Ladle into bowls. Garnish with toasted French bread and melted mozzarella cheese. Yield: 4 servings.

**Approx Per Serving:** Cal 191; Prot 10 g; Carbo 20 g; Fiber 2 g;
 T Fat 7 g; Chol 22 mg; Sod 713 mg.

*Joann Tourville, WEIU Friend*

1907  *The Legal Aid Department made a persistent campaign against fraudulent advertisements that offer home work to women.*

## Oxtail Soup St. Botolph

1/2 cup chopped salt pork
5 pounds oxtails
2 tablespoons flour
1 teaspoon salt
1/4 teaspoon pepper
1 medium onion, chopped
2 medium carrots, chopped

1 small turnip, chopped
1 cup chopped celery
1 clove of garlic, minced
3 bay leaves
1 cup red wine
1 cup tomato juice
5 cups beef broth

Sauté salt pork in Dutch oven until brown. Cut oxtails at joints. Coat with mixture of flour, salt and pepper. Add to Dutch oven. Cook until brown, stirring occasionally. Add onion, carrots, turnip, celery, garlic and bay leaves. Cook for 5 minutes, stirring constantly. Add wine, tomato juice and beef broth; mix well. Bring to a boil. Bake, covered, at 450 degrees for 2 hours. Serve hot. Yield: 4 servings.

**Approx Per Serving:** Cal 192; Prot 7 g; Carbo 17 g; Fiber 4 g;
T Fat 7 g; Chol 12 mg; Sod 1044 mg.
Nutritional analysis does not include oxtails.

*Mario L. Bouello, St. Botolph's Restaurant*

## Potato Soup

1 pound mushrooms, chopped
4 teaspoons butter
1/2 stalk celery, chopped
2 onions, chopped
3 carrots, chopped
5 pounds potatoes, peeled,
chopped

1  5-ounce can evaporated milk
1/2 teaspoon salt
1/2 teaspoon pepper
1 1/2 pounds Velveeta cheese,
cubed

Brown mushrooms in butter in large stockpot, stirring frequently. Add celery, onions, carrots, potatoes and enough water to cover vegetables. Simmer, covered, until vegetables are tender, stirring occasionally. Stir in evaporated milk, salt, pepper and cheese. Heat to serving temperature. May use Mexican Velveeta cheese or add clams. Yield: 12 servings.

**Approx Per Serving:** Cal 516; Prot 20 g; Carbo 57 g; Fiber 6 g;
T Fat 24 g; Chol 73 mg; Sod 986 mg.

*Michelle Camp, WEIU Friend*

1908  *The School of Salesmanship graduated 47 women into permanent positions in leading department stores.*

## ARLENE'S CURRIED PUMPKIN MUSHROOM SOUP

8 ounces mushrooms, sliced
1 small onion, chopped
2 tablespoons margarine
2 tablespoons flour
1 teaspoon curry powder
3 cups chicken broth
2 cups puréed pumpkin

1 tablespoon honey
1/2 teaspoon cinnamon
1/4 teaspoon nutmeg
1 teaspoon salt
1/4 teaspoon pepper
1 cup half and half

Sauté mushrooms and onion in margarine in large skillet for 7 minutes or until soft. Stir in flour and curry powder. Add chicken broth a small amount at a time, mixing well after each addition. Add pumpkin, honey, cinnamon, nutmeg, salt and pepper; mix well. Simmer for 45 minutes to 1 hour or until thickened to desired consistency. Stir in half and half. Heat to serving temperature. Serve hot or cold. Garnish with nutmeg, sour cream or yogurt. *The Union was an invaluable resource to me when I was unemployed.* Yield: 6 servings.

**Approx Per Serving:** Cal 234; Prot 6 g; Carbo 16 g; Fiber 3 g;
        T Fat 17 g; Chol 45 mg; Sod 808 mg.

*Ellen Elk, WEIU Friend*

## SPINACH AND GARLIC SOUP

12 ounces garlic
Thyme to taste
1 teaspoon sage
1 bay leaf
2 tablespoons olive oil
2 quarts chicken stock

4 ounces fresh bread crumbs
Salt and pepper to taste
4 ounces chopped spinach,
    blanched
2 cups whipping cream

Sauté garlic with thyme, sage and bay leaf in olive oil in 4-quart saucepan. Add chicken stock. Simmer for 15 to 20 minutes. Add bread crumbs to thicken; beat with mixer to purée. Pour soup into fine sieve, pressing through with spoon. Combine with salt and pepper in saucepan. Stir in spinach and cream. Heat to serving temperature. This recipe is from the Mediterranean region where I worked for 5 years. It is simple, tasty and healthy. Yield: 8 servings.

**Approx Per Serving:** Cal 379; Prot 10 g; Carbo 24 g; Fiber 1 g;
        T Fat 28 g; Chol 83 mg; Sod 888 mg.

*Serge Wechseler, Silks Restaurant at Stonehedge Inn*

# Rice and Shrimp Soup

1/2 cup chopped onion
1/2 cup chopped green bell
  pepper
1/4 cup water
1  28-ounce can tomatoes,
  chopped
1/2 teaspoon minced garlic
Hot pepper sauce to taste
1/4 teaspoon rosemary

1/4 teaspoon paprika
1/4 teaspoon pepper
1 1/2 cups water
1  6 1/4-ounce package
  quick-cooking long grain and
  wild rice mix
16 ounces peeled medium
  shrimp

Combine onion, green pepper and 1/4 cup water in large saucepan. Simmer for 3 minutes or until tender. Add undrained tomatoes, garlic, hot pepper sauce, rosemary, paprika and pepper; mix well. Add water and both packets from rice mix. Bring to a boil. Add shrimp. Simmer for 4 to 5 minutes or until rice is tender. Ladle into soup bowls. Serve with additional hot pepper sauce. Yield: 6 servings.

**Approx Per Serving:** Cal 199; Prot 16 g; Carbo 31 g; Fiber 2 g;
  T Fat 1 g; Chol 118 mg; Sod 352 mg.

*Annette O'Connor, WEIU Friend*

# Butternut Squash Soup

1 large onion, coarsely chopped
6 tablespoons butter
1 large butternut squash,
  peeled, coarsely chopped
4 cups chicken stock
Juice and rind of 1 orange

2 Bosc pears, peeled, coarsley
  chopped
Salt and freshly ground pepper
  to taste
Nutmeg and allspice to taste

Cook onion in butter in large saucepan until soft, stirring frequently. Add squash. Cook for 5 minutes, stirring frequently. Add chicken stock, juice and rind of orange, pears, salt, pepper, nutmeg and allspice. Simmer, covered, for 30 minutes or until orange rind and squash are tender. Purée in blender or food processor. Pour into saucepan. Heat to serving temperature. *I have used this recipe as the first course of Thanksgiving dinner since I discovered it about 8 years ago. It always gets rave reviews.* Yield: 6 servings.

**Approx Per Serving:** Cal 232; Prot 5 g; Carbo 27 g; Fiber 6 g;
  T Fat 13 g; Chol 32 mg; Sod 620 mg.

*Sarie Booy, WEIU Member*

# TOMATO ALFREDO SOUP

1 pound lean ground beef
1 medium Spanish onion,
  chopped
1  28-ounce can tomato purée
1  28-ounce can beef broth
1 broth can water
1 tablespoon salt
1/4 teaspoon white pepper

1 1/2 tablespoons sugar
1 teaspoon oregano
2 teaspoons dried basil
1/2 cup fresh basil leaves,
  chopped
1 cup grated Parmesan cheese
1 cup sour cream
1 cup half and half

Brown ground beef with onion in 4-quart skillet, stirring frequently; drain. Add tomato purée, beef broth and water; mix well. Bring to a boil. Add salt, white pepper, sugar, oregano, dried basil, fresh basil, Parmesan cheese and sour cream. Simmer over low heat for 1 1/4 hours, stirring occasionally. Add half and half. Simmer for 20 minutes longer, stirring occasionally. Store in refrigerator for 24 hours to enhance flavor. Heat to serving temperature. Ladle into bowls. Garnish with additional fresh chopped basil. Serve with tossed salad and fresh French bread. Yield: 10 servings.

**Approx Per Serving:** Cal 294; Prot 15 g; Carbo 13 g; Fiber 2 g;
  T Fat 21 g; Chol 71 mg; Sod 1111 mg.

*Dennis J. McMath, The Tavern Club Restaurant*

# TOMATO BISQUE

1/2 cup chopped onion
1/4 cup chopped green onions
1/4 cup chopped celery
1/4 cup butter
3 tomatoes, chopped
1  10-ounce can beef bouillon

2 teaspoons salt
1/4 teaspoon basil
1/4 cup flour
1/4 cup butter, softened
1/4 cup dry vermouth
1 cup half and half

Sauté onion, green onions and celery in 1/4 cup butter in skillet until celery is tender. Add tomatoes, beef bouillon, salt and basil. Simmer for 30 minutes. Cool slightly. Purée in blender. Pour through sieve into saucepan. Bring to a boil. Blend flour into remaining 1/4 cup butter in bowl. Stir a small amount at a time into hot soup until soup is thickened. Add vermouth and half and half. Heat to serving temperature; do not boil. Garnish with sour cream and chopped parsley. This is nice to start off a winter dinner. Yield: 8 servings.

**Approx Per Serving:** Cal 253; Prot 3 g; Carbo 13 g; Fiber 3 g;
  T Fat 21 g; Chol 64 mg; Sod 774 mg.

*Dorothea J. Mahoney, WEIU Friend*

## CHILLED TOMATO AND DILL SOUP

4 medium onions, finely
  chopped
3 tablespoons vegetable oil
3 pounds fresh tomatoes,
  coarsely chopped
1/4 cup catsup
2 cups ice water

2 1/2 tablespoons finely chopped
  fresh dill
1 teaspoon salt
1/4 teaspoon Tabasco
1/2 cup sour cream
6 sprigs fresh dill

Sauté onions in oil in saucepan for 5 minutes or until tender and golden brown. Add tomatoes. Cook over medium heat for 20 to 30 minutes or until tender, stirring frequently. Put mixture through Foley food mill or purée in blender. Combine with catsup, ice water, dill, salt and Tabasco sauce in bowl; mix well. Chill in refrigerator for 4 hours or until very cold. Serve in glass bowls. Garnish with sour cream and sprig of fresh dill. Yield: 6 servings.

**Approx Per Serving:** Cal 194; Prot 4 g; Carbo 21 g; Fiber 5 g;
  T Fat 12 g; Chol 9 mg; Sod 507 mg.

*Sara Cowles Walden, WEIU Member*

## TOMATO ORANGE SOUP

2 pounds fresh tomatoes,
  peeled, chopped
1 onion, chopped
1 quart chicken stock
1 medium carrot, scraped, thinly
  sliced
1 bay leaf
1 strip lemon rind

1/2 teaspoon freshly ground
  pepper
3 tablespoons sugar
Chopped basil to taste
3 tablespoons melted butter
3 tablespoons flour
Juice of 2 oranges
2 tablespoons chopped parsley

Combine tomatoes, onion, chicken stock, carrot, bay leaf, lemon rind, pepper, sugar and basil in 3-quart saucepan; mix well. Simmer for 30 to 35 minutes, stirring frequently. Blend melted butter and flour in skillet. Add 1/2 cup soup. Simmer for 1 minute, stirring constantly. Add to soup. Simmer for 2 minutes, stirring frequently. Cool slightly. Discard lemon rind and bay leaf. Purée a small amount of soup at a time in blender container. Pour into saucepan. Add orange juice; mix well. Adjust seasoning. Heat to serving temperature. Add parsley. Ladle into bowls. Garnish with sour cream. Yield: 8 servings.

**Approx Per Serving:** Cal 101; Prot 5 g; Carbo 19 g; Fiber 3 g;
  T Fat 1 g; Chol 1 mg; Sod 287 mg.

*Alice P. Williams, WEIU Friend*

# VEGETABLE CHOWDER

1 cup chopped onion
1 cup chopped celery
1 cup chopped carrots
1/2 cup chopped green bell
  pepper
2 tablespoons butter
1 cup chopped potato
1 1/2 cups chopped turnips
1 cup chopped cabbage

4 cups water
1/4 cup chopped fresh parsley
1/4 teaspoon curry powder
1/4 teaspoon nutmeg
1/4 teaspoon tarragon
Salt and pepper to taste
2 tablespoons flour
4 cups milk

Sauté onion, celery, carrots and green pepper in butter in stockpot until onions are golden. Add potato, turnips and water. Simmer for 40 minutes or until vegetables are tender, stirring occasionally. Add cabbage. Simmer for 5 minutes longer, stirring occasionally. Add parsley, curry powder, nutmeg, tarragon, salt and pepper. Add mixture of flour and milk to chowder. Heat to serving temperature; do not boil. May chill overnight to enhance flavor and reheat. *This was served every Thursday in Union restaurants.* Yield: 10 servings.

**Approx Per Serving:** Cal 129; Prot 5 g; Carbo 16 g; Fiber 2 g;
    T Fat 6 g; Chol 19 mg; Sod 92 mg.

*Helen H. Hodgdon, Former WEIU Food Shop Director*

# WINTER VEGETABLE SOUP

2 cups chopped onions
1/4 cup butter
2 tablespoons flour
6 cups chicken broth
2 cups chopped potatoes
Small bunch parsley, tied
2 bay leaves
Salt and white pepper to taste

1 cup chopped turnip
1 cup chopped celery
1/2 to 1 cup whipping cream
3 or 4 carrots, julienned
6 large mushrooms, thinly sliced
2 large leeks, julienned
1 tablespoon butter

Sauté onions in 1/4 cup butter in stockpot until tender. Add flour, mixing well. Cook for 2 minutes, stirring constantly. Add chicken broth gradually, stirring constantly. Add potatoes, parsley, bay leaves, salt and white pepper. Simmer, uncovered, until potatoes are tender-crisp. Cook turnip in a small amount of salted water in saucepan until tender; drain. Add celery and turnip to soup; mix well. Add whipping cream; mix well. Discard parsley and bay leaves. Adjust seasoning. Sauté carrots, mushrooms and leeks in remaining 1 tablespoon butter in skillet until tender; do not brown. Ladle soup into bowls; top with sautéed vegetables. May serve over toast points. Yield: 6 servings.

**Approx Per Serving:** Cal 415; Prot 10 g; Carbo 37 g; Fiber 6 g;
    T Fat 26 g; Chol 81 mg; Sod 935 mg.

*Barbara Mohrman, WEIU President, Board of Trustees*

**The Horn Bookshop for Boys and Girls**
*Founded in 1916, the Bookshop evolved into the* **Horn Book Magazine.**

# Meat and Meatless Main Dishes

## *To Roast Veal:*

Take a piece suitable for baking, cut gashes an inch long, and put in bits of salt pork cut in thin slices; cook in a slow oven about 2 hours; when done melt butter in size of an egg and pour over the top. This is delicious.

*P.G.*
*from The Kirmess Cookbook, 1887*

# BEEF WITH BROCCOLI

1 tablespoon soy sauce
1 tablespoon rice wine or dry
  sherry
1 tablespoon cornstarch
1 teaspoon water
8 to 12 ounces flank steak

3 tablespoons oil
1 cup broccoli flowerets
1½ tablespoons oyster sauce
1 tablespoon soy sauce
¼ cup beef stock or water

Combine 1 tablespoon soy sauce, wine, cornstarch and water in bowl; mix well. Cut steak into 1x2-inch pieces ⅛ inch thick. Add to marinade; mix well. Marinate for 20 to 30 minutes. Stir in 1 tablespoon oil. Heat 1 tablespoon oil in skillet over high heat. Add beef mixture. Stir-fry just until beef is cooked through. Remove with slotted spoon. Add remaining 1 tablespoon oil and broccoli to skillet. Stir-fry until broccoli is done to taste. Combine oyster sauce, 1 tablespoon soy sauce and beef stock in bowl; mix well. Pour into skillet; add beef. Cook until heated through, stirring to coat beef well. Serve over rice. Oyster sauce can be purchased at most supermarkets and Asian markets. Yield: 2 servings.

**Approx Per Serving:** Cal 452; Prot 35 g; Carbo 7 g; Fiber 1 g;
  T Fat 31 g; Chol 97 mg; Sod 1095 mg.
Nutritional information does not include oyster sauce.

*Stanley Wong, WEIU Friend*

# CHUTNEY POT ROAST

1  3½-pound arm or blade pot
   roast
2 tablespoons shortening
1½ teaspoons salt

⅛ teaspoon pepper
½ cup chutney
¼ cup water

Brown roast in shortening in heavy saucepan; drain. Season roast with salt and pepper. Add mixture of chutney and water. Simmer, tightly covered, for 3 to 3½ hours or until tender. May thicken pan juices with flour if desired. May roast in oven if preferred. Serve with buttered Brussels sprouts, peanut-garnished rice and Waldorf salad. Yield: 8 servings.

**Approx Per Serving:** Cal 328; Prot 43 g; Carbo 0 g; Fiber 0 g;
  T Fat 16 g; Chol 131 mg; Sod 469 mg.
Nutritional information does not include chutney.

*Mrs. Charles Inches, WEIU Friend*

1908  *The Research Department studied child labor in Massachusetts,*
      *employees' insurance against illness, and opportunities for*
      *educated women in careers other than teaching.*

## GRILLED PEPPERED STEAK WITH MAPLE CIDER GLAZE

2 cups veal stock
1/4 cup pure maple syrup
1 cup apple cider
1/4 cup balsamic vinegar
Salt and freshly cracked pepper
1 small red onion, finely
  chopped
1/2 green bell pepper, finely
  chopped

4 apples, peeled, finely chopped
1/4 cup butter
1/4 cup roasted chopped pecans
1/4 cup pure maple syrup
3 tablespoons cider vinegar
2 tablespoons chopped fresh
  sage
4  12-ounce New York  sirloin
  steaks

Combine veal stock, 1/4 cup maple syrup and apple cider in saucepan; mix well. Simmer for 30 to 40 minutes or until reduced by 2/3. Stir in balsamic vinegar. Simmer for 10 minutes longer. Season with salt and pepper; set aside. Sauté onion, bell pepper and apples for 3 to 4 minutes in butter in skillet. Add pecans, 1/4 cup maple syrup, cider vinegar, sage, salt and pepper. Cook for 2 minutes longer. Adjust salt and pepper. Rub steaks with cracked pepper. Grill over medium-high heat for 4 to 5 minutes on each side. Place on serving plates. Spoon glaze over steaks. Serve with Apple Pecan Relish. Yield: 4 servings.

**Approx Per Serving:** Cal 786; Prot 60 g; Carbo 58 g; Fiber 4 g;
  T Fat 35 g; Chol 185 mg; Sod 632 mg.

*Chris Schlesinger, East Coast Grill Restaurant*

## LONDON BROIL FOR TWO

2 tablespoons minced shallots
1 1/2 tablespoons olive oil
1 tablespoon soy sauce
Juice of 1/2 lemon

1/2 teaspoon thyme
1/8 teaspoon cayenne pepper
12 ounces London broil

Combine shallots, olive oil, soy sauce, lemon juice, thyme and cayenne pepper in bowl; mix well. Trim beef; score lightly on both sides. Spread both sides with marinade; place in broiler pan. Marinate, covered with plastic wrap, in refrigerator for several hours to overnight. Preheat broiler. Broil steak very close to heat source for 3 to 4 minutes on 1 side. Turn steak. Broil for just a few minutes or until seared on outside and rare in center. Slice diagonally cross grain. Place on serving plate; pour pan juices over top. Garnish with parsley. Serve with buttered parsley potatoes and Brussels sprouts or snow peas. Accompany with a robust Burgundy.
Yield: 2 servings.

**Approx Per Serving:** Cal 328; Prot 33 g; Carbo 3 g; Fiber <1 g;
  T Fat 20 g; Chol 96 mg; Sod 568 mg.

*Paul Leahy, WEIU Trustee*

# SHISH KABOBS

1/2 cup corn oil
1/2 cup lemon juice
1 medium onion, chopped
10 cloves of garlic
1/2 teaspoon oregano
1 teaspoon dry mustard
1 teaspoon salt
1/8 teaspoon pepper

1 1/2 pounds beef cubes
8 small onions
2 medium tomatoes, cut into
  wedges
2 medium green bell peppers,
  cut into pieces
8 small mushrooms

Combine oil, lemon juice, chopped onion, garlic, oregano, dry mustard, salt and pepper in bowl; mix well. Add beef, coating well. Marinate in refrigerator for 4 hours to overnight. Drain, reserving marinade; discard garlic. Cook small onions in boiling salted water in saucepan for 5 minutes. Alternate beef, tomatoes, green peppers, onions and mushrooms on skewers. Brush vegetables with marinade. Grill until done to taste, basting with reserved marinade as desired. Yield: 6 servings.

**Approx Per Serving:** Cal 402; Prot 25 g; Carbo 21 g; Fiber 4 g;
T Fat 25 g; Chol 64 mg; Sod 402 mg.

*Anita MacKinnon, WEIU Employee*

# BURGUNDY BEEFBURGERS

1 cup fresh bread crumbs
1/4 cup Burgundy
2 pounds ground beef
1 egg
2 scallions, sliced

1 1/2 teaspoons salt
Pepper to taste
1/2 cup butter
2 scallions, sliced
1/4 cup Burgundy

Combine bread crumbs with 1/4 cup wine in bowl; mix well. Let stand for several minutes. Add ground beef, egg, 2 scallions, salt and pepper; mix well. Shape into 8 patties. Place on rack in broiler pan. Melt butter in saucepan. Add 2 scallions and 1/4 cup wine. Brush over patties. Broil patties for 8 to 10 minutes per side, basting with sauce. This is a good recipe for tailgate parties or picnics at the beach. Yield: 8 servings.

**Approx Per Serving:** Cal 369; Prot 23 g; Carbo 3 g; Fiber <1 g;
T Fat 28 g; Chol 132 mg; Sod 600 mg.

*Jean McMurtry, WEIU Member*

1908   *An exhibit of needlework from the Handwork Shop was
sent to the Convention of the National Society for the
Promotion of Industrial Education, which was held in Chicago.*

# FRENCH BURGERS

1 egg
1½ pounds ground beef
1  4-ounce can mushroom
  pieces, drained

2 tablespoons chopped parsley
Garlic salt and pepper to taste
½ cup (about) red wine

Beat egg with fork in bowl. Add ground beef, mushrooms, parsley, garlic salt and pepper; mix well. Add as much wine as can be absorbed for desired consistency. Shape into patties. Grill until done to taste. Serve with thickly sliced French bread. Yield: 6 servings.

**Approx Per Serving:** Cal 214; Prot 18 g; Carbo 2 g; Fiber <1 g;
  T Fat 14 g; Chol 94 mg; Sod 65 mg.

*Judy Blackburn, WEIU Employee*

# BROILED HAMBURGERS WITH VINAIGRETTE SAUCE

½ yellow onion, finely chopped
1 tablespoon peanut oil
½ clove of garlic, minced
12 ounces ground sirloin

⅛ teaspoon thyme
⅛ teaspoon cayenne pepper
2 tablespoons Vinaigrette Sauce

Sauté onion in peanut oil until onion is translucent. Add garlic. Sauté for 1 minute. Shape ground sirloin into 2 ovals. Spread with onion mixture; sprinkle with thyme and cayenne pepper. Fold over to enclose filling, shaping into patties and sealing edges. Place on rack in broiler pan. Broil until done to taste. Spoon 1 tablespoon Vinaigrette Sauce onto each patty; garnish with parsley. Yield: 2 servings.

**Approx Per Serving:** Cal 434; Prot 37 g; Carbo 3 g; Fiber <1 g;
  T Fat 30 g; Chol 98 mg; Sod 100 mg.
  Nutritional analysis includes Vinaigrette Sauce.

*Paul Leahy, WEIU Trustee*

# VINAIGRETTE SAUCE

1 tablespoon French mustard
1½ tablespoons red wine
  vinegar
3 ounces virgin olive oil

3 ounces peanut oil
½ clove of garlic, minced
Tabasco sauce to taste

Combine mustard, vinegar, olive oil, peanut oil, garlic and Tabasco sauce in covered jar; shake to mix well. Store indefinitely in refrigerator. Use with beef, chicken or grilled tomatoes. Yield: 12 tablespoons.

**Approx Per Tablespoon:** Cal 127; Prot <1 g; Carbo <1 g; Fiber <1 g;
  T Fat 14 g; Chol 0 mg; Sod 16 mg.

*Paul Leahy, WEIU Trustee*

# GREEK-STYLE MOUSSAKA

4　1-pound eggplant
Salt to taste
1/2 cup flour
1/2 cup oil
3 pounds ground beef
1 onion, chopped
1 cup chopped green bell pepper
6 stalks celery, chopped
2 sprigs of parsley, chopped
1 clove of garlic, chopped
1 cup wine
1 cup tomato paste

2 cups water
6 eggs, beaten
1/2 cup grated Parmesan cheese
1 cup shortening
1 cup flour
1 quart milk, warmed
6 eggs, beaten
1/2 cup grated Parmesan cheese
1 teaspoon nutmeg
1 teaspoon salt
1/2 teaspoon white pepper

Slice eggplant lengthwise into 3/4-inch slices. Soak in salted water to cover in bowl for 20 minutes. Drain and pat dry. Coat with 1/2 cup flour. Fry in oil in skillet for 5 minutes on each side; drain. Brown ground beef with onion, green pepper, celery, parsley and garlic in skillet, stirring frequently; drain. Stir in wine, tomato paste and water. Simmer for 15 minutes. Cool to room temperature. Stir in 6 eggs and 1/2 cup cheese. Alternate layers of eggplant and meat sauce in 12x15-inch baking pan. Melt shortening in saucepan. Stir in 1 cup flour. Cook for several minutes, stirring constantly. Stir in milk. Cook over low heat until thickened, stirring constantly. Stir a small amount of hot mixture into 6 eggs; stir eggs into hot mixture. Add 1/2 cup cheese, nutmeg, 1 teaspoon salt and pepper. Pour over layers in baking pan. Bake at 375 degrees for 40 minutes. Cut into 4x4-inch squares. Serve with rice pilaf. Yield: 10 servings.

**Approx Per Serving:** Cal 830; Prot 39 g; Carbo 35 g; Fiber 8 g;
　　T Fat 60 g; Chol 345 mg; Sod 597 mg.
　　Nutritional information includes entire amount of oil
　　for frying eggplant.

*Raymond Bandar, Averof Restaurant*

1909　*The Research Department supported four college fellowships—
one each at Columbia, Radcliffe, Simmons, and Wellesley.*

# MEATBALLS PIEDMONT

2 pounds ground beef
1/2 clove of garlic, crushed
1 medium onion, finely chopped
1 cup bread crumbs
1 tablespoon Worcestershire
  sauce
Dash of Tabasco sauce
1/4 teaspoon each savory,
  oregano and paprika
2 teaspoons salt
1/4 cup (about) flour

4 slices bacon, chopped
3/4 cup Burgundy
1 cup strong coffee
1 teaspoon sugar
1 teaspoon salt
1 1/2 tablespoons flour
1/4 cup water
1   16-ounce package fettucini,
  cooked
1 cup sour cream

Combine ground beef, garlic, onion, bread crumbs, Worcestershire sauce, Tabasco sauce, savory, oregano, paprika and 2 teaspoons salt in bowl; mix well. Shape into 2-inch meatballs. Coat with flour. Cook bacon in skillet until crisp; remove with slotted spoon. Add meatballs to drippings in skillet. Cook until lightly browned on all sides. Add wine, coffee, sugar and 1 teaspoon salt; mix well. Simmer for 15 minutes. Blend 1 1/2 tablespoons flour with water in cup. Stir with bacon into meatballs. Simmer for 5 minutes. Serve on fettucini; top with sour cream. Yield: 8 servings.

**Approx Per Serving:** Cal 613; Prot 33 g; Carbo 59 g; Fiber 1 g;
    T Fat 25 g; Chol 90 mg; Sod 512 mg.

*Margot Kittredge, WEIU Member*

# MAJOR GREY MEAT LOAF

2 pounds lean ground beef
2 tablespoons oil
1 large onion, finely chopped
2 cloves of garlic, minced
1/2 cup bread crumbs

1/2 cup Major Grey chutney
1/4 cup plain yogurt
2 to 3 teaspoons curry powder
Salt and pepper to taste
2 eggs, beaten

Combine ground beef and oil in large bowl; mix well. Mix onion, garlic, bread crumbs, chutney, yogurt, curry powder, salt and pepper in bowl, chopping large pieces of mango in chutney if necessary. Add eggs; mix well. Add to ground beef; mix well. Shape into loaf and place in lightly greased 5x9-inch loaf pan. Score top in pattern with tines of fork. Bake, covered with foil, at 350 degrees for 45 minutes. Bake, uncovered, for 15 minutes longer. Remove to serving plate. May cool for 20 to 30 minutes, cover with foil and weight with heavy object; store in refrigerator for 2 to 3 days and serve cold as paté. Yield: 6 servings.

**Approx Per Serving:** Cal 462; Prot 36 g; Carbo 9 g; Fiber 1 g;
    T Fat 31 g; Chol 184 mg; Sod 190 mg.
    Nutritional information does not include chutney.

*Serena Gibson, WEIU Friend*

## EASY AND ELEGANT MEAT LOAF

1 pound lean ground beef
1 egg
1 onion, chopped
1 cup milk

1 cup corn bread stuffing mix
1/2 cup Dijon mustard
1/2 cup light mayonnaise

Combine ground beef, egg, onion, milk and stuffing mix in bowl; mix well. Pack into loaf pan. Bake at 325 degrees for 40 to 45 minutes or until done to taste. Remove to serving plate. Combine mustard and mayonnaise in small bowl; mix well. Serve with meat loaf. Garnish with parsley. Yield: 6 servings.

Approx Per Serving: Cal 309; Prot 19 g; Carbo 15 g; Fiber 1 g;
　　T Fat 18 g; Chol 90 mg; Sod 536 mg.

*Mrs. Hollis Plimpton, WEIU Trustee, Former WEIU President*

## MOM'S MEAT LOAF

1 pound ground beef
1 medium onion, chopped
1/2 cup bread crumbs
1 egg
Oregano, garlic salt, salt and
　pepper to taste

1/4 cup catsup
1/4 cup water
1/4 cup catsup
2 tablespoons mustard
2 tablespoons brown sugar

Combine ground beef, onion, bread crumbs, egg, oregano, garlic salt, salt, pepper and 1/4 cup catsup in bowl; mix well. Place in 9x11-inch baking dish. Pour water around loaf. Spread 1/4 cup catsup and mustard over top; sprinkle with brown sugar. Bake at 350 degrees for 40 to 45 minutes or until done to taste. Serve with mashed potatoes, brown gravy and green peas. May serve cold in sandwiches. Yield: 6 servings.

Approx Per Serving: Cal 247; Prot 17 g; Carbo 17 g; Fiber 1 g;
　　T Fat 12 g; Chol 85 mg; Sod 409 mg.

*Gina O'Connor, WEIU Friend*

**1910** *The Room Registry maintained a list of close to 400 rooms available for rent in Boston, Brookline, and Cambridge.*

# CHEATIN' CHILI

2 pounds lean ground beef
2 large onions, chopped
3 tablespoons butter
2  10-ounce cans tomato soup

3  16-ounce cans kidney beans
2 tablespoons (or more) chili
   powder
Salt and pepper to taste

Brown ground beef with onion in butter in saucepan, stirring frequently; drain. Add tomato soup, kidney beans, chili powder, salt and pepper; mix well. Simmer, covered, for 30 to 40 minutes or until done to taste. Serve with tortilla chips, shredded Cheddar cheese and additional chopped onion if desired. Yield: 8 servings.

**Approx Per Serving:** Cal 478; Prot 32 g; Carbo 39 g; Fiber 14 g;
    T Fat 22 g; Chol 86 mg; Sod 1241 mg.

*Molly Dow, WEIU Friend*

# SPAGHETTI SAUCE

1 pound lean ground beef
1 large onion, finely chopped
1 or 2 cloves of garlic, minced
2  16-ounce cans tomatoes,
   crushed
1  8-ounce can tomato sauce
2  6-ounce cans tomato paste

3 small mushrooms, chopped
1 cup canned beef bouillon
2 tablespoons parsley flakes
1 tablespoon brown sugar
1 teaspoon each oregano, basil
   and salt
1/4 teaspoon pepper

Brown ground beef with onion and garlic in large skillet, stirring until ground beef is crumbly; drain. Combine with tomatoes, tomato sauce, tomato paste, mushrooms, bouillon, parsley flakes, brown sugar, oregano, basil, salt and pepper in large saucepan. Simmer, covered, for 6 to 8 hours, stirring frequently. Serve over spaghetti. Yield: 6 servings.

**Approx Per Serving:** Cal 263; Prot 19 g; Carbo 24 g; Fiber 5 g;
    T Fat 12 g; Chol 50 mg; Sod 1042 mg.

*Sidney A. Dimond, WEIU Friend*

**1910** *An Industrial Credit Union was incorporated in November.*

## GRILLED LEG OF LAMB

1 medium onion, chopped
3 large cloves of garlic, chopped
¾ cup olive oil
½ cup white wine
¼ cup chopped fresh parsley
Juice of 1 lemon
1 bay leaf, crushed

2 tablespoons Dijon mustard
½ teaspoon each marjoram,
  rosemary, thyme and pepper
1 teaspoon each basil, oregano
  and salt
1 6 to 7-pound leg of lamb,
  boned, butterflied

Combine onion, garlic, olive oil, wine, parsley, lemon juice, bay leaf, mustard, marjoram, rosemary, thyme, pepper, basil, oregano and salt in plastic bag. Add lamb; seal securely. Marinate for up to 3 days. Drain, reserving marinade. Let stand at room temperature for 1 hour. Grill for 30 to 40 minutes for rare or until done to taste, basting with reserved marinade. Yield: 6 servings.

**Approx Per Serving:** Cal 945; Prot 97 g; Carbo 4 g; Fiber 1 g;
    T Fat 56 g; Chol 315 mg; Sod 664 mg.

*Markie Phillips, WEIU Trustee*

## ROSEMARY LEG OF LAMB

5 cloves of garlic, cut into slivers
3 or 4 sprigs of rosemary, cut
  into 20 pieces

1 6-pound leg of lamb
Salt and pepper to taste

Place garlic and rosemary in slits in leg of lamb. Sprinkle with salt and pepper. Place in roasting pan; add water to depth of ¼ inch. Roast at 350 degrees for 30 minutes per pound. Serve with mint jelly or mint sauce. May roast potatoes and onions with lamb if desired. Yield: 10 servings.

**Approx Per Serving:** Cal 408; Prot 58 g; Carbo <1 g; Fiber <1 g;
    T Fat 17 g; Chol 189 mg; Sod 144 mg.

*Sarah Fraser Robbins, WEIU Lecturer*

1910  *Practice training for vocational teachers and institutional managers plus vocational advising and placing of trained women in careers other than teaching were significant developments.*

## ORIENTAL PORK CHOPS

1 egg
3 tablespoons soy sauce
1 tablespoon dry sherry
⅛ teaspoon ginger

½ teaspoon garlic powder
4 thick lean pork chops
½ cup (about) bread crumbs

Combine egg, soy sauce, wine, ginger and garlic powder in bowl; mix well. Dip pork chops into egg mixture; coat with bread crumbs. Place in baking pan. Bake at 350 degrees for 50 minutes, turning after 30 minutes. Yield: 4 servings.

**Approx Per Serving:** Cal 308; Prot 36 g; Carbo 11 g; Fiber 1 g;
     T Fat 12 g; Chol 152 mg; Sod 959 mg.

*R. Harding Ford, WEIU Friend*

## HAM JAMBALAYA

3 onions, sliced
1 green bell pepper, chopped
1 clove of garlic, minced
¼ cup butter
2 cups chopped cooked ham
3½ cups crushed canned
   tomatoes

½ cup dry white wine
½ teaspoon thyme
¼ teaspoon basil
¼ teaspoon paprika
¼ teaspoon Tabasco sauce
1 cup uncooked rice

Sauté onions, green pepper and garlic in butter in skillet for 10 minutes. Add ham, tomatoes, wine, thyme, basil, paprika and Tabasco sauce; mix well. Bring to a boil. Add rice; reduce heat. Simmer, covered, for 25 minutes. Serve with garlic bread and salad. Yield: 6 servings.

**Approx Per Serving:** Cal 326; Prot 17 g; Carbo 38 g; Fiber 4 g;
     T Fat 11 g; Chol 46 mg; Sod 920 mg.

*Sarah Sullivan, WEIU Friend*

1910   *The Research Department gave fellowships to Radcliffe and Wellesley to study the employment of women in the manufacture of women's wear and opportunities for women in real estate and agriculture.*

## Sausage Jambalaya

2 large chicken breasts, boned
1 pound hot Italian sausage,
　chopped
1 large green bell pepper,
　chopped
1 large onion, chopped
1 cup uncooked rice
1　14-ounce can chicken broth

1　28-ounce can tomatoes,
　crushed
2 tablespoons chopped parsley
1 teaspoon cumin
1 teaspoon chili powder
1 teaspoon pepper
1 pound shrimp, cooked

Rinse chicken and pat dry. Brown sausage in saucepan; remove with slotted spoon. Cut chicken into pieces. Add to drippings in skillet. Cook until brown; remove. Add green pepper and onion. Sauté until tender. Add rice, chicken broth, tomatoes, parsley, cumin, chili powder, pepper and sausage; mix well. Simmer for 30 minutes. Add chicken. Simmer for 10 minutes. Add shrimp. Cook until heated through. Yield: 6 servings.

**Approx Per Serving:** Cal 447; Prot 38 g; Carbo 34 g; Fiber 2 g;
　　T Fat 17 g; Chol 205 mg; Sod 878 mg.

*Claire Labbe, WEIU Friend*

## Fettucini Carbonara

6 ounces hot link sausage
2 ounces dry red wine
1 tablespoon olive oil
8 ounces mushrooms, cut into
　quarters
4 ounces zucchini, chopped
1/4 cup chopped green onions

1/4 cup butter
2 cups whipping cream
1　16-ounce package fettucini,
　cooked
Salt and pepper to taste
1/2 cup grated Parmesan cheese

Cook sausage in wine in covered saucepan until wine has evaporated. Cut cooled sausage into slices. Sauté in olive oil in 12-inch sauté pan until brown. Add mushrooms and zucchini. Sauté until light brown. Add green onions and remove from heat. Heat butter and cream in 6-quart saucepan. Add sausage mixture and pasta; mix well. Stir in salt, pepper and cheese. Cook until heated through and thickened to desired consistency, stirring gently. Serve with additional Parmesan cheese. Yield: 4 servings.

**Approx Per Serving:** Cal 1101; Prot 25 g; Carbo 93 g; Fiber 6 g;
　　T Fat 70 g; Chol 208 mg; Sod 467 mg.

*Clement Cizewsky, WEIU Friend*

# Award-Winning Roast Stuffed Loin of Veal

2 tablespoons minced carrot
2 tablespoons minced celery
2 tablespoons minced onion
2 tablespoons olive oil
¼ cup Port
1 teaspoon minced garlic
2 tablespoons minced fresh
  thyme
8 ounces ground veal
1 tablespoon minced broadleaf
  parsley

2 eggs, slightly beaten
1 cup bread crumbs
1　2-pound boneless veal loin,
  butterflied
2 teaspoons salt
2 teaspoons freshly ground
  pepper
6 ounces fresh spinach leaves
Demi-Glacé

Sauté carrot, celery and onion in olive oil in skillet over medium heat until tender. Add Port; stir to deglaze. Add garlic and half the thyme. Cool to room temperature. Combine ground veal, parsley, eggs and bread crumbs in bowl; mix well. Fry a small amount of mixture in skillet to test seasonings and adjust seasonings. Open veal loin fat side down on work surface. Season with remaining thyme, salt and pepper; line with spinach leaves. Shape veal mixture into roll; place in center of loin. Roll loin to enclose filling. Place fat side up on rack in roasting pan. Roast at 375 degrees for 40 minutes or to 145 degrees on meat thermometer. Let stand for 10 minutes. Slice roast. Ladle 1 ounce Demi-Glacé onto each serving plate. Place 2 slices veal in sauce. Garnish with fresh thyme. This recipe was a finalist in the second annual Chefs Awards. The Catered Affair received a 1989 Certificate of Achievement from The American Institute of Wine and Food and the Massachusetts Chapter of the National Multiple Sclerosis Society. Yield: 6 servings.

## Demi-Glacé

4 pounds beef bones
4 pounds veal bones
½　6-ounce can tomato paste
1 medium onion
8 ounces carrots
3 stalks celery
2 tablespoons olive oil

½ bunch fresh thyme
½ bunch parsley
2 bay leaves
2 teaspoons peppercorns
1 clove of garlic
1 cup red wine
Grated zest of 1 orange

Roast bones in roasting pan at 425 degrees for 1 hour or until dark brown; drain. Spread with tomato paste. Chop unpeeled vegetables coarsely. Sauté in olive oil in large stockpot until tender and light brown. Add bones and enough cold water to cover by 2 inches. Deglaze roasting pan with a small amount of water. Add to stockpot. Stir in thyme, parsley, bay leaves, peppercorns and garlic. Simmer, covered, for 6 hours. Strain into clean stockpot; skim surface. Stir in wine. Cook until reduced to 12 to 16 ounces, skimming as necessary. Add orange zest. Remove bay leaves.

**Approx Per Serving:** Cal 382; Prot 48 g; Carbo 15 g; Fiber 2 g;
  T Fat 13 g; Chol 247 mg; Sod 999 mg.
  Nutritional information does not include Demi-Glacé.

*Joseph Occhipinti, The Catered Affair*

# HAM AND VEAL LOAF

2 pounds ground ham
1 pound ground pork
1 pound ground veal
2 eggs
1 cup milk
1 cup bread crumbs
¼ teaspoon ground cloves

12 candied cherry halves
½ cup packed brown sugar
1 tablespoon mustard
¼ cup cider vinegar
¼ cup water
Several whole cloves

Combine ground ham, ground pork, ground veal, eggs, milk, bread crumbs and ground cloves in bowl; mix well. Shape into ham shape; place in baking pan. Score top into diamonds; top with cherry halves. Bake at 350 degrees for 50 minutes. Combine brown sugar, mustard, vinegar, water and whole cloves in saucepan. Bring to a boil. Cook for 5 minutes. Pour over ham loaf. Bake for 30 minutes longer, basting frequently. *This recipe is from my mother's family, the Meads, who were original subscribers of Horseneck, now Greenwich, Connecticut. It probably travelled with them by ox cart to Meadville, Pennsylvania.* Yield: 12 servings.

**Approx Per Serving:** Cal 309; Prot 37 g; Carbo 16 g; Fiber <1 g;
T Fat 10 g; Chol 135 mg; Sod 1143 mg.

*Evelyn W. Farnum, WEIU Trustee*

# VEAL ROLL-UPS

2 tablespoons grated Parmesan
cheese
2 tablespoons chopped parsley
Salt and pepper to taste
8  2-ounce veal scallops
4  1-ounce slices mozzarella
cheese, cut into halves

4  ½-ounce slices prosciutto,
cut into halves
2 tablespoons butter
¼ cup olive oil
2 tablespoons butter
½ cup dry white wine
4 lemon slices

Mix Parmesan cheese, parsley, salt and pepper in bowl. Pound veal very thin with meat mallet. Sprinkle with Parmesan mixture. Layer ½ slice mozzarella cheese and ½ slice proscuitto on each veal scallop. Roll to enclose filling; secure with wooden picks. Melt 2 tablespoons butter with olive oil in 12-inch skillet. Brown roll-ups in oil mixture; remove to dish. Add 2 tablespoons butter and wine to skillet, stirring to deglaze. Add roll-ups. Simmer for 15 minutes. Serve with lemon slices. Yield: 4 servings.

**Approx Per Serving:** Cal 481; Prot 34 g; Carbo 1 g; Fiber 0 g;
T Fat 35 g; Chol 159 mg; Sod 499 mg.

*Salvatore J. Tecce, Joe Tecce's Restaurant*

# VEAL WITH RASPBERRIES AND ROSEMARY

2 pounds veal loin or rib eye
1/2 cup olive oil
2 tablespoons minced shallots
2 tablespoons minced garlic
1 tablespoon minced rosemary
5 pounds veal bones
1 pound mirepoix
1 tablespoon finely chopped
   shallots

1 teaspoon finely chopped garlic
1 tablespoon olive oil
1 cup Chambord
1/4 cup balsamic vinegar
Salt and pepper to taste
1 cup fresh raspberries

Trim veal, discarding fat and silvery membrane. Cut into 4 steaks. Combine 1/2 cup olive oil, 2 tablespoons shallots, 2 tablespoons garlic and 1 tablespoon rosemary in bowl; mix well. Rub into steaks. Chill, covered, for 4 hours. Roast veal bones in baking pan in 450-degree oven for 10 minutes. Combine with mirepoix and water to cover in 8-quart stockpot. Simmer for 4 hours. Strain, discarding bones and mirepoix; return stock to stockpot. Cook until reduced to 1 quart. Sauté 1 tablespoon shallots and 1 teaspoon garlic in 1 tablespoon olive oil in saucepan for 1 minute. Add Chambord and balsamic vinegar. Simmer for 4 minutes. Strain into saucepan. Strain stock into saucepan. Reduce to 12 ounces. Add salt, pepper and raspberries. Broil veal steaks for 6 minutes on each side or until done to taste. Spoon sauce over top. Yield: 4 servings.

**Approx Per Serving:** Cal 520; Prot 50 g; Carbo 2 g; Fiber <1 g;
   T Fat 34 g; Chol 205 mg; Sod 128 mg.
   Nutritional information does not include sauce.

*Karen Kostigen, WEIU Member*

# VENISON STEAKS

4  3/4-inch venison steaks
1  16-ounce bottle of Holland
   House Red Wine and Herb
   Marinade
5 tablespoons olive oil

2 tablespoons flour
Juice of 1 lemon
1 cup (about) water
1 cup sour cream
1 tablespoon red cooking wine

Combine steaks with wine marinade in shallow dish. Marinate for 24 hours, turning several times. Drain, discarding marinade; pat steaks dry. Brown in olive oil in skillet over medium-high heat for 3 minutes on each side. Remove to serving plate. Sprinkle flour into drippings in skillet. Stir in lemon juice, water, sour cream and wine. Cook until thickened and smooth, stirring constantly. Serve with steaks. Yield: 4 servings.

**Approx Per Serving:** Cal 748; Prot 78 g; Carbo 5 g; Fiber <1 g;
   T Fat 45 g; Chol 191 mg; Sod 209 mg.
   Nutritional information does not include marinade.

*Franklin W. Hobbs, WEIU Trustee*

## BAKED CHEESE OMELET

½ cup sifted flour
1 teaspoon baking powder
12 eggs, beaten
Salt and pepper to taste
5 or 6 drops of Tabasco sauce

16 ounces Muenster cheese, shredded
2 cups cottage cheese
¼ cup melted butter

Preheat oven to 400 degrees. Sift flour with baking powder. Season eggs with salt and pepper in bowl. Add Tabasco sauce, flour mixture, shredded cheese, cottage cheese and melted butter; mix well. Pour into buttered 9-by-13-inch baking dish. Bake for 15 minutes. Reduce temperature to 325 degrees. Bake for 10 minutes or until browned and puffed.
Yield: 8 servings.

**Approx Per Serving:** Cal 458; Prot 29 g; Carbo 9 g; Fiber <1 g;
    T Fat 33 g; Chol 397 mg; Sod 763 mg.

*Jamie Rose Therrien, WEIU Employee*

## CHEESE TART

10 ounces Edam cheese
¼ cup melted butter
1 cup soft bread crumbs

3 medium tomatoes, sliced
8 small mushroom caps
1 tablespoon melted butter

Shred enough cheese to measure 1 cup. Slice remaining cheese. Combine shredded cheese, ¼ cup butter and breadcrumbs in bowl; mix well. Press firmly over bottom and side of greased 9-inch pie plate. Layer sliced cheese, tomatoes and mushroom caps in prepared pie plate. Brush with remaining 1 tablespoon butter. Bake at 350 degrees for 20 minutes.
Yield: 6 servings.

**Approx Per Serving:** Cal 280; Prot 13 g; Carbo 6 g; Fiber 1 g;
    T Fat 23 g; Chol 68 mg; Sod 567 mg.

*Michele Fallon, WEIU Friend*

1910   *Members of the Boston Symphony Orchestra gave five Sunday
       Musicales at the Union.*

## EGGS À LA BILL

2 eggs, beaten
2 tablespoons milk
Salt and pepper to taste

2 tablespoons orange juice
1 tablespoon butter

Combine eggs, milk, salt, pepper and orange juice in bowl; mix well. Melt butter in skillet. Add eggs. Cook until set, stirring frequently with fork. Serve with 2 slices toast and sausage or bacon. Yield: 1 serving.

**Approx Per Serving:** Cal 292; Prot 14 g; Carbo 6 g; Fiber <1 g;
T Fat 24 g; Chol 461 mg; Sod 248 mg.

*Massachusetts Governor William Weld, WEIU Friend*

## TIMBALLO DI MELENZANA

8 ounces wild mushrooms, sliced
1 tablespoon olive oil
8 ounces goat cheese, crumbled
6 ounces marscapone cheese
4 ounces grated Romano cheese
1 teaspoon freshly ground
  pepper

3 eggs, beaten
2 tablespoons chopped parsley
2 tablespoons chopped basil
Salt to taste
3 eggplant, peeled, sliced
1/2 cup flour
1/4 cup olive oil

Sauté mushrooms in 1 tablespoon olive oil in skillet. Combine with cheeses, pepper, eggs, parsley, basil and salt to taste in bowl; mix well. Chill for 1 hour. Season eggplant with salt; drain. Dust with flour. Sauté in 1/4 cup olive oil. Let stand until cool. Layer eggplant slices and 2 tablespoons cheese mixture in greased soufflé cups. Top with eggplant slice. Place in large baking dish half filled with water. Bake in preheated 375-degree oven for 20 minutes. Let stand for 5 minutes. Unmold onto serving plate. Drizzle with extra virgin olive oil or tomato sauce if desired. Yield: 12 servings.

**Approx Per Serving:** Cal 257; Prot 11 g; Carbo 12 g; Fiber 3 g;
T Fat 19 g; Chol 96 mg; Sod 405 mg.

*Tommy Golden, Davio's Restaurant*

1912  *Classes in physical education became the latest experiment in the Union's social work.*

# QUICK E-Z PASTA

2 quarts water
1 teaspoon salt
1 tablespoon oil
4 ounces uncooked linguine
1/4 cup ricotta cheese
1/4 cup mixed chives, basil and
    parsley

2 tablespoons butter
2 tablespoons (heaping)
    Parmesan cheese
Salt and pepper to taste

Preheat 2 soup plates in 250-degree oven. Bring water with salt and oil to a boil in large saucepan. Add linguine. Cook for 8 to 10 minutes or just until tender. Remove soup plates from oven. Spoon half the ricotta cheese, herbs, butter and Parmesan cheese into each. Drain pasta. Place in soup plates. Season with salt and pepper. Toss and serve. *This recipe originally came from the son of Enrico Caruso.* Yield: 2 servings.

**Approx Per Serving:** Cal 479; Prot 15 g; Carbo 46 g; Fiber 3 g;
    T Fat 26 g; Chol 54 mg; Sod 1380 mg.

*Annette Athanas, WEIU Friend*

# CHRISTIANE'S LENTILS

1 cup lentils
1 can consommé
1/2 consommé can water
1 clove
1 onion, peeled

1 carrot, peeled, chopped
1 stalk celery, chopped
1 tablespoon balsamic vinegar
2 or 3 mint sprigs, snipped

Sort lentils. Rinse with cold water; drain. Combine lentils, consommé and water in sauce pan. Insert clove into onion. Add onion, carrot and celery. Cook for 12 minutes or until lentils are tender. Add vinegar and mint. The mint adds a very pleasant *Je ne sais quoi.* Yield: 8 servings.

**Approx Per Serving:** Cal 96; Prot 8 g; Carbo 16 g; Fiber 3 g;
    T Fat <1 g; Chol <1 mg; Sod 107 mg.

*Helen Cotton, WEIU Member*

1912  *A company of experienced amateurs, known as "The Children's Players," put on two plays, "The Forest Ring" and "The Naughty Little Princess." The proceeds went to support research work at the Union.*

## Pasta with Fresh Tomatoes

2 pounds very ripe tomatoes,
  chopped
2 cloves of garlic, minced
20 fresh basil leaves, minced
1/4 teaspoon oregano
1 tablespoon chopped parsley
1/4 teaspoon freshly ground
  pepper

1 teaspoon salt
5 tablespoons olive oil
8 ounces whole milk mozzarella
  cheese, chopped
6 quarts water
2 tablespoons salt
16 ounces uncooked ziti

Combine tomatoes, garlic, basil, oregano and parsley in bowl. Add pepper, salt, olive oil and cheese; mix well. Let stand at room temperature for 1 hour. Bring salted water to a boil in large saucepan. Add ziti. Cook just until tender; drain well. Add to tomato mixture; mix well. Serve immediately on warm plates. Yield: 8 servings.

**Approx Per Serving:** Cal 387; Prot 14 g; Carbo 49 g; Fiber 4 g;
    T Fat 15 g; Chol 22 mg; Sod 383 mg.

*Massachusetts Lt. Governor Paul Cellucci, WEIU Friend*

## Spaghetti Soufflé

1 cup milk, scalded
1 cup soft bread crumbs
1/2 cup shredded sharp Cheddar
  cheese
1 teaspoon margarine
3 tablespoons chopped green
  bell pepper

1 tablespoon chopped onion
1/8 teaspoon mace or nutmeg
Salt and pepper to taste
1 1/2 cups cooked spaghetti
4 eggs yolks, beaten
4 egg whites, stiffly beaten

Combine hot milk, bread crumbs, cheese, margarine, green pepper, onion, seasonings and spaghetti in large bowl. Stir in beaten egg yolks. Fold in stiffly beaten egg whites gently. Pour into ungreased 1-quart casserole. Place in larger pan half filled with hot water. Bake at 350 degrees for 30 minutes or until set. Serve with cheese sauce. *This was a popular luncheon dish served in WEIU restaurants.* Yield: 4 servings.

**Approx Per Serving:** Cal 285; Prot 15 g; Carbo 24 g; Fiber 1 g;
    T Fat 14 g; Chol 236 mg; Sod 252 mg.

*Helen H. Hodgdon, Former WEIU Food Shop Director*

# SPINACH PIE

6 cups sifted flour
1 teaspoon baking powder
1/2 cup corn oil
1 3/4 cups (about) warm water
3 10-ounce packages fresh
  spinach
16 ounces cottage cheese with
  chives

1 1/2 cups feta cheese, crumbled
7 eggs, well beaten
1 tablespoon flour
1 pound butter, melted
2 tablespoons shortening,
  melted
2 tablespoons corn oil

Sift 6 cups sifted flour and baking powder together into large bowl. Add oil; mix well. Add water gradually, mixing well after each addition. Dough will be soft and slightly sticky. Knead for 10 minutes or longer or until very smooth. Let rest in covered bowl for 3 to 4 hours. Immerse spinach 1 package at a time in cold water. Remove stems; drain and chop spinach. Place in large saucepan. Cook over low heat until wilted; drain and set aside. Combine spinach, cottage cheese, feta cheese and eggs in bowl; mix well. Knead dough for 3 minutes. Cut into three 3-inch round balls and fourteen 2 1/2-inch balls. Roll 3-inch balls 1 at a time on floured surface with 36-inch long rolling pin into 17-inch circles. Stack in 17-inch baking pan, sprinkling each layer with remaining 1 tablespoon flour. Bake at 350 degrees for 8 minutes. Separate layers; cool on large towel. Roll seven 2 1/2-inch balls into 8-inch circles on floured surface. Stack circles, brushing with mixture of butter, shortening and oil between each layer. Roll stack into 21-inch circle on floured surface. Spread with butter mixture. Place in 17-inch baking pan. Brush 1 baked layer with butter. Place in prepared pan. Top with 1/3 of the spinach mixture. Repeat layers with remaining baked layers and spinach mixture, ending with spinach mixture. Roll remaining 2 1/2-inch balls into 8-inch circles. Stack circles, brushing each with butter mixture. Roll into 17-inch circle. Place on top of spinach mixture, swirling top. Brush with remaining butter mixture. Bring overhanging edge of bottom pastry up, tucking to make crust. Bake at 350 degrees for 45 minutes or until puffed and brown. Let stand until settled. Cut into squares. Serve warm. Yield: 15 servings.

**Approx Per Serving:** Cal 678; Prot 20 g; Carbo 40 g; Fiber 3 g;
  T Fat 50 g; Chol 210 mg; Sod 924 mg.

*Boston City Councillor David Scondras, WEIU Friend*

1912   *The WEIU training course for teachers of salesmanship
appeared in the Simmons College catalogue. Students for the
classes came from as far away as Milwaukee.*

# ZESTY TOFU CASSEROLE

½ cup chopped onion
½ cup chopped red bell pepper
1 tablespoon oil
1  28-ounce can tomatoes
½ teaspoon sugar
¼ teaspoon dried basil
⅛ teaspoon pepper

2 tablespoons chopped parsley
1 medium eggplant, sliced
1 medium zucchini, sliced
1 tablespoon oil
1 pound tofu
1 cup shredded reduced-fat
   Cheddar cheese

Sauté onion and red pepper in 1 tablespoon oil in skillet until tender, stirring frequently. Add tomatoes, sugar, basil, pepper and parsley; mix well. Simmer for 30 minutes. Place eggplant and zucchini slices on oiled baking sheet. Brush with remaining 1 tablespoon oil. Broil 5 inches from heat source for 5 minutes or until brown, turning once. Cut tofu into ½x2-inch slices. Layer vegetables, tofu and cheese ½ at a time. Pour tomato sauce over top. Bake at 350 degrees for 30 to 40 minutes or until bubbly. *This Union recipe won a prize.* Yield: 6 servings.

**Approx Per Serving:** Cal 204; Prot 11 g; Carbo 15 g; Fiber 6 g;
    T Fat 13 g; Chol 15 mg; Sod 300 mg.

*Helen H. Hodgdon, Former WEIU Food Shop Director*

# VEGETABLE PIE

2 cups chopped fresh broccoli
½ cup chopped onion
½ cup chopped green bell
   pepper
1 cup shredded Cheddar cheese

1½ cups milk
¾ cups baking mix
3 eggs, beaten
1 teaspoon salt
¼ teaspoon pepper

Cook broccoli in a small amount of water in saucepan until tender; drain. Combine broccoli, onion, green pepper and cheese in greased 10-inch pie plate. Combine milk, baking mix, eggs, salt and pepper in bowl; mix well. Pour over broccoli mixture. Bake at 400 degrees for 35 to 40 minutes or until golden brown. Yield: 6 servings.

**Approx Per Serving:** Cal 303; Prot 13 g; Carbo 27 g; Fiber 1 g;
    T Fat 16 g; Chol 135 mg; Sod 938 mg.

*Jane Murphy, WEIU Friend*

**1913**  *The Bureau of Research made a study of social conditions in the North End for the North Bennett Street Industrial School.*

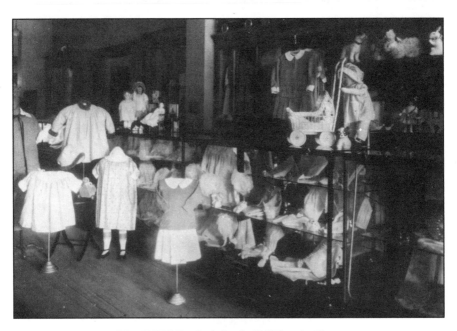

**The WEIU's Original Children's Shop**
*Today the Children's Shop is one of five different shops at the WEIU.*

**The Needlework Shop**
*The WEIU operates the country's oldest Needlework
Design Studio and Shop.*

# Poultry and Seafood Main Dishes

### ROAST TURKEY

Remove neck, liver, and heart, and rinse turkey in cold water. Drain well and pat dry. Fill the cavity loosely with stuffing. Do not pack tightly, as the stuffing expands when cooked. Rub with melted butter.

Roast bird at 325 degrees for approximately 15 to 20 minutes per pound. Remember to baste frequently.

*from **A WEIU Thanksgiving Dinner Menu**, 1981*

## ELEANOR SHORT'S CHICKEN ALOHA

1½ cups sliced celery
1 green bell pepper, cut into
 strips
3 tablespoons butter
3 cups chopped cooked chicken
¼ cup soy sauce

1  21-ounce can pineapple pie
 filling
⅓ cup water
2 teaspoons instant chicken
 bouillon

Sauté celery and green pepper in butter in skillet until tender-crisp. Add chicken, soy sauce, pie filling, water and instant bouillon; mix well. Cook until heated through. Serve over chow mein noodles. *This is a recipe from Eleanor Ballou Short (Smith '19) who lived on a pineapple plantation in Hawaii. It was a favorite for church suppers, receptions and care baskets.* Yield: 8 servings.

**Approx Per Serving:** Cal 204; Prot 13 g; Carbo 22 g; Fiber 2 g;
 T Fat 8 g; Chol 50 mg; Sod 679 mg.

*Jan White, Former WEIU Trustee*

## CHICKEN WITH ARTICHOKES AND MUSHROOMS

6  6-ounce chicken breast filets
1  6-ounce can artichoke hearts
8 ounces fresh mushrooms
2 cups flour
1 teaspoon each onion powder,
 nutmeg, thyme, salt and
 pepper

½ cup oil
2 cloves of garlic, finely chopped
1 cup dry white wine
Juice of 1 lemon
½ cup chopped fresh parsley

Rinse chicken and pat dry. Pound ½ inch thick with meat mallet. Cut artichokes and mushrooms into quarters. Mix flour, onion powder, nutmeg, thyme, salt and pepper in shallow dish. Coat chicken with mixture. Cook in hot oil in large skillet until golden brown on both sides; remove to warm platter. Sauté garlic and mushrooms in pan drippings in skillet. Add wine, stirring to deglaze skillet. Stir in lemon juice, parsley and artichokes. Add chicken. Simmer until liquid is reduced to desired consistency. Place chicken on warm serving platter; spoon sauce over top. Yield: 6 servings.

**Approx Per Serving:** Cal 505; Prot 35 g; Carbo 38 g; Fiber 2 g;
 T Fat 20 g; Chol 74 mg; Sod 107 mg.

*Jack B. Dailey, The College Club Restaurant*

# BREADED CHICKEN

8 chicken breast filets
2 eggs, beaten
1/3 cup melted butter

1 teaspoon salt
8 ounces butter crackers, finely
crushed

Rinse chicken and pat dry. Combine eggs, butter and salt in bowl; whisking until smooth. Dip chicken in cracker crumbs, then in egg mixture, and then in crumbs again. Arrange in 9x13-inch glass dish sprayed with nonstick cooking spray, placing meatier portions toward outside. Microwave on High for 13 to 15 minutes or until tender, rotating dish 1/2 turn after 7 minutes. May use other pieces of chicken as preferred. Yield: 8 servings.

**Approx Per Serving:** Cal 322; Prot 23 g; Carbo 20 g; Fiber <1 g;
 T Fat 19 g; Chol 123 mg; Sod 686 mg.

*Helen Clough, WEIU Member*

# CHINESE NOODLES WITH CHICKEN

1/3 pound chicken breast filets
1   16-ounce package Chinese
 noodles
1 tablespoon oil
2   14-ounce cans chicken broth
2 slices fresh ginger
1 tablespoon oil
1 clove of garlic, crushed

2 stalks celery, sliced
1 medium onion, chopped
2 medium carrots, julienned
4 ounces mushrooms, sliced
1 scallion, sliced
1/3 pound bean sprouts
2 tablespoons cornstarch

Rinse chicken and pat dry; slice into thin strips. Break noodles into 1 tablespoon hot oil in saucepan. Sauté until light brown. Remove to large platter. Heat chicken broth in saucepan. Pour half the broth over noodles. Let stand, covered, while preparing chicken. Brown ginger in 1 tablespoon oil in skillet. Add garlic and chicken. Sauté until chicken begins to brown. Remove ginger and garlic with slotted spoon. Add celery, onion and carrots. Cook for 4 to 5 minutes. Add mushrooms and scallion. Cook for 4 minutes. Add bean sprouts. Cook for 1 minute. Stir in remaining broth and cornstarch; mix well. Cook for 3 minutes, stirring constantly. Spoon over noodles. May buy Chinese noodles in the refrigerator section of the market. Yield: 6 servings.

**Approx Per Serving:** Cal 127; Prot 9 g; Carbo 11 g; Fiber 3 g;
 T Fat 6 g; Chol 11 mg; Sod 448 mg.
 Nutritional information does not include Chinese noodles.

*Laurel Sgan, Former WEIU Employee*

## CHICKEN AND JALAPEÑO PANCAKES

| | |
|---|---|
| 2 pounds chicken breast filets | 1 cup heavy cream |
| 1/2 teaspoon salt | 4 canned jalapeño peppers, |
| 1/4 teaspoon white pepper |   seeded, rinsed, chopped |
| 2 tablespoons butter | 1 recipe Pancakes |
| 3 tablespoons flour | 1 cup shredded Swiss cheese |
| 1 cup chicken stock | |

Rinse chicken and pat dry. Season with salt and pepper. Melt butter in 10-inch skillet. Add chicken with tongs, turning to coat well with butter; reduce heat. Simmer, covered, until chicken is cooked through, turning once or twice. Remove and cut into 1/4-inch cubes. Stir flour into drippings in skillet. Add chicken stock gradually, stirring constantly. Cook until thickened, stirring constantly. Add cream. Cook until sauce is reduced to 1 1/2 cups. Combine with chicken and peppers in bowl; mix well. Spoon 1/4 cup filling onto each Pancake; roll to enclose filling. Arrange in greased 9x13-inch baking pan; sprinkle with cheese. Bake at 325 degrees for 10 minutes. Increase oven temperature to 500 degrees. Bake for 5 minutes longer or until cheese is melted and light brown. Yield: 8 servings.

**Approx Per Serving:** Cal 403; Prot 24 g; Carbo 11 g; Fiber <1 g;
    T Fat 29 g; Chol 180 mg; Sod 813 mg.
Nutritional information includes Pancakes.

### Pancakes

| | |
|---|---|
| 1/2 cup flour | 1 egg yolk |
| 2/3 cup milk | 6 tablespoons melted butter |
| 1 egg | 1/4 teaspoon salt |

Combine flour, milk, egg, egg yolk, butter and salt in blender container; process until smooth. Let rest for 1 hour or longer. Heat 6-inch nonstick crêpe pan. Add 2 tablespoons batter at a time, tilting to coat well. Bake until pancakes are lightly browned on both sides. Fill immediately or store in refrigerator or freezer until needed. Yield: 8 servings.

**Approx Per Serving:** Cal 135; Prot 3 g; Carbo 7 g; Fiber <1 g;
    T Fat 11 g; Chol 79 mg; Sod 158 mg.

*Dorothea J. Mahoney, WEIU Friend*

1913  *Three other "Appointment Bureaus" were established in New York, Philadelphia, and Chicago. The Union's was the first in the country to advise women on business and professional opportunities.*

## CREOLE STEWED CHICKEN

3 pounds cut-up chicken
2 cups sliced onions
2 large tomatoes, cut into wedges
3 tablespoons chopped scallions
6 tablespoons minced parsley
4 cloves of garlic, minced
2 tablespoons white wine
  vinegar
1 teaspoon thyme

6 tablespoons Worcestershire
  sauce
1 teaspoon salt
Freshly ground pepper to taste
3 tablespoons oil
6 tablespoons brown sugar
6 tablespoons catsup
2 cups water

Rinse chicken and pat dry. Combine onions, tomatoes, scallions, parsley, garlic, vinegar, thyme, Worcestershire sauce, salt and pepper in bowl; mix well. Add chicken. Marinate in refrigerator for 1 hour to overnight. Drain, reserving marinade. Heat oil in heavy saucepan. Stir in brown sugar until dissolved. Add chicken. Cook until chicken is brown on all sides; drain on paper towels. Stir reserved marinade, catsup and water into skillet. Arrange chicken in skillet. Simmer, covered, for 1 hour, stirring occasionally. Serve with rice. Yield: 6 servings.

**Approx Per Serving:** Cal 389; Prot 35 g; Carbo 27 g; Fiber 2 g;
  T Fat 16 g; Chol 101 mg; Sod 790 mg.

*Chobee Hoy, WEIU Friend*

## LEMON CHICKEN

1 chicken, cut up
1 lemon
2/3 cup flour
1 teaspoon each paprika and salt
1/2 cup oil

1 lemon, sliced
2 tablespoons brown sugar
2 cups chicken broth
1 tablespoon angostura bitters

Rinse chicken and pat dry. Squeeze juice of 1 lemon over chicken. Combine flour, paprika and salt in bag. Add chicken; shake to coat well. Brown in oil in skillet. Remove to baking dish. Top with sliced lemon. Combine brown sugar with chicken broth in bowl, stirring to dissolve brown sugar. Add bitters. Pour over chicken. Bake, covered, at 375 degrees for 1 hour. Arrange chicken on serving plate; pour pan juices over top. Yield: 5 servings.

**Approx Per Serving:** Cal 554; Prot 43 g; Carbo 20 g; Fiber 1 g;
  T Fat 33 g; Chol 122 mg; Sod 1709 mg.

*Mrs. Arthur C. Babson, WEIU Trustee and Former President*

## LEMON-HERBED CHICKEN

6 chicken breast filets
1 cup flour
2 tablespoons chopped parsley
1 teaspoon garlic powder
1/2 teaspoon salt

1/2 teaspoon white pepper
3 tablespoons unsalted butter
1/2 cup Chablis
1 lemon, cut into wedges

Rinse chicken and pat dry. Pound thin with meat mallet. Mix flour, parsley, garlic powder, salt and pepper in bowl. Add chicken, coating well. Cook in butter in skillet until golden brown on both sides. Add wine; reduce heat. Cook until of desired consistency. Place chicken on serving platter. Spoon sauce over top. Serve with lemon wedges. Yield: 6 servings.

**Approx Per Serving:** Cal 238; Prot 22 g; Carbo 17 g; Fiber 1 g;
T Fat 7 g; Chol 65 mg; Sod 283 mg.

*Anthony M. Sammarco, WEIU Lecturer*

## LEMON CHICKEN WITH THYME

4 boneless chicken breasts,
    skinned
3 tablespoons flour
1/2 teaspoon salt
1/4 teaspoon pepper
2 tablespoons olive oil
1 tablespoon margarine

1 medium onion, chopped
1 cup chicken broth
1/2 teaspoon thyme
3 tablespoons lemon juice
1 lemon, cut into wedges
2 tablespoons chopped parsley

Rinse chicken and pat dry; cut into halves. Mix flour, salt and pepper in bag. Add chicken, shaking to coat well. Shake to remove excess flour, reserving remaining flour. Brown chicken on 1 side in 1 tablespoon olive oil in skillet over medium heat. Add remaining 1 tablespoon olive oil; turn chicken. Cook until brown; remove to warm plate. Add margarine and onion to skillet. Cook for 2 to 3 minutes. Stir in reserved flour. Cook for 1 minute. Add broth, thyme and 2 tablespoons lemon juice. Bring to a boil, stirring constantly. Add chicken. Cook until chicken is tender. Remove chicken to serving plates. Stir remaining 1 tablespoon lemon juice into juices in skillet. Pour over chicken. Top with lemon wedges and parsley. Yield: 4 servings.

**Approx Per Serving:** Cal 226; Prot 22 g; Carbo 9 g; Fiber 1 g;
T Fat 11 g; Chol 49 mg; Sod 550 mg.

*Ruth L. Elsemore, WEIU Friend*

# CHICKEN MOUSSAKA

1 cup chopped onion
1/4 cup butter
1 tablespoon oil
2 large eggplant
1  28-ounce can
  tomato-mushroom sauce
1 cup water

1 pound chicken breast filets
2 tablespoons butter
Oregano, basil and hot pepper
  to taste
1 pound potatoes, peeled, sliced
  1/4 inch thick
2 cups Béchamel sauce

Sauté onion in 1/4 cup butter and oil in 6-quart saucepan. Peel eggplant and cut into 1-inch cubes. Add to onions in saucepan. Cook until lightly browned. Add tomato sauce and water. Simmer for several minutes. Rinse chicken and pat dry, discarding skin and fat. Cut into 1-inch pieces. Sauté in 2 tablespoons butter in skillet until brown. Add chicken, oregano, basil and hot pepper to eggplant in saucepan. Simmer for 30 to 45 minutes or until eggplant is tender. Cook potatoes in water to cover in saucepan until tender; drain. Layer potatoes and chicken mixture in baking dish. Top with Béchamel sauce. Bake at 350 degrees for 45 minutes to 1 hour; do not overbake. Serve with Greek salad, pita bread, Greek cheese, Greek olives and a good wine. Yield: 8 servings.

**Approx Per Serving:** Cal 301; Prot 19 g; Carbo 34 g; Fiber 7 g;
  T Fat 11 g; Chol 46 mg; Sod 909 mg.

*Marie Cosindas, Montilio's Restaurant*

# JOAN'S CHICKEN À L'ORANGE

4 chicken breasts
2 tablespoons butter
2 tablespoons oil
Salt and pepper to taste

1  6-ounce can orange juice
  concentrate
Tabasco sauce to taste

Rinse chicken and pat dry. Sauté in butter and oil in skillet for 1 to 3 minutes or until golden brown. Sprinkle with salt and pepper. Add orange juice concentrate and Tabasco sauce. Simmer, covered, for 30 minutes. Serve with rice. Yield: 4 servings.

**Approx Per Serving:** Cal 273; Prot 21 g; Carbo 16 g; Fiber <1 g;
  T Fat 13 g; Chol 65 mg; Sod 105 mg.

*Betsy Boveroux, WEIU Trustee*

119

## CHICKEN BREASTS WITH ORANGE AND SHERRY SAUCE

1/2 cup orange juice
1/2 cup soy sauce
1/2 cup sherry
2 cloves of garlic
1/2 teaspoon ginger
8 chicken breast filets

5 tablespoons flour
Salt and pepper to taste
1/4 cup butter
8 ounces fresh mushrooms, cut
into halves or thirds

Mix orange juice, soy sauce, sherry, garlic and ginger in bowl. Rinse chicken and pat dry. Add to marinade. Marinate in refrigerator for several hours to overnight. Drain, reserving marinade. Coat chicken with mixture of flour, salt and pepper. Brown in butter in large saucepan over medium heat for 5 minutes; remove to warm plate. Add reserved marinade to saucepan. Cook over high heat, stirring to deglaze saucepan. Cook for 3 to 5 minutes or until thickened to desired consistency. Reduce heat. Add chicken to sauce. Simmer for 20 minutes or until tender. Add mushrooms. Cook for 5 minutes longer. Place chicken on warm serving platter; spoon mushrooms and sauce over chicken. Yield: 6 servings.

**Approx Per Serving:** Cal 271; Prot 29 g; Carbo 11; Fiber 1 g;
    T Fat 9 g; Chol 86 mg; Sod 1514 mg.

*James Vorenberg, WEIU Friend*

## PLANTATION CHICKEN CASSEROLE

1/4 cup cornmeal
1 teaspoon salt
1 cup boiling water
2 eggs, beaten

1 cup milk
1 teaspoon baking powder
2 tablespoons melted butter
2 cups chopped cooked chicken

Mix cornmeal and salt in bowl. Add boiling water, mixing until smooth. Cool to room temperature. Add mixture of eggs and milk; mix gently. Stir in baking powder, butter and chicken. Spoon into greased 1-quart baking dish. Bake at 375 degrees for 40 to 45 minutes or until set and brown. May substitute turkey for chicken. Yield: 4 servings.

**Approx Per Serving:** Cal 268; Prot 22 g; Carbo 10 g; Fiber 1 g;
    T Fat 15 g; Chol 181 mg; Sod 772 mg.

*Barbara Merullo, WEIU Employee*

**1913** *There were eight conferences on different vocations opened to women at the Union—among them were journalism, secretarial work, agriculture, business, applied science, architecture, and medicine.*

# POLLO BORRACHO

72 chicken thighs
3/4 cup oil
3/4 cup butter
1½ pounds ham, coarsely
  chopped
2 pounds seedless raisins
1½ quarts Sauterne
1½ teaspoons garlic powder

3/4 teaspoon each cinnamon,
  cloves, coriander and cumin
1 tablespoon salt
1 teaspoon pepper
3 cups toasted slivered almonds
3 cups stuffed olives, cut into
  halves

Rinse chicken and pat dry. Sauté in oil and butter in large Dutch oven or roaster. Add ham, raisins, wine, garlic powder, cinnamon, cloves, coriander, cumin, salt and pepper; mix well. Bake, covered, at 300 degrees for 1 to 1½ hours or until chicken is tender. Cool to room temperature. Bone chicken, leaving meat as intact as possible. Add to Dutch oven with almonds and olives. Chill in refrigerator. Reheat at 300 degrees for 35 to 45 minutes. Yield: 40 servings.

**Approx Per Serving:** Cal 343; Prot 13 g; Carbo 23 g; Fiber 3 g;
    T Fat 21 g; Chol 41 mg;: Sod 778 mg.

*Willona H. Sinclair, WEIU Friend*


# CHICKEN SNOW'S EDGE

4 pounds chicken breast filets
2 bunches fresh broccoli
1 pound fresh mushrooms,
  sliced
2  10-ounce cans sliced water
  chestnuts, drained
3 cups lite sour cream
2  10-ounce cans
  reduced-sodium cream of
  chicken soup

2  10-ounce cans reduced-
  sodium cream of mushroom
  soup
1 cup lite mayonnaise
1 tablespoon (about) curry
  powder
Salt and pepper to taste
1½ pounds sharp Cheddar
  cheese, shredded
2 cups seasoned croutons

Rinse chicken well. Poach in a small amount of water in saucepan for 20 minutes; drain. Cool to room temperature. Shred into 2-inch strips. Steam broccoli until tender; drain. Cut into stalks. Sauté mushrooms in nonstick skillet sprayed with cooking spray. Layer broccoli, chicken and water chestnuts in 2 baking dishes. Combine sour cream, soups, mayonnaise, curry powder, salt and pepper in bowl; mix well. Spoon over layers. Top with cheese, croutons and mushrooms. Bake at 350 degrees for 45 minutes. The recipe can be reduced by ½. *We serve this at our ski house, "Snow's Edge" in Waterville, New Hampshire. I can make it in advance, ski all day and still serve up a "party" dish. I add a tossed salad, French bread and a white wine.* Yield: 16 servings.

**Approx Per Serving:** Cal 475; Prot 32 g; Carbo 21 g; Fiber 3 g;
    T Fat 30 g; Chol 111 mg; Sod 857 mg.

*Mrs. Adolfo R. Garcia, WEIU Member*

# No-Fail Chicken Stir-Fry

1 pound chicken breasts
1/4 cup oil
1 large yellow onion, coarsely chopped
3 cups sliced carrots
1 stalk celery, coarsely chopped
3 cloves of garlic, crushed
1 lemon

1/4 teaspoon each ginger, freshly ground black pepper and white pepper
1 large red bell pepper, cut into 1 1/2-inch strips
3 cups broccoli flowerets
3 tablespoons soy sauce

Rinse chicken and pat dry; cut into strips. Heat oil in wok preheated over medium-high heat or to 375 degrees. Add onion. Stir-fry for 1 minute. Add carrots and celery. Stir-fry for 2 minutes. Add garlic. Stir-fry for 1 minute. Add chicken. Stir-fry for 2 to 3 minutes or until opaque. Squeeze lemon juice over chicken. Stir-fry for 1 minute. Add ginger, freshly ground black pepper and white pepper; mix well. Add bell pepper, broccoli and soy sauce. Stir-fry for 2 minutes. Reduce heat. Simmer, covered, for 5 minutes. Serve over rice. May vary amounts and ingredients such as snow peas, bean sprouts or water chestnuts to taste. Yield: 6 servings.

**Approx Per Serving:** Cal 203; Prot 16 g; Carbo 13 g; Fiber 4 g;
    T Fat 10 g; Chol 33 mg; Sod 591 mg.

*Cynthia Matthews Roy, WEIU Friend*

# Chicken Tarragon

2 whole boneless chicken breasts
1/4 cup flour
1/2 teaspoon paprika
Salt and pepper to taste
3 1/2 tablespoons butter

1/4 cup heavy cream
1/2 teaspoon Dijon mustard
1 tablespoon dry white wine
1 tablespoon tarragon
1/4 teaspoon parsley

Rinse chicken and pat dry; cut into halves. Pound 1/4 inch thick with meat mallet. Mix flour, paprika, salt and pepper in bowl. Coat chicken well with mixture. Sauté in 2 1/2 tablespoons butter in 8 to 10-inch skillet for 15 minutes; remove to plate. Add remaining 1 tablespoon butter, cream, mustard, wine, tarragon and parsley. Simmer for 5 to 10 minutes or until of desired consistency. Add chicken. Cook until heated through. Place chicken on serving plate; spoon sauce over top. Serve with roasted potatoes and asparagus. *The Union is my favorite place to find beautiful gifts for my friends.* Yield: 4 servings.

**Approx Per Serving:** Cal 265; Prot 21 g; Carbo 6 g; Fiber <1 g;
    T Fat 17 g; Chol 97 mg; Sod 153 mg.

*Emma H. Rymer, WEIU Friend*

## CHICKEN LIVERS IN WINE SAUCE

12 chicken livers
1/4 cup chopped onion
1 tablespoon oil
8 ounces mushrooms, sliced
2 tablespoons flour

3/4 cup beef consommé
3/4 cup Sherry or Madeira
1 tablespoon oil
Chopped parsley, salt and
   pepper to taste

Rinse livers and pat dry. Cut into halves with scissors, discarding membrane. Sauté onion in 1 tablespoon oil in skillet until golden brown. Add mushrooms. Sauté until tender. Sprinkle with flour. Cook for several minutes, stirring constantly. Add consommé. Bring to a rolling boil. Add wine; remove from heat. Sauté livers in 1 tablespoon oil in skillet. Add wine sauce, parsley, salt and pepper. Cook until heated through. Serve on toast points, garnished with additional chopped parsley. *This dish was always cooked to order in the Union kitchen, with the chef and her assistant working quickly to produce this favorite entrée. They finished it under the broiler and heaven help you if it were served lukewarm.* Yield: 4 servings.

**Approx Per Serving:** Cal 281; Prot 23 g; Carbo 8 g; Fiber 1 g;
   T Fat 12 g; Chol 537 mg; Sod 196 mg.

*Helen H. Hodgdon, Former WEIU Food Shop Director*

## CORNISH HENS WITH SPINACH STUFFING

1  10-ounce package frozen
   chopped spinach
1 cup low-fat cottage cheese
1/4 cup grated Parmesan cheese
1 egg
1 clove of garlic, crushed
1/4 cup chopped walnuts
1/8 teaspoon salt

1/4 teaspoon pepper
2 Cornish game hens
1 lemon, cut into halves
Freshly ground pepper to taste
2 tablespoons olive oil
1/4 teaspoon each oregano,
   rosemary and basil

Cook spinach using package directions; drain and press to remove moisture. Combine with cottage cheese, Parmesan cheese, egg, garlic, walnuts, salt and pepper in bowl; mix well. Rinse hens inside and out; sprinkle cavities with juice of 1/2 lemon and pepper to taste. Separate skin gently from tops of breasts, thighs and legs. Spoon stuffing evenly between skin and chicken. Place in roasting pan. Brush with olive oil; sprinkle with crushed oregano, rosemary and basil. Drizzle with juice of remaining 1/2 lemon. Roast at 350 degrees for 45 minutes to 1 hour or until done to taste. Serve with risotto or wild rice, broiled tomato halves and fresh broccoli. Yield: 4 servings.

**Approx Per Serving:** Cal 334; Prot 39 g; Carbo 6 g; Fiber 1 g;
   T Fat 17 g; Chol 127 mg; Sod 500 mg.

*Marie Crocetti, WEIU Member*

# PHEASANT TERRINE

1 onion, chopped
6 shallots, chopped
3 bay leaves
1 carrot
3 sprigs of rosemary
1/2 cup brandy
1/2 cup red wine
Meat of 2 pheasants, about 3
   pounds

1 pound lean ground pork
2 pounds fresh pork fat
1 cup pistachios
1 teaspoon each cinnamon,
   nutmeg, allspice and pepper
Ground cloves to taste
2 tablespoons salt
12 eggs
6 slices bacon

Combine onion, shallots, bay leaves, carrot, rosemary, brandy and wine in bowl; mix well. Add pheasant, pork and pork fat. Marinate in refrigerator for 24 hours. Put mixture through meat grinder. Combine with pistachios, cinnamon, nutmeg, allspice, pepper, cloves and salt in bowl; mix well. Beat in eggs 1 at a time. Fry a small amount of mixture in skillet to test seasonings; adjust seasonings. Line terrine mold with bacon. Pack pheasant mixture into prepared mold; fold bacon over top. Place in larger pan of water. Bake at 350 degrees to 140 degrees on meat thermometer. Cool in pan of water for 1 hour; remove from water. Chill, weighted, in pan overnight. Unmold onto serving plate. Serve with mustard and chutney. Yield: 16 servings.

**Approx Per Serving:** Cal 760; Prot 43 g; Carbo 6 g; Fiber 1 g;
   T Fat 68 g; Chol 550 mg; Sod 1501 mg.

*Ross Cameron, Back Bay Bistro Restaurant*

# SAUTÉED COD CHEEKS EN PIPERADE

1/2 onion, chopped
1 1/2 tablespoons olive oil
1 clove of garlic, finely chopped
1/2 green bell pepper, chopped
1/2 red bell pepper, chopped
1/2 yellow bell pepper, chopped
Chopped fresh basil, tarragon
   and oregano to taste

1 large tomato, peeled, seeded,
   chopped
Salt and freshly ground pepper
   to taste
2 pounds cod cheeks
Juice of 1/2 lemon
1/2 cup flour
1 1/2 teaspoons olive oil

Sauté onion in 1 1/2 tablespoons olive oil in saucepan. Add garlic, bell peppers, basil, tarragon and oregano; mix well. Sauté for 3 minutes. Add tomato, salt and pepper; keep warm. Sprinkle cod cheeks with lemon juice, salt and pepper. Coat with flour. Sauté in 1 1/2 teaspoons olive oil in skillet for 8 to 10 minutes or until fish flakes easily. Serve with peppers. Yield: 4 servings.

**Approx Per Serving:** Cal 303; Prot 35 g; Carbo 17 g; Fiber 2 g;
   T Fat 10 g; Chol 78 mg; Sod 169 mg.

*Christoph Leu, Turner Fisheries Restaurant*

## SALMON WITH POLISH FIREWATER

1 pound salmon
1 carrot, grated

1 tomato, chopped
1 cup Firewater

Place salmon in baking dish. Top with carrot and tomato. Pour 1 cup Firewater over salmon. Bake at 400 degrees for 18 minutes or until fish flakes easily. Yield: 4 servings.

**Approx Per Serving:** Cal 282; Prot 19 g; Carbo 4 g; Fiber 1 g;
    T Fat 6 g; Chol 50 mg; Sod 111 mg.
    Nutritional information includes Firewater.

*Daniel S. Holmes, Downtown Café*

## POLISH FIREWATER

1 liter 80-proof vodka
2 tablespoons red pepper
1/2 cup tomato sauce
4 cloves of garlic, minced
1 Mexican pepper, chopped
1 tablespoon chopped onion
3 pods cardamom

1 tablespoon rosemary
12 capers
1/8 teaspoon each anise, caraway
    seed and sage
1 slice lemon
1 tablespoon grated carrot
1 tablespoon paprika

Combine all ingredients in covered jar; shake to mix well. Let stand for 1 month. Use to cook salmon or to flame crêpes. May serve over ice in place of Bloody Marys. Yield: 4 1/2 cups.

**Approx Per Cup:** Cal 556; Prot <1 g; Carbo 3 g; Fiber <1 g;
    T Fat <1 g; Chol 0 mg; Sod 248 mg.

*Daniel S. Holmes, Downtown Café*

## BARBECUED SWORDFISH

1/2 cup orange juice
1/2 cup soy sauce
1/4 cup catsup
1/4 cup chopped parsley
2 tablespoons lemon juice
2 cloves of garlic, minced

1 teaspoon oregano
1/2 teaspoon dry mustard
1 teaspoon freshly ground
    pepper
2 pounds 1-inch swordfish
    steaks

Combine orange juice, soy sauce, catsup, parsley, lemon juice, garlic, oregano, dry mustard and pepper in shallow dish. Add fish. Marinate in refrigerator for 4 hours, turning occasionally. Remove rack from grill. Preheat grill on High. Reduce heat to Medium-Low; replace rack. Drain fish, reserving marinade. Place fish on oiled grill; close grill. Grill for 5 to 6 minutes on each side or until fish flakes easily, brushing occasionally with reserved marinade. Serve with rice salad and white wine. May substitute cod, halibut or salmon for swordfish. Yield: 6 servings.

**Approx Per Serving:** Cal 225; Prot 33 g; Carbo 8 g; Fiber <1 g;
    T Fat 6 g; Chol 61 mg; Sod 1631 mg.

*Ron Noble, WEIU Employee*

# PARTY TUNA CASSEROLE

3 cups uncooked noodles
Salt to taste
1 7-ounce can tuna
1/2 cup mayonnaise
1 cup sliced celery
1/3 cup finely chopped onion
1/4 cup chopped green bell
  pepper

1/4 cup chopped pimento
1 teaspoon salt
1 10-ounce can cream of celery
  soup
1/2 cup milk
1 cup shredded sharp Cheddar
  cheese
1/2 cup slivered almonds

Cook noodles in salted water to cover in saucepan until tender; drain. Combine with tuna, mayonnaise, celery, onion, green pepper, pimento and salt in bowl; mix well. Heat soup and milk in saucepan. Stir in cheese until melted. Add to noodle mixture; mix well. Spoon into ungreased 1 1/2-quart baking dish. Sprinkle with almonds. Bake at 425 degrees for 20 minutes or until bubbly. Yield: 8 servings.

**Approx Per Serving:** Cal 361; Prot 16 g; Carbo 22 g; Fiber 2 g;
  T Fat 24 g; Chol 42 mg; Sod 827 mg.

*Eileen F. Quinn, WEIU Friend*

# TUNA-STUFFED ZUCCHINI

10 medium-small zucchini
1 16-ounce can water-pack
  tuna, drained
1 medium onion, chopped
1 bunch parsley, chopped
20 fresh basil leaves, chopped
1 tablespoon olive oil
1 tablespoon margarine

1 1/2 cups (or less) Italian bread
  crumbs
1 egg
1/2 teaspoon salt
1/4 teaspoon pepper
1/2 cup grated Parmesan cheese
2 tablespoons oil

Cut zucchini into halves lengthwise. Parboil in water in 6-quart saucepan for 10 minutes; drain and remove carefully. Cool to room temperature. Scoop pulp into colander to drain; reserve shells. Sauté tuna, zucchini pulp, onion, parsley and basil in 1 tablespoon olive oil and margarine in large skillet until onion is tender; remove from heat. Stir in bread crumbs, egg, salt, pepper and cheese. Spoon into reserved zucchini shells. Chill, covered with waxed paper, for 4 hours. Fry stuffing side down in 2 tablespoons oil in skillet; turn zucchini. Fry until heated through. Serve immediately with salad and white wine. This recipe is from my grandmother who was from northern Italy. Yield: 20 servings.

**Approx Per Serving:** Cal 96; Prot 10 g; Carbo 8 g; Fiber 1 g;
  T Fat 3 g; Chol 25 mg; Sod 294 mg.

*G. Marie Whitty, WEIU Member*

# FISH STEW PROVENÇAL

1 pound potatoes, peeled, thinly
  sliced
1 leek, thinly sliced
3 small carrots, sliced
1 large clove of garlic, minced
Grated rind of 2 oranges
1 small fennel bulb, thinly sliced
3 bay leaves

2 quarts fish stock
2 cups dry white wine
2 pounds monkfish or other
  white fish
2 plum tomatoes, chopped
2 or 3 large fresh basil leaves,
  minced

Combine potatoes, leek, carrots, garlic, orange rind, fennel, bay leaves, fish stock and wine in 8-quart stockpot. Bring to a boil over high heat. Reduce heat to medium. Simmer just until vegetables are tender. Add fish. Simmer for 5 minutes or until fish flakes easily, skimming frequently. Add tomatoes and basil. Discard bay leaves. May substitute water for fish stock. Serve with toasted garlic bread, green salad and a simple dessert. Yield: 6 servings.

**Approx Per Serving:** Cal 358; Prot 34 g; Carbo 27 g; Fiber 4 g;
    T Fat 6 g; Chol 76 mg; Sod 122 mg.

*Lisa Geissenhainer, WEIU Friend*

# SPAGHETTI WITH CLAM SAUCE

8 ounces uncooked spaghetti
1  6-ounce can minced clams
2 teaspoons cornstarch
3 small cloves of garlic, crushed
2 tablespoons chopped green
  onions
2 teaspoons parsley flakes

1/2 teaspoon Italian seasoning
6 tablespoons butter
1  4-ounce can shrimp, drained,
  chopped
2 tablespoons butter
1 cup shredded mozzarella
  cheese

Cook spaghetti using package directions; rinse and drain. Drain clams, reserving liquid. Add enough water to reserved liquid to measure 1 cup. Blend cornstarch into liquid. Sauté garlic, green onions, parsley flakes and Italian seasoning in 6 tablespoons butter in 1½-quart saucepan for 5 minutes or until green onions are soft. Stir in clam liquid. Cook over medium heat until thickened, stirring constantly. Cook for 2 minutes longer. Stir in clams and shrimp. Cook until heated through. Toss spaghetti with 2 tablespoons butter in bowl; sprinkle with cheese. Pour clam sauce over top. Yield: 4 servings.

**Approx Per Serving:** Cal 608; Prot 32 g; Carbo 48 g; Fiber 3 g;
    T Fat 31 g; Chol 170 mg; Sod 407 mg.

*D'Arcy Goldman, WEIU Trustee*

## MARYLAND LUMP CRAB CAKES

1 egg
2 ounces mayonnaise
1 tablespoon finely chopped
parsley
2 teaspoons Worcestershire sauce
1 teaspoon Dijon mustard
1 teaspoon salt

1 teaspoon white pepper
3 ounces fine bread crumbs
1 pound Maryland lump crab
meat
6 ounces flaked crab meat
2 tablespoons drawn butter

Combine egg, mayonnaise, parsley, Worcestershire sauce, mustard, salt and pepper in bowl; mix well. Mix in bread crumbs. Fold in crab meat gently. Shape into 6 patties. Sauté in drawn butter in skillet until light brown. Serve with spicy mustard sauce. Yield: 6 servings.

**Approx Per Serving:** Cal 228; Prot 21 g; Carbo 11 g; Fiber 1 g;
T Fat 11 g; Chol 127 mg; Sod 815 mg.

*Carl J. Davis, Union Oyster House Restaurant*


## DEVILED CRAB

1 pound crab meat
³/₄ cup cracker crumbs
³/₄ cup finely chopped celery
³/₄ cup finely chopped onion
¹/₂ cup melted butter
¹/₄ cup milk

1 tablespoon chopped green bell
pepper
2 tablespoons chopped parsley
1 teaspoon dry mustard
¹/₂ teaspoon salt

Mix crab meat, cracker crumbs, celery and onion in bowl. Add butter and milk; mix until moistened. Stir in remaining ingredients. Spoon into 2-quart baking dish. Bake at 350 degrees for 30 minutes. Yield: 6 servings.

**Approx Per Serving:** Cal 257; Prot 13 g; Carbo 10 g; Fiber 1 g;
T Fat 18 g; Chol 107 mg; Sod 629 mg.

*Elizabeth Forsyth, WEIU Friend*


## DIET CRAB MEAT QUICHE

6 ounces Alaskan crab meat
5 ounces nonfat Swiss cheese,
crumbled
1   12-ounce can evaporated milk
3 eggs, slightly beaten

Nutmeg and cayenne pepper to
taste
¹/₂ teaspoon salt
¹/₈ teaspoon pepper

Layer crab meat and cheese in pie plate sprayed with nonstick cooking spray. Combine evaporated milk, eggs, nutmeg, cayenne pepper, salt and pepper in bowl; mix well. Pour over layers. Bake at 400 degrees for 30 minutes. Let stand for 10 minutes before serving. Yield: 6 servings.

**Approx Per Serving:** Cal 100; Prot 11 g; Carbo 6 g; Fiber 0 g;
T Fat 3 g; Chol 131 mg; Sod 330 mg.
Nutritional information does not include nonfat Swiss cheese.

*Lois L. Lindauer, The Diet Workshop, Inc.*

## CORN AND CRAB STEW

½ cup chopped onion
½ cup chopped celery
1 tablespoon butter
12 ounces potatoes, chopped, cooked
1 cup clam juice
1 cup water

¼ teaspoon red pepper flakes
Salt and pepper to taste
1 cup corn kernels
1 cup cooked crab meat
Cilantro and coriander to taste
1 cup half and half

Sauté onion and celery in butter in saucepan. Add potatoes, clam juice, water, red pepper flakes, salt and pepper. Bring to a boil. Stir in corn, crab meat, cilantro and coriander. Simmer for 5 minutes. Stir in half and half. Heat just to serving temperature. *I buy all my needlework supplies and many lovely gifts at the Union shop.* Yield: 2 servings.

**Approx Per Serving:** Cal 545; Prot 22 g; Carbo 70 g; Fiber 7 g; T Fat 22 g; Chol 117 mg; Sod 797 mg.

*Mrs. Peter C. Mackin, WEIU Friend*

## LOBSTER AND CRAB CAKES

⅓ cup finely chopped onion
⅓ cup each finely chopped red and green bell pepper
⅓ cup finely chopped celery
2 tablespoons Worcestershire sauce
1 tablespoon Tabasco sauce
1 tablespoon lemon juice

1 teaspoon each salt and pepper
1 cup chopped lobster meat
1 cup chopped king crab meat
1¾ cups mayonnaise
2 eggs
1 cup (or more) dry bread crumbs
2 tablespoons butter

Combine onion, bell peppers, celery, Worcestershire sauce, Tabasco sauce, lemon juice, salt and pepper in bowl; mix well. Fold in lobster, crab meat, mayonnaise and eggs. Add 1 cup bread crumbs or enough to make of desired consistency; mix gently. Shape into 12 patties. Coat with remaining bread crumbs. Sauté in butter in skillet until golden brown. Serve with caper mayonnaise. Yield: 12 servings.

**Approx Per Serving:** Cal 300; Prot 7 g; Carbo 8 g; Fiber <1 g; T Fat 27 g; Chol 73 mg; Sod 365 mg.

*Leah Kesten, The Captain's Table Restaurant*

**1913** *The social service agent in charge of helping handicapped or untrained women find employment helped 1,847 women find work.*

# GRILLED LOBSTER

2 1-pound lobsters
3 tablespoons butter, softened
2 to 3 tablespoons fresh bread
  crumbs
Chopped parsley and garlic to
  taste
Salt and pepper to taste
3 tablespoons melted butter

2 tablespoons whiskey
1 shallot, chopped
1 tablespoon butter
1¹/₂ ounces whiskey
1 cup lobster stock
Juice of 1 lemon
2 tablespoons butter

Remove claws from lobsters. Boil in water to cover in saucepan for 5 minutes; drain. Remove meat from shells; set aside. Split lobsters into halves, discarding sand sack and brain. Remove tomalley and eggs to small bowl. Add 3 tablespoons butter, bread crumbs, parsley, garlic, salt and pepper; mix well. Brush lobster meat with 3 tablespoons melted butter and 2 tablespoons whiskey; sprinkle with salt and pepper. Place cut side down on hot grill. Grill until shell is red halfway up; turn lobsters. Spoon stuffing mixture into cavities of lobsters. Grill, covered, for 5 minutes. Sauté shallot in 1 tablespoon butter in saucepan until tender. Add 1¹/₂ ounces whiskey. Ignite with match; let flame die down. Stir in lobster stock, lemon juice and salt. Cook until reduced by half. Stir in 2 tablespoons butter. Add claw meat. Place lobsters on serving plates; spoon sauce over top. *My first "experience" in the cooking world was making pecan rolls, apple pies and date nut bread for the Union in 1989.* Yield: 2 servings.

**Approx Per Serving:** Cal 719; Prot 70 g; Carbo 9 g; Fiber 1 g;
    T Fat 38 g; Chol 438 mg; Sod 1448 mg.

*Lydia Shire, Biba Restaurant*

# LOBSTER MERRYMOUNT

3 cups flaked lobster meat
1 cup heavy cream
1 cup milk
1 cup soft bread crumbs
2 eggs, slightly beaten
2 tablespoons butter
¹/₂ teaspoon lemon juice

1 teaspoon prepared mustard
Cayenne pepper to taste
1 teaspoon salt
¹/₄ teaspoon pepper
1 cup dry bread crumbs
2 tablespoons melted butter

Combine lobster meat, cream, milk and soft bread crumbs in large saucepan. Bring to a boil, stirring constantly. Stir a small amount of hot mixture into eggs; stir eggs into hot mixture. Pour into double boiler. Add 2 tablespoons butter, lemon juice, mustard, cayenne pepper, salt and pepper; mix well. Cook until thickened, stirring constantly. Spoon into lightly buttered baking dish. Top with mixture of dry bread crumbs and melted butter. Bake at 325 degrees for 30 minutes. Yield: 8 servings.

**Approx Per Serving:** Cal 343; Prot 13 g; Carbo 23 g; Fiber 1 g;
    T Fat 22 g; Chol 151 mg; Sod 680 mg.

*Nancy Rust Fitts, WEIU Employee*

## AGNES GLENNON'S LOBSTER NEWBURG

3 tablespoons flour
1/4 teaspoon salt
1/8 teaspoon pepper
1/4 cup melted margarine
1 cup half and half, warmed
2 ounces (about) Velveeta
cheese, chopped

3 tablespoons undiluted tomato
soup
1 pound knuckle lobster meat
2 tablespoons sherry
Nutmeg to taste

Blend flour, salt and pepper into melted margarine in medium saucepan. Cook for 2 minutes, stirring constantly. Add half and half gradually. Cook until thickened, stirring constantly. Stir in cheese until melted. Add soup and lobster meat. Chill overnight to improve flavor. Heat just to serving temperature in double boiler. Stir in wine and nutmeg. Serve with tiny peas and molded salad. May substitute milk for part of the half and half. *This was a favorite recipe of Agnes Glennon who was the chef for the executives of a company in Cambridge for many years.* Yield: 4 servings.

**Approx Per Serving:** Cal 423; Prot 21 g; Carbo 9 g; Fiber <1 g;
    T Fat 33 g; Chol 159 mg; Sod 744 mg.

*Mrs. Robert K. Quinn, WEIU Member*

## SCALLOPS AND PASTA

1 red bell pepper, chopped
1 green bell pepper, chopped
1 bunch scallions, chopped
1 clove of garlic, chopped
2 tablespoons olive oil

1 pound scallops
Fresh tarragon or basil to taste
Salt and pepper to taste
12 cherry tomatoes
1/2 cup black olives

Sauté bell peppers, scallions and garlic in olive oil in large skillet. Add scallops, tarragon, salt and pepper. Sauté until scallops are cooked through. Add tomatoes and olives. Serve over desired amount of hot cooked linguini. Serve with Parmesan cheese. Yield: 4 servings.

**Approx Per Serving:** Cal 187; Prot 23 g; Carbo 12 g; Fiber 4 g;
    T Fat 8 g; Chol 40 mg; Sod 403 mg.

*Diane Goldman, WEIU Employee*

**1913**  *In this year, 18,000 school lunches were served to 16 schools.*

## BAY SCALLOPS SAUTÉ AU SHERRY

2 pounds bay scallops
1/2 cup flour
Oil for frying
Salt and pepper to taste

1/4 cup butter
1/4 cup sherry
Juice of 1/2 lemon
Chopped parsley to taste

Drain scallops and pat dry. Coat with flour, shaking to remove excess. Fry lightly 1/2 at a time in 1/4 inch oil in iron skillet for 5 minutes. Do not overcook. Remove to warm plate; sprinkle with salt and pepper. Drain skillet. Heat butter in skillet until light brown; remove from heat. Stir in sherry, lemon juice and parsley. Pour over scallops. Yield: 4 servings.

Approx Per Serving: Cal 383; Prot 43 g; Carbo 18 g; Fiber 1 g;
T Fat 14 g; Chol 111 mg; Sod 456 mg.
Nutritional information does not include oil for frying.

*William Harrington, Algonquin Club Restaurant*

## BOURBON SHRIMP

1 shallot, minced
1 clove of garlic, crushed
3/4 cup white wine
6 jumbo shrimp, shelled,
  deveined

2 tablespoons bourbon
1 cup heavy cream
1/2 teaspoon Dijon mustard

Combine 3/4 of the shallot, garlic and wine in saucepan. Simmer until wine has nearly evaporated. Add shrimp. Cook until shrimp are pink, stirring constantly. Add bourbon; ignite with match. Stir in cream. Simmer for 2 minutes, stirring gently. Stir in mustard. Top with remaining shallot. Serve over angel hair pasta or rice. Yield: 2 servings.

Approx Per Serving: Cal 575; Prot 17 g; Carbo 5 g; Fiber <1 g;
T Fat 45 g; Chol 296 mg; Sod 218 mg.

*Judith R. Haberkorn, WEIU Member*

**1913** *A fellowship was given to Sybil Foster to study silversmithing at the Museum School. She was to pay particular attention to the making of table silver and articles other than jewelry to then sell in the Handwork Shop at the Union.*

## SHRIMP AND CRAB MEAT PIE

2 eggs
1/2 cup mayonnaise
2 tablespoons flour
1/2 cup milk
6 medium mushrooms, sliced
8 ounces crab meat

8 ounces cooked shrimp
Salt and pepper to taste
1 unbaked pie shell
1/2 cup fine bread crumbs
2 tablespoons melted butter
1/2 cup shredded Cheddar cheese

Beat eggs in medium bowl. Add mayonnaise, flour and milk; mix well. Stir in mushrooms, crab meat, shrimp, salt and pepper. Spoon into pie shell. Top with mixture of bread crumbs and melted butter. Bake at 350 degrees for 30 minutes. Sprinkle with cheese. Bake for 6 to 8 minutes longer or until cheese melts. Let stand for 8 to 10 minutes before serving. Serve with green salad and crusty rolls or bread. Yield: 6 servings.

**Approx Per Serving:** Cal 528; Prot 24 g; Carbo 23 g; Fiber 1 g;
T Fat 38 g; Chol 222 mg; Sod 677 mg.

*Mary Maynard, WEIU Member*

## LEMON GINGER SCAMPI

1/4 cup avocado oil
2 cloves of garlic, minced
1 tablespoon Tamari sauce
Juice of 1/2 large lemon
1/2 teaspoon minced fresh ginger

2 pounds 21 to 24-count shrimp,
peeled
1 1/2 teaspoons freshly ground
pepper

Combine avocado oil, garlic, Tamari sauce, lemon juice and ginger in bowl. Add shrimp; mix well. Marinate for 30 minutes. Preheat broiler for 10 minutes. Drain shrimp; arrange on rack in broiler pan. Sprinkle with pepper. Broil 5 inches from heat source for 5 to 7 minutes or until done to taste, turning once. Garnish with parsley. Yield: 6 servings.

**Approx Per Serving:** Cal 202; Prot 25 g; Carbo 1 g; Fiber <1 g;
T Fat 10 g; Chol 236 mg; Sod 271 mg.
Nutritional information includes entire amount of marinade but does not include Tamari sauce.

*Stephen E. Lizio, Be Our Guest Caterer*

**The Handwork Department**
*The WEIU taught classes on handwork; finished items
were sold in the Gift Shop.*

**The Appointment Bureau**
*Training classes for clerical workers were sponsored by
the WEIU's Appointment Bureau in the 1920s.*

# Vegetable and Side Dishes

### BAKED BEANS

Every Yankee housekeeper knows how to bake beans but I will give my way for the rest of mankind. Pick over a quart of pea beans; wash and soak overnight in plenty of cold water. In the morning put into a kettle on the back of stove, pour on a teakettleful of boiling water and let them stand 20 minutes. Prepare ½ pound of fat pork. Put into a cup one even teaspoonful of dry mustard, 2 teaspoonfuls of salt, 2 tablespoonfuls of molasses, mix well and fill the cup with boiling water. Pour over the beans which have been placed in the pot, with pork in the centre. Fill the pot with boiling water, cover, and bake eight or ten hours.

*Mrs. Ellen S. Coffin*
*from* **The Kirmess Cookbook,** *1887*

# BAKED BEANS

1 10-ounce package dried navy beans
4 ounces sliced bacon, chopped
1/2 yellow onion, chopped
8 cups water
1/4 cup molasses

1/4 cup packed brown sugar
1 cup catsup
1 tablespoon prepared mustard
Salt and freshly ground pepper to taste

Soak beans in water to cover in saucepan overnight; drain. Brown bacon in saucepan. Add onion. Cook for 5 minutes. Add water, molasses, brown sugar, catsup, mustard and beans. Bring to a boil; reduce heat. Simmer for 3 to 4 hours or until beans are tender, adding additional water if necessary. Season with salt and pepper. Yield: 4 servings.

**Approx Per Serving:** Cal 326; Prot 10 g; Carbo 63 g; Fiber 8 g;
T Fat 5 g; Chol 7 mg; Sod 922 mg.

*Chris Schlesinger, East Coast Grill Restaurant*

# PENNSYLVANIA RED CABBAGE

2 tablespoons bacon drippings
1/4 cup packed brown sugar
1/4 cup vinegar
1/4 cup water
1 1/4 teaspoons salt

1/2 to 1 teaspoon caraway seed
Pepper to taste
4 cups shredded red cabbage
2 cups chopped unpeeled apples

Heat bacon drippings in skillet. Stir in brown sugar, vinegar, water, salt, caraway seed and pepper. Add cabbage and apple, stirring to coat. Cook, covered, over low heat for 30 minutes, stirring occasionally. May substitute oil for bacon drippings. Yield: 8 servings.

**Approx Per Serving:** Cal 83; Prot 1 g; Carbo 13 g; Fiber 2 g;
T Fat 4 g; Chol 21 mg; Sod 377 mg.

*Jack Hutter, WEIU Friend*

1913  *The Food Laboratory made cakes for the Union's lunchrooms as well as becoming a laboratory for testing food and estimating costs. Special attention was given to the production of food on a large scale.*

# MARINATED CARROTS

2 pounds carrots, peeled
1 onion, sliced into rings
1 green bell pepper, cut into
   strips
1/2  10-ounce can tomato soup
1 cup sugar

1/2 cup white vinegar
1/2 teaspoon salt
Pepper to taste
1/2 teaspoon dry mustard
1/4 cup oil

Cook carrots in a small amount of water in saucepan until tender; drain.
Cut into matchsticks. Combine with onion rings and green pepper in
bowl. Combine soup, sugar, vinegar, salt, pepper, dry mustard and oil in
bowl; mix well. Add to carrot mixture; mix well. Marinate in refrigerator
for several days. Serve hot or cold. Yield: 8 servings.

**Approx Per Serving:** Cal 473; Prot 8 g; Carbo 99 g; Fiber 22 g;
   T Fat 9 g; Chol 0 mg; Sod 494 mg.

*Saul Scheff, WEIU Friend*

# CARROT RING

2 tablespoons butter
2 tablespoons flour
1/2 cup milk
1/2 teaspoon salt

4 egg yolks, beaten
2 cups mashed cooked carrots
4 egg whites, stiffly beaten

Melt butter in saucepan. Add flour; mix well. Stir in milk. Cook until
thickened, stirring constantly; remove from heat. Add salt. Stir a small
amount of hot mixture into egg yolks; stir egg yolks into hot mixture. Add
carrots; mix well. Fold in egg whites gently. Pour into buttered ring mold.
Place mold in larger pan filled with 1 inch hot water. Bake at 325 degrees
for 30 minutes or until set. Let stand for several minutes. Invert onto hot
serving platter. Fill center with green peas, creamed mushrooms, or
asparagus tips. Yield: 8 servings.

**Approx Per Serving:** Cal 79; Prot 4 g; Carbo 7 g; Fiber 2 g;
   T Fat 3 g; Chol 108 mg; Sod 237 mg.

*Mrs. George R. Rowland, WEIU Friend*

**1914**  *At the invitation of Harvard Medical School, the New England
Kitchen opened a lunchroom in one of its buildings.*

## FRENCH PEAS

1/4 cup butter
1/2 cup chopped onion
2  6-ounce cans artichoke
   hearts, drained

2  6-ounce cans tiny peas,
   drained
Salt and pepper to taste

Melt butter in saucepan. Add onion. Sauté for 3 minutes or until golden. Add artichoke hearts; mix gently. Place peas in buttered baking dish. Spoon artichokes and onions over peas. Let stand, covered with foil, for 8 hours. Bake, covered, at 375 degrees for 35 to 45 minutes or until heated through. Yield: 4 servings.

**Approx Per Serving:** Cal 205; Prot 6 g; Carbo 21 g; Fiber 4 g;
    T Fat 12 g; Chol 31 mg; Sod 339 mg.

*Marianne B. Abrams, WEIU Trustee*

## POTATO FILLING

8 potatoes, peeled, chopped
2 onions, chopped
1 cup chopped celery
1 teaspoon salt
8 slices bread

1/2 cup (or more) milk
3 eggs
1/2 cup butter, softened
1/4 cup chopped parsley

Cook potatoes, onions and celery with salt in a small amount of water in saucepan until potatoes are tender; drain. Soak bread in milk in bowl. Add to potato mixture; mix well. Add eggs, butter and parsley; mix well. Add any remaining milk if needed for desired consistency. Spoon into large casserole. Bake at 350 degrees for 45 to 60 minutes or until set. Yield: 8 servings.

**Approx Per Serving:** Cal 451; Prot 10 g; Carbo 69 g; Fiber 6 g;
    T Fat 16 g; Chol 113 mg; Sod 569 mg.

*Eleanor Hutter, WEIU Friend*

**1914**  *By this time, catering had become a recognized profession for women.*

## SPINACH WITH ARTICHOKES

2  10-ounce packages fresh
   spinach
2  12-ounce jars marinated
   artichoke hearts, drained,
   chopped

8 ounces cream cheese, softened
1/2 cup melted butter
1/4 cup milk
2 tablespoons plus 1/2 cup
   grated Parmesan cheese

Wash spinach; remove stems and heavy veins. Place in glass baking dish. Microwave on High for 1 1/2 minutes. Layer artichoke hearts and spinach in 9x13-inch baking dish. Combine cream cheese, butter, milk and 2 tablespoons Parmesan cheese in bowl; mix well. Spoon over spinach. Sprinkle with remaining 1/2 cup Parmesan cheese. Bake, covered with foil, for 30 minutes. Broil, uncovered, for 1 to 2 minutes or until brown. Yield: 10 servings.

**Approx Per Serving:** Cal 267; Prot 7 g; Carbo 8 g; Fiber 6 g;
   T Fat 26 g; Chol 54 mg; Sod 644 mg.

*Joan Kittredge, WEIU Friend*

## SPINACH AND ARTICHOKE CASSEROLE

1  10-ounce package frozen
   artichokes
2  10-ounce packages frozen
   chopped spinach
1/2 cup melted margarine

8 ounces cream cheese, softened
1 tablespoon lemon juice
2 cups herb-seasoned stuffing
   mix
2 tablespoons margarine

Cook artichokes using package directions; drain. Place in shallow casserole. Cook spinach using package directions; drain. Combine with melted margarine, cream cheese and lemon juice in bowl; mix well. Spoon over artichokes. Sprinkle stuffing mix over top; dot with 2 tablespoons margarine. Bake at 350 degrees for 25 minutes. Yield: 6 servings.

**Approx Per Serving:** Cal 348; Prot 8 g; Carbo 17 g; Fiber 6 g;
   T Fat 29 g; Chol 83 mg; Sod 408 mg.

*Mrs. R. Forbes Perkins, WEIU Trustee*

1916   *The Food Laboratory made 26 different kinds of cakes—18 loaves
and 8 individual cakes—amounting to an output of 109,000 cakes
for the year.*

## SUMMER SQUASH CASSEROLE

6 medium summer squash,
  sliced 1/2 inch thick
1/4 cup butter, sliced
1/2 cup shredded Cheddar cheese
1 medium onion, sliced

Salt and pepper to taste
1/2 cup half and half
1/2 cup seasoned bread crumbs
1/4 cup melted butter

Steam squash for 10 minutes; remove seed. Layer squash, sliced butter, cheese, onion, salt and pepper 1/2 at a time in 4-quart casserole. Pour half and half over layers. Sprinkle with mixture of bread crumbs and melted butter. Bake at 350 degrees for 30 minutes or until crumbs are brown. Yield: 8 servings.

**Approx Per Serving:** Cal 224; Prot 4 g; Carbo 11 g; Fiber 2 g;
  T Fat 19 g; Chol 55 mg; Sod 194 mg.

*Mrs. George Lovejoy, WEIU Member*

## TOMATOES FLORENTINE

1  10-ounce package frozen
  spinach
1/2 cup soft bread crumbs
1/2 cup seasoned dry bread
  crumbs
1/2 cup finely chopped green
  onions
3 eggs, slightly beaten

1/4 cup melted butter
1/3 cup freshly grated Parmesan
  cheese
4 slices crisp-fried bacon,
  crumbled
Pepper to taste
8 thick tomato slices

Cook spinach using package directions; drain. Combine with bread crumbs, green onions, eggs, butter, cheese, bacon and pepper in bowl; mix well. Arrange tomato slices in greased 9x9-inch glass baking dish. Spoon spinach mixture on top of each slice. Bake at 350 degrees for 15 minutes or until light brown. Yield: 8 servings.

**Approx Per Serving:** Cal 161; Prot 7 g; Carbo 9 g; Fiber 2 g;
  T Fat 11 g; Chol 101 mg; Sod 276 mg.

*Betsy Ryan, WEIU Friend*

**1916** *Bertha Mahoney Miller founded the Union's Bookshop for Boys and Girls.*

# PICCALILLI

2 quarts chopped green tomatoes
3 small onions, chopped
1/4 cup salt
1 green bell pepper, chopped
1 red bell pepper, chopped

2 cups chopped celery
1 1/4 cups packed brown sugar
1 1/2 cups vinegar
1/4 cup mixed pickling spices

Combine tomatoes, onions and salt in bowl. Let stand overnight; drain. Combine with peppers, celery, brown sugar and vinegar in saucepan. Add spices tied in cheesecloth bag. Simmer for 2 1/2 hours or until tender. Remove spice bag. Pour into hot sterilized jars, leaving 1/2-inch headspace. Seal with 2-piece lids. Yield: 40 servings.

**Approx Per Serving:** Cal 39; Prot <1 g; Carbo 10 g; Fiber <1 g; T Fat <1 g; Chol 0 mg; Sod 651 mg.

*Anita MacKinnon, WEIU Employee*

# PINEAPPLE BREAD PUDDING

1/2 cup butter, softened
4 1/2 teaspoons artificial
  sweetener
4 eggs

1  16-ounce can crushed
  pineapple
8 slices bread, cubed

Cream butter and artificial sweetener in mixer bowl until light and fluffy. Add eggs; mix well. Add undrained pineapple; fold in bread cubes. Pour into greased 1 1/2-quart casserole. Bake at 350 degrees for 1 hour or until light brown. This tastes sinfully rich. Yield: 6 servings.

**Approx Per Serving:** Cal 321; Prot 6 g; Carbo 34 g; Fiber 1 g; T Fat 19 g; Chol 112 mg; Sod 345 mg.

*Michelle Camp, WEIU Friend*

# GRITS SOUFFLÉ

2 cups quick-cooking grits
8 cups boiling water
1 cup melted butter
4 ounces Boursin cheese

1 teaspoon Worcestershire sauce
1 teaspoon Tabasco sauce
2 eggs, beaten
1/2 teaspoon dillweed

Add grits to boiling water in saucepan. Cook for 3 minutes or until water is almost absorbed. Reserve 2 tablespoons melted butter. Add remaining butter, cheese, Worcestershire sauce, Tabasco sauce and eggs to grits; mix well. Spoon into 9x13-inch baking dish. Drizzle with reserved 2 tablespoons butter; sprinkle with dillweed. Bake at 300 degrees for 1 hour. Yield: 12 servings.

**Approx Per Serving:** Cal 279; Prot 4 g; Carbo 21 g; Fiber 3 g; T Fat 20 g; Chol 87 mg; Sod 174 mg.

*Evelyn W. Farnum, WEIU Trustee*

# RICE ALFREDO

¼ cup butter
1 cup half and half
3 cups hot cooked rice

½ cup grated Parmesan cheese
½ teaspoon salt
¾ teaspoon seasoned pepper

**M**elt butter in saucepan. Add half and half. Cook until heated through. Add rice, cheese and seasonings; toss gently. This recipe is as delicious as fettucini Alfredo and can be served as a side dish or entrée. Yield: 8 servings.

**Approx Per Serving:** Cal 197; Prot 5 g; Carbo 20 g; Fiber <1 g;
    T Fat 11 g; Chol 31 mg; Sod 288 mg.

*Evelyn W. Farnum, WEIU Trustee*

# GREEN RICE

2 cups cooked rice
⅔ cup olive oil
1 clove of garlic, chopped
1 medium onion, chopped
1 medium green bell pepper,
    chopped
½ cup minced parsley

1 cup shredded sharp Cheddar
    cheese
1   4-ounce can green chilies,
    chopped
1   12-ounce can evaporated milk
2 eggs, beaten

**C**ombine rice and olive oil in bowl; mix well. Add garlic, onion, green pepper, parsley, cheese, green chilies and evaporated milk; mix well. Add eggs; mix well. Spoon into buttered 2-quart casserole. Bake at 350 degrees for 1¼ hours. May be made the day ahead, stored in refrigerator, and baked before serving. Yield: 12 servings.

**Approx Per Serving:** Cal 228; Prot 7 g; Carbo 14 g; Fiber 1 g;
    T Fat 16 g; Chol 47 mg; Sod 105 mg.

*Willona H. Sinclair, WEIU Friend*

**1916** *The Lunch Room had to enforce meatless and wheatless days to observe national conservation measures during World War I.*

# Rice Pilaf

1/4 cup uncooked orzo
2 cups chicken stock
3 tablespoons butter
1/2 teaspoon salt
1/2 teaspoon pepper

Pinch of dried mint
Pinch of dried basil
1 teaspoon parsley flakes
1 cup uncooked rice

Brown orzo in saucepan over low heat, shaking saucepan constantly. Add chicken stock, butter, salt, pepper, mint, basil and parsley flakes. Bring to a boil. Rinse rice 3 times. Add to saucepan; cover. Bring to a boil; reduce heat. Simmer for 20 minutes. Cook for 2 to 3 minutes longer or until liquid is absorbed. Remove cover; mix well. Let stand for 5 to 6 minutes. Rice Pilaf is a staple of Armenian cookery and has many variations. This basic recipe may be embellished with tomatoes, mushrooms, vermicelli or many other ingredients. Yield: 3 servings.

**Approx Per Serving:** Cal 386; Prot 9 g; Carbo 57 g; Fiber 1 g;
T Fat 13 g; Chol 32 mg; Sod 973 mg.

*Virginia A. Tashjian, WEIU Friend*

# Cheese Sauce

3 tablespoons margarine
2 tablespoons flour
1 tablespoon dry mustard
1 teaspoon onion juice
2 cups evaporated milk

1/2 teaspoon Worcestershire
sauce
8 ounces sharp Cheddar cheese,
shredded
Pinch of cayenne pepper

Melt margarine in saucepan over low heat. Stir in flour. Cook for several minutes. Add dry mustard, onion juice, evaporated milk, Worcestershire sauce, cheese and cayenne pepper; mix well. Cook over low heat until cheese melts; do not boil. May be used as sauce for Welsh Rarebit. Yield: 48 servings.

**Approx Per Serving:** Cal 41; Prot 2 g; Carbo 1 g; Fiber <1 g;
T Fat 3 g; Chol 8 mg; Sod 49 mg.

*Helen H. Hodgdon, former WEIU Food Shop Director*

1916  *In this year, 13,500 pounds of candy were made in the Candy Kitchen.*

## UNCLE BOUNCE'S MUSTARD

2 2-ounce cans dry mustard  
2 cups wine vinegar  
2 eggs, beaten  

8 envelopes artificial sweetener  
1¹/₂ cups mayonnaise  

Combine dry mustard and vinegar in 2-quart glass bowl; mix well. Let stand overnight. Add eggs and sweetener. Beat for 1 minute. Microwave on High for 2 minutes; mix well. Microwave on High for 2 minutes, stirring once. Add mayonnaise; beat until blended. Chill in refrigerator. May add sour cream for lighter taste. *This recipe was discovered by former WEIU member Betty Arnold's son, Uncle Bounce. The entire family uses it faithfully, and we have many requests for it.* Yield: 32 servings.

**Approx Per Serving:** Cal 83; Prot 1 g; Carbo 1 g; Fiber <1 g;  
T Fat 9 g; Chol 19 mg; Sod 107 mg.

*Robin Hoefer, WEIU Friend*

## EXTRA ZINGY MUSTARD SAUCE

1 cup dry mustard  
1 cup malt vinegar  

1 cup sugar  
3 eggs  

Place dry mustard in double boiler. Stir in vinegar gradually. Let stand, covered, overnight. Beat sugar and eggs in mixer bowl until light and fluffy. Add to mustard mixture; mix well. Cook over hot water until thickened, stirring constantly. Pour into hot sterilized jars; seal with 2-piece lids. Store in refrigerator for 3 days before using. Fill jars to top as mustard will settle as it cools. *I remember coming to the Union as a little girl with my uncle to buy delicious cookies.* Yield: 32 servings.

**Approx Per Serving:** Cal 40; Prot 1 g; Carbo 8 g; Fiber <1 g;  
T Fat 1 g; Chol 20 mg; Sod 105 mg.

*Gail Perrin, Food Editor, **The Boston Globe***

## SPAETZLE

2 cups flour  
1 teaspoon salt  
2 eggs, beaten  

³/₄ cup milk  
¹/₂ cup fine dry bread crumbs  
¹/₄ cup melted butter  

Mix flour and salt in bowl. Add mixture of eggs and milk; mix well. Pour into colander with large holes. Press through colander into large saucepan of boiling salted water. Cook for 5 minutes, stirring constantly; drain. Pour into serving dish. Sprinkle mixture of bread crumbs and melted butter over top. Spaetzle may be patted thin on floured surface and cut instead of pressing through sieve. Yield: 6 servings.

**Approx Per Serving:** Cal 297; Prot 9 g; Carbo 39 g; Fiber 1 g;  
T Fat 11 g; Chol 96 mg; Sod 518 mg.

*Jack Hutter, WEIU Friend*

## CALDWELL'S CURRY POWDER

| | |
|---|---|
| ½ cup coriander seed | 1 tablespoon cardamom pods or |
| ¼ cup ground turmeric | 1 teaspoon cardamom seed |
| 1 tablespoon cumin seed | 1 teaspoon peppercorns |
| 1  4-inch cinnamon stick | 2 bay leaves |
| 5 whole cloves | 1 teaspoon ground ginger |

Combine coriander seed, turmeric, cumin seed, cinnamon stick, cloves, cardamom, peppercorns, bay leaves and ginger in shallow baking pan. Bake at 300 degrees for 25 minutes, stirring occasionally. Process in blender or food processor until finely ground. Store in airtight containers. Makes a great holiday or hostess gift. Yield: 16 servings.

Nutritional analysis for this recipe is not available.

*Ann W. Caldwell, WEIU Trustee*

## FRESH TOMATO VINAIGRETTE

| | |
|---|---|
| 1 teaspoon mixed salt and | 2 tomatoes, peeled, seeded, |
| pepper | finely chopped |
| 2 cloves of garlic, minced | 1 tablespoon balsamic vinegar |
| 1½ cups chopped red onions | 3 cups tomato juice |
| 6 scallions, finely chopped | 2 drops of Tabasco sauce |
| 1 tablespoon minced chives | |

Combine salt and pepper, garlic, onions, scallions, chives, tomatoes, vinegar, tomato juice and Tabasco sauce in bowl. Mix with wire whisk. Chill, tightly covered, overnight. Serve with fish, poultry, veal or vegetables. Yield: 10 servings.

**Approx Per Serving:** Cal 29; Prot 1 g; Carbo 7 g; Fiber 2 g;
  T Fat 2 g; Chol 0 mg; Sod 482 mg.

*F. Christopher Heyl, WEIU Friend*

**1917** *John F. Kennedy, 35th President of the United States, was born in Brookline.*

**The Business Agency in the 1920s**
The Business Agency was one of the first vocational centers for women in the U.S.

# Breads

## OMELET CORN CAKE

A coffee-cup of granulated Indian meal, a cup and a half of sour milk, 2 eggs, a tablespoon of sugar, a heaping tablespoon of butter and a teaspoon of salt. Mix the eggs in the meal, then add the other ingredients, the soda last, beating all the while very thoroughly. Bake in a quick oven and serve at once.

*Mrs. M. E. York*
*from* **The Kirmess Cookbook,** *1887*

# POPPY SEED COFFEE CAKE

1  2¹/₄-ounce jar poppy seed
1 cup buttermilk
¹/₂ teaspoon almond extract
1¹/₂ cups sugar
1 cup unsalted butter, softened
4 egg yolks
2¹/₂ cups flour

1 teaspoon baking powder
1 teaspoon soda
¹/₂ teaspoon salt
4 egg whites, stiffly beaten
¹/₂ cup sugar
1 teaspoon cinnamon

Combine poppy seed, buttermilk and almond extract in small bowl; mix well and set aside. Cream 1¹/₂ cups sugar and butter in mixer bowl until light and fluffy. Beat in egg yolks. Mix flour, baking powder, soda and salt together. Add to creamed mixture alternately with poppy seed mixture, mixing well after each addition. Fold in stiffly beaten egg whites gently. Layer batter and mixture of ¹/₂ cup sugar and cinnamon ¹/₂ at a time in greased 10-inch tube pan. Bake at 350 degrees for 45 minutes or until coffee cake tests done. Cool in pan for 5 to 10 minutes. Invert onto serving plate. Serve as dessert for brunch or with tea or coffee. Yield: 12 servings.

**Approx Per Serving:** Cal 394; Prot 6 g; Carbo 54 g; Fiber 1 g;
    T Fat 18 g; Chol 113 mg; Sod 233 mg.

*Mary S. Hurley, WEIU Friend*

# SOUR CREAM COFFEE CAKE

¹/₂ cup butter, softened
1 cup sugar
2 eggs
1 cup sour cream
¹/₂ teaspoon vanilla extract
2¹/₄ cups flour

1 teaspoon soda
¹/₂ teaspoon baking powder
¹/₂ teaspoon salt
¹/₂ cup sugar
2 teaspoons cinnamon
¹/₂ cup chopped walnuts

Cream butter and sugar in mixer bowl. Add eggs, sour cream and vanilla; mix well. Add flour, soda, baking powder and salt; mix well. Mix ¹/₂ cup sugar, cinnamon and walnuts in small bowl. Layer half the batter and ¹/₃ of the walnut mixture in greased bundt pan. Add layers of remaining batter and remaining walnut mixture. Bake at 350 degrees for 40 to 45 minutes or until coffee cake tests done. Cool in pan for 5 to 10 minutes. Invert onto serving plate. Yield: 12 servings.

**Approx Per Serving:** Cal 337; Prot 5 g; Carbo 45 g; Fiber 1 g;
    T Fat 16 g; Chol 65 mg; Sod 190 mg.

*Elizabeth J. Haddad, WEIU Executive Director*

## SOMERSET CORN DODGERS

9 cups water
1½ cups unsalted butter

1 tablespoon salt
3½ cups cornmeal

Combine water, butter and salt in saucepan. Bring to a boil. Boil until butter melts; pour into mixer bowl. Add cornmeal gradually, beating until smooth. Drop by spoonfuls onto greased baking sheet. Drop baking sheet onto work surface to flatten corn dodgers. Bake at 500 degrees or until golden brown on bottom; turn. Bake until crisp and golden brown. Serve hot with butter or jam. Yield: 48 servings.

**Approx Per Serving:** Cal 89; Prot 1 g; Carbo 8 g; Fiber <1 g;
T Fat 6 g; Chol 16 mg; Sod 134 mg.

*Dennis Michel, Somerset Club Restaurant*

## DENTIST'S DREAM FRENCH TOAST

5 eggs
1 cup whipping cream
3 tablespoons sugar
¼ teaspoon cinnamon

1 teaspoon vanilla extract
¼ cup butter
6 slices whole wheat bread

Beat eggs in bowl. Add whipping cream, sugar, cinnamon and vanilla; mix well. Melt butter a small amount at a time in hot skillet. Dip bread slice into egg mixture; place in butter in skillet. Fry until light brown on both sides, turning once. Repeat with remaining butter, bread and egg mixture. Place on serving plate. Garnish with dusting of confectioners' sugar. Dig in—then call the dentist! Yield: 6 servings.

**Approx Per Serving:** Cal 362; Prot 8 g; Carbo 21 g; Fiber 1 g;
T Fat 28 g; Chol 253 mg; Sod 243 mg.

*U. S. Representative Joseph P. Kennedy II, WEIU Friend*

1919   *The Research Department had four fellows—two from the University of Wisconsin, one from Mt. Holyoke, and one from Radcliffe. The subject investigated was "How Self-Supporting Women May Provide for Their Old Age."*

## FRENCH TOAST WITH APPLE SLICES

1½ cups low-fat milk
½ teaspoon vanilla extract
2 cinnamon sticks
2 tablespoons grated lemon zest
4 eggs, beaten
8  1-inch slices French bread
4 tart green apples

1 tablespoon margarine
¼ cup honey
½ teaspoon grated lemon zest
1 tablespoon lemon juice
¼ teaspoon cinnamon
4 ounces low-fat Cheddar
  cheese, cut into ¼-inch cubes

Combine milk, vanilla, cinnamon sticks and 2 tablespoons lemon zest in saucepan. Simmer for 10 minutes. Discard cinnamon sticks. Let stand until cooled to room temperature. Whisk eggs into milk mixture. Dip bread slices into mixture; arrange in 9x13-inch dish. Pour remaining milk mixture over bread. Chill for 15 minutes to overnight. Cut unpeeled apples into bite-sized pieces. Sauté apples in margarine in skillet for 3 minutes. Add honey, ½ teaspoon lemon zest, lemon juice and cinnamon; mix well. Simmer until apples are tender; remove from heat. Stir in cheese. Preheat large nonstick skillet over medium-high heat. Place bread slices in skillet. Cook until golden brown on both sides, turning once. Place on plates. Spoon apple mixture over top. Yield: 8 servings.

**Approx Per Serving:** Cal 306; Prot 12 g; Carbo 40 g; Fiber 3 g;
    T Fat 11 g; Chol 126 mg; Sod 366 mg.

*Jack Hutter, WEIU Friend*

## CHEESY APPLE WALNUT BREAD

6 tablespoons margarine,
  softened
½ cup sugar
2 eggs
1 cup coarsely shredded tart
  apple
¾ cup finely chopped walnuts

½ cup shredded Cheddar cheese
1 cup whole wheat flour
1 cup unbleached flour
2 teaspoons baking powder
¼ teaspoon salt
¼ cup skim milk
¼ cup finely chopped walnuts

Cream margarine and sugar in mixer bowl until light and fluffy. Beat in eggs. Add apple, ¾ cup walnuts and cheese; mix well. Mix flours, baking powder and salt together. Add half the flour mixture to apple mixture; stir until moistened. Stir in skim milk and remaining flour mixture. Pour into greased 5x9-inch loaf pan. Sprinkle remaining ¼ cup walnuts on top. Bake at 375 degrees for 35 to 40 minutes or until loaf tests done. Remove to wire rack to cool. Yield: 12 servings.

**Approx Per Serving:** Cal 260; Prot 6 g; Carbo 28 g; Fiber 2 g;
    T Fat 15 g; Chol 41 mg; Sod 211 mg.

*Alexis N. Voulgaris, WEIU Friend*

## GREAT-GRANDMOTHER'S BANANA BREAD

½ cup butter, softened
1 cup sugar
2 eggs, beaten
½ cup sour cream
2 bananas, mashed

1 teaspoon vanilla extract
2 cups bread flour
2 teaspoons baking powder
1 teaspoon soda
½ cup chopped pecans

Cream butter and sugar in bowl until light and fluffy. Add eggs, sour cream, bananas and vanilla; mix well. Add mixture of flour, baking powder and soda; mix well. Stir in pecans. Pour into greased 5x9-inch loaf pan. Bake at 350 degrees for 45 minutes or until loaf tests done. *Warm bread didn't last long when teenage boys were hungry, so their smart Yankee mother always baked two loaves and hid one to have for dinner.* Yield: 12 servings.

**Approx Per Serving:** Cal 293; Prot 4 g; Carbo 39 g; Fiber 1 g;
T Fat 14 g; Chol 60 mg; Sod 205 mg.

*Jan White, Former WEIU Trustee*

## WHOLE WHEAT BANANA BREAD

2 cups mashed very ripe bananas
¾ cup sugar
2 eggs
2 cups whole wheat flour

1 teaspoon soda
¾ cup chopped pecans
½ teaspoon vanilla extract

Grease 4x9-inch loaf pan well; line bottom with waxed paper. Combine bananas and sugar in mixer bowl; beat until well blended. Beat in eggs. Add mixture of flour and soda; beat until smooth. Stir in pecans and vanilla. Pour into prepared loaf pan. Bake at 325 degrees for 1 hour or until loaf tests done. *This bread was often used in WEIU lunch boxes and also for tea sandwiches. Note that no shortening is used in this recipe so it is a firm bread that slices very well.* Yield: 12 servings.

**Approx Per Serving:** Cal 204; Prot 5 g; Carbo 35 g; Fiber 4 g;
T Fat 7 g; Chol 36 mg; Sod 81 mg.

*Helen H. Hodgdon, Former WEIU Food Shop Director*

**1919** *The Book Caravan traveled for three months in Massachusetts, Maine, New Hampshire, and Vermont, stopping at 49 places. It ended its sojourn at Lake Placid for the New York State Library meeting.*

# BLUEBERRY BREAD

½ cup melted butter
1½ cups sugar
3 eggs
3 cups flour
1 teaspoon baking powder
1 teaspoon soda

½ teaspoon salt
1 teaspoon vanilla extract
1 cup sour cream
2 cups drained canned
  blueberries

Combine butter, sugar and eggs in bowl; blend well. Add mixture of flour, baking powder, soda and salt; mix well. Blend in vanilla and sour cream. Fold in blueberries gently. Pour into greased 5x9-inch loaf pan. Bake at 350 degrees for 40 minutes or until loaf tests done. Cool in pan for several minutes. Remove to wire rack to cool completely. *Several years ago I enjoyed a trip to Charleston, South Carolina for the Festival of Houses. While there, I stayed at the Indigo Inn where a different freshly baked fruit bread was featured each morning for breakfast. On leaving, I told the manager how much I had enjoyed the breads and he gave me recipes of all of them. The Blueberry Bread is one of my favorites.* Yield: 12 servings.

**Approx Per Serving:** Cal 424; Prot 6 g; Carbo 67 g; Fiber 2 g;
    T Fat 15 g; Chol 93 mg; Sod 314 mg.

*Mary Maynard, WEIU Member*

# HAZELNUT AND GINGER CARROT BREAD

2 tablespoons grated dried
  gingerroot
1½ cups boiling water
2 large carrots, grated

10 hazelnuts, chopped
2 cups whole wheat flour
1 teaspoon baking powder
1 egg

Combine gingerroot and boiling water in bowl; steep for several minutes. Add carrots and hazelnuts. Stir in flour and baking powder. Add egg; mix well. Spoon into well greased 5x9-inch loaf pan; spread batter into corners. Bake at 350 degrees for 45 to 90 minutes or until loaf tests done. Cool in pan for several minutes. Remove to wire rack to cool completely. Bread may be eaten fresh but flavors improve with standing. Serve plain or with yogurt or all-fruit jam. May substitute other types of flour for whole wheat or substitute 1 cup oats for 1 cup flour for chewy consistency. Yield: 12 servings.

**Approx Per Serving:** Cal 97; Prot 4 g; Carbo 16 g; Fiber 3 g;
    T Fat 3 g; Chol 18 mg; Sod 38 mg.

*Eva M. Schlesinger, WEIU Friend*

## SPECIAL CRANBERRY WALNUT BREAD

2 cups sifted flour
1 cup sugar
1½ teaspoons baking powder
½ teaspoon soda
1 teaspoon salt
¼ cup butter

1 egg, beaten
1 teaspoon grated orange rind
¾ cup orange juice
1 cup golden raisins
1 cup chopped cranberries
1 cup chopped walnuts

Sift flour, sugar, baking powder, soda and salt into large bowl. Cut in butter until crumbly. Add egg, orange rind and orange juice all at once; stir just until moistened. Fold in raisins, cranberries and walnuts. Spoon into greased 5x9-inch loaf pan. Bake at 350 degrees for 1 hour and 10 minutes or until loaf tests done. Remove from pan. Cool on wire rack. Yield: 12 servings.

**Approx Per Serving:** Cal 291; Prot 5 g; Carbo 47 g; Fiber 2 g; T Fat 11 g; Chol 28 mg; Sod 295 mg.

*Dawn S. Adelson, WEIU Employee*

## IRISH BREAD

¾ cup sugar
6 tablespoons butter, softened
4 cups flour
4 teaspoons baking powder

⅛ teaspoon salt
2 cups milk
1   15-ounce package raisins
½ teaspoon caraway seed

Cream sugar and butter in bowl until light and fluffy. Sift flour, baking powder and salt into bowl. Add milk; mix well. Add to creamed mixture; mix well. Stir in raisins and caraway seed. Pour into greased and floured 5x9-inch loaf pan. Score loaf once in each direction to form cross. Bake at 350 degrees for 1 hour. This is my mother's traditional recipe, a staple at all our family gatherings. A buttered slice is wonderful with a cup of tea. *My mother came to this country when she was sixteen (about 1913) and worked in private homes until 1925. My first recollection of The Union was having her tell me about the place where rolls were ordered for special dinner parties for one of the homes where she worked. I am sure she would be pleased and probably amused to know one of her recipes is included in a Union cookbook.* Yield: 12 servings.

**Approx Per Serving:** Cal 383; Prot 7 g; Carbo 75 g; Fiber 3 g; T Fat 8 g; Chol 21 mg; Sod 202 mg.

*Mary A. Heneghan, WEIU Member*

# MOLASSES BREAD

4 cups whole wheat flour
2 cups milk
1 cup molasses

1 teaspoon soda
1/8 teaspoon salt

Combine flour, milk, molasses, soda and salt in bowl; mix well. Pour into greased 5x9-inch loaf pan. Bake at 350 degrees for 1 hour or until loaf tests done. Cool in pan for several minutes. Remove to wire rack to cool completely. Yield: 12 servings.

**Approx Per Serving:** Cal 215; Prot 7 g; Carbo 45 g; Fiber 5 g;
T Fat 2 g; Chol 6 mg; Sod 134 mg.

*Mrs. J. Norton Wood, WEIU Member*

# ZUCCHINI BREAD

2 cups sugar
1 cup oil
3 eggs
1 teaspoon vanilla extract
2 cups shredded unpeeled
zucchini
3 cups flour

1 teaspoon soda
1/4 teaspoon baking powder
1/2 teaspoon salt
1 teaspoon cinnamon
1 teaspoon cloves
1 teaspoon ginger
1 cup chopped walnuts

Combine sugar, oil, eggs, vanilla and zucchini in large bowl; mix well. Sift flour, soda, baking powder, salt and spices together. Add to zucchini mixture; mix well. Stir in walnuts. Pour into 2 greased and floured 5x9-inch loaf pans. Bake at 325 degrees for 1 hour or until loaves test done. Cool in pans for 20 minutes. Remove to wire rack to cool completely. Bread does not slice well when freshly baked but does freeze well. Yield: 24 servings.

**Approx Per Serving:** Cal 246; Prot 3 g; Carbo 30 g; Fiber 1 g;
T Fat 13 g; Chol 27 mg; Sod 92 mg.

*Karen Kosko, WEIU Member*

**1921** *The Protection Committee turned its legal work over to the Legal Aid Society in Boston as the Society had a woman lawyer on its staff and a small claims court had been established.*

# UNION MUFFINS

| | |
|---|---|
| ½ cup margarine, softened | 1 tablespoon baking powder |
| ¾ cup sugar | ½ cup milk |
| 2 eggs, beaten | ½ cup sugar |
| 2½ cups flour | ¼ teaspoon nutmeg |
| ½ teaspoon salt | ½ teaspoon cinnamon |

Cream margarine and ¾ cup sugar in bowl until light and fluffy. Beat in eggs. Add mixture of flour, salt and baking powder alternately with milk, mixing well after each addition. Fill greased muffin cups ⅔ full. Sprinkle mixture of ½ cup sugar, nutmeg and cinnamon over top. Bake at 400 degrees for 20 minutes. These muffins were made 16 dozen at a time. The batter was prepared in late afternoon, refrigerated and baked in the morning. When pans are removed from the oven they should be placed on a wet towel to generate steam and help to remove the muffins from the pans. May make Apple Muffins by stirring ¾ cup chopped apple into tops of batter-filled muffin cups and sprinkling with spiced sugar mixture. May make Blueberry Muffins by stirring 1 cup floured blueberries into batter and sprinkling with spiced sugar mixture before baking. Yield: 14 servings.

**Approx Per Serving:** Cal 226; Prot 4 g; Carbo 36 g; Fiber 1 g; T Fat 8 g; Chol 32 mg; Sod 237 mg.

*Helen H. Hodgdon, Former WEIU Food Shop Director*

# COTTAGE CHEESE PANCAKES

| | |
|---|---|
| 6 eggs | ⅛ teaspoon salt |
| 1 cup cottage cheese | Sugar to taste |
| 3 tablespoons melted butter | ½ cup flour |

Beat eggs in bowl. Add cottage cheese, butter, salt and sugar; mix well. Add flour; mix well. Drop by tablespoonfuls onto hot greased griddle. Bake until brown on both sides, turning once. *My WEIU keynote address, "Give Them the Business," resulted in a special issue of the New England Journal of Public Policy, Spring/Summer 1990, entitled "Women and Economic Empowerment," with 26 articles by leading New England women. See what WEIU started?* Yield: 4 servings.

**Approx Per Serving:** Cal 306; Prot 17 g; Carbo 14 g; Fiber <1 g; T Fat 19 g; Chol 351 mg; Sod 456 mg.

*Dawn-Marie Driscoll, WEIU Friend*

# POPOVER PANCAKE

½ cup flour
½ cup milk
2 eggs
¼ cup butter

2 tablespoons confectioners'
    sugar
Juice of ½ lemon

Combine flour, milk and eggs in bowl; beat lightly. Batter will be slightly lumpy. Heat butter in 8x12-inch baking pan. Pour batter into pan. Bake at 450 degrees for 20 minutes or until puffed and golden. Sprinkle with confectioners' sugar and lemon juice. Bake for 2 to 3 minutes longer or until glazed. Serve with honey, jam or marmalade. May serve as side dish instead of potatoes. Yield: 4 servings.

**Approx Per Serving:** Cal 233; Prot 6 g; Carbo 18 g; Fiber <1 g;
    T Fat 16 g; Chol 142 mg; Sod 144 mg.

*Judy Blackburn, WEIU Employee*

# EASY HERBED POPOVERS

2 eggs, beaten
1 cup flour
1 cup milk

½ teaspoon salt
Rosemary to taste

Combine eggs, flour, milk and salt in bowl. Beat with egg beater until well mixed. Fill well greased muffin cups ¾ full. Sprinkle pinch of rosemary over each. Place in cold oven. Bake at 450 degrees for 30 minutes; do not open oven door. Yield: 8 servings.

**Approx Per Serving:** Cal 95; Prot 4 g; Carbo 14 g; Fiber <1 g;
    T Fat 3 g; Chol 57 mg; Sod 164 mg.

*Diane Dalton, WEIU Friend*

**1922** *There were nine art exhibits in the Bookshop for Boys and Girls—among those on exhibit were George Bellow's drawings for "Where the Wind Bloweth" and Gustave Tenggrens' drawings for "Heidi." Lucy Wheelock, for whom Wheelock College was named, was an advisor to the Bookshop.*

## APPLE AND WALNUT SCONES

2¹/₄ cups flour  
¹/₂ cup sugar  
2 teaspoons baking powder  
¹/₂ teaspoon salt  
¹/₂ cup butter  
2 eggs, beaten  
¹/₄ cup milk  

2 teaspoons vanilla extract  
1 teaspoon grated lemon rind  
1 cup chopped apple  
1 cup chopped walnuts  
¹/₂ cup packed brown sugar  
1 teaspoon cinnamon  

Combine flour, sugar, baking powder and salt in bowl; mix well. Cut in butter until crumbly. Mix eggs with milk, vanilla and lemon rind in bowl. Stir into flour mixture; dough will be sticky. Stir in apples. Grease an 11-inch circle on baking sheet. Pat dough into 9-inch circle on baking sheet. Sprinkle with mixture of walnuts, brown sugar and cinnamon. Cut circle into 8 wedges with sharp knife. Bake at 375 degrees for 30 to 35 minutes or until light brown. Serve warm or cool. Yield: 8 servings.

**Approx Per Serving:** Cal 361; Prot 8 g; Carbo 58 g; Fiber 2 g; T Fat 11 g; Chol 54 mg; Sod 245 mg.

*Lisa Rein-Woisin, WEIU Employee*

## ENGLISH MUFFIN LOAVES

2 envelopes dry yeast  
3 cups flour  
1 tablespoon sugar  
2 teaspoons salt  
¹/₄ teaspoon soda  

2 cups milk  
¹/₂ cup water  
3 cups flour  
2 to 3 tablespoons cornmeal  

Combine dry yeast, 3 cups flour, sugar, salt and soda in large bowl. Heat milk and water in saucepan until very warm. Add to flour mixture; beat until well mixed. Stir in remaining 3 cups flour. Spoon into two 4x8-inch loaf pans greased and sprinkled with ²/₃ of the cornmeal. Sprinkle remaining cornmeal on top. Let rise, covered, for 45 minutes. Bake at 400 degrees for 25 minutes. Remove from pans immediately. Cool on wire rack. Yield: 20 servings.

**Approx Per Serving:** Cal 159; Prot 5 g; Carbo 31 g; Fiber 1 g; T Fat 1 g; Chol 3 mg; Sod 235 mg.

*Persis Blanchard, WEIU Employee*

## HERBED SOUR CREAM BREAD

2 envelopes dry yeast
1/2 cup lukewarm water
1 cup sour cream, at room
  temperature
6 tablespoons margarine,
  softened
1/3 cup sugar

2 teaspoons salt
1/2 teaspoon dry marjoram leaves
1/2 teaspoon dry oregano leaves
1/2 teaspoon dry thyme leaves
2 eggs, at room temperature
3³/4 to 4³/4 cups flour

Dissolve yeast in lukewarm water in warm large bowl. Add sour cream, margarine, sugar, salt, marjoram, oregano, thyme and eggs; mix well. Add 3 cups flour; beat until well blended. Stir in enough remaining flour to make soft dough. Let rise, covered, in warm place for 50 minutes or until doubled in bulk. Stir dough down. Spoon into 2 buttered 1-quart casseroles. Let rise, covered, for 50 minutes or until doubled in bulk. Bake at 375 degrees for 15 minutes. Reduce temperature to 350 degrees. Bake for 20 minutes longer. Cool on wire racks. *Those who knew Leota Janke, former president of the WEIU, during her leadership in the 1980s know that this recipe reflects her hospitality and fabulous cooking skills.* Yield: 24 servings.

**Approx Per Serving:** Cal 155; Prot 4 g; Carbo 22 g; Fiber 1 g;
  T Fat 6 g; Chol 22 mg; Sod 223 mg.

*Anne Stuart Galli, WEIU Member*

## OATMEAL BREAD

1 cup quick-cooking oats
3¹/2 tablespoons shortening
1 tablespoon salt
2 cups boiling water
1/2 cup molasses

1/4 cup boiling water
1 envelope dry yeast
5 to 6 cups flour
1 to 2 tablespoons butter

Combine oats, shortening and salt in large bowl. Stir in 2 cups boiling water. Let stand until cooled to lukewarm. Blend molasses and 1/4 cup boiling water in small bowl. Let stand until cooled to lukewarm. Stir in yeast until dissolved. Add to oats mixture; mix well. Add enough flour to make firm dough. Knead on floured surface until smooth and elastic. Place in greased bowl, turning to coat surface. Let rise, covered, until doubled in bulk. Shape into 2 loaves; place in buttered 5x9-inch loaf pans. Bake at 400 degrees for 10 minutes. Reduce temperature to 325 degrees. Bake for 30 minutes longer. Brush tops of hot loaves with butter. *My mother's recipe has always been a favorite with my family, and now my grandchildren are asking me to teach them how to make it.* Yield: 24 servings.

**Approx Per Serving:** Cal 158; Prot 4 g; Carbo 30 g; Fiber 1 g;
  T Fat 2 g; Chol 0 mg; Sod 274 mg.

*Helen L. Steverman, WEIU Friend*

# OLIVE FOCACCIA

2 envelopes dry yeast
1 tablespoon sugar
2 cups warm water
6½ cups flour
4 teaspoons kosher salt

1½ cups pitted calamata olives
⅔ cup olive oil
¼ cup (about) cornmeal
¼ cup rosemary

Combine yeast, sugar and warm water in small bowl. Let stand for 5 minutes or until mixture is foamy. Combine half the flour and half the salt in food processor; mix for several seconds. Add half the yeast mixture gradually, processing constantly until mixture pulls from side of container. Add half the olives and 2 tablespoons olive oil. Process for 1 minute. Turn dough onto lightly floured surface. Repeat with remaining yeast mixture, flour, salt, olives and 2 tablespoons olive oil. Combine both dough portions. Knead together for 5 minutes. Place in oiled bowl, turning to coat surface. Let rise, covered with plastic wrap, for 1½ hours or until doubled in bulk. Divide into 8 portions. Roll each into 8-inch circle. Make indentations over surface with knuckles. Brush with remaining olive oil; sprinkle with additional kosher salt and rosemary. Place on baking sheets sprinkled with cornmeal. Bake at 400 degrees for 20 minutes. Serve as appetizer with a hearty red wine or with a winter antipasto supper. *I first heard of the Union while I was a student in search of a job, and am now happy to support such a fine example of the strength of women.* Yield: 10 servings.

**Approx Per Serving:** Cal 498; Prot 10 g; Carbo 67 g; Fiber 4 g;
    T Fat 23 g; Chol 0 mg; Sod 1539 mg.

*Teresa Spillane, WEIU Friend*

# WHOLE WHEAT BATTER BREAD

1½ envelopes dry yeast
¼ teaspoon ginger
2 tablespoons molasses
½ cup lukewarm water

3½ cups whole wheat flour
¼ cup all-purpose flour
2 teaspoons salt
1½ cups lukewarm water

Combine yeast, ginger, molasses and ½ cup lukewarm water in small bowl. Let proof for 10 minutes. Combine flours and salt in large mixer bowl. Add 1½ cups lukewarm water and yeast mixture; mix with paddle attachment of heavy-duty mixer or beat with spoon. Dough will be sticky; do not knead. Spoon into buttered 5x9-inch loaf pan. Let rise, covered with plastic wrap, for 30 minutes. Bake at 450 degrees for 10 minutes. Reduce temperature to 425 degrees. Bake for 35 minutes longer. Baking bread is one of life's pleasures for me but it does require a commitment of time not always available. This is a recipe that is ready in an hour. Yield: 12 servings.

**Approx Per Serving:** Cal 136; Prot 5 g; Carbo 29 g; Fiber 5 g;
    T Fat 1 g; Chol 0 mg; Sod 360 mg.

*Barbara Haber, Curator, Schlesinger Library*

**The WEIU's Cake Decorating Kitchen**
*Employees decorate cakes to be sold in WEIU's food shop.*

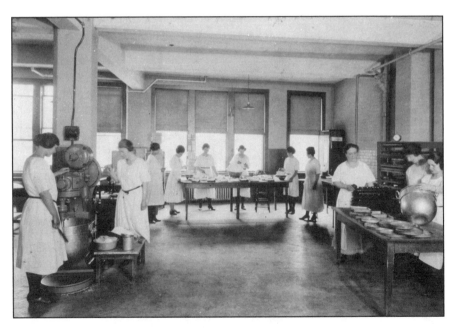

**A Well-Equipped WEIU Kitchen**
*Food preparation is an important part of the WEIU's
long and varied history.*

# Desserts

## NANTUCKET SPONGE CAKE

Weigh eight eggs (unbroken), take their weight of flour and half their weight of fine sugar; break the yolks of the eggs in the sugar, and add a tablespoon of cold water, beat very thoroughly; then add the whites, beaten to a stiff froth; then add the flour all at once, stirring very lightly; bake in a hot oven.

*Mrs. M. E. York*
*from **The Kirmess Cookbook**, 1887*

# APPLE BETTY

4 cups chopped peeled apples    ½ teaspoon cinnamon
¼ cup orange juice    ¼ teaspoon nutmeg
1 cup sugar    ½ cup butter
¾ cup flour

Mound apples in center of greased 9x9-inch baking dish. Drizzle orange juice over apples. Combine sugar, flour, cinnamon and nutmeg in small bowl. Cut in butter until crumbly. Sprinkle over apples. Bake at 375 degrees for 35 minutes or until apples are tender and topping is golden brown. Yield: 6 servings.

**Approx Per Serving:** Cal 368; Prot 2 g; Carbo 57 g; Fiber 2 g;
    T Fat 16 g; Chol 41 mg; Sod 131 mg.

*Michele Norton, WEIU Friend*

# APPLE PUDDING CAKE

½ cup margarine    1 egg
2 Granny Smith apples    1 28-ounce can chunky
1 cup self-rising flour       applesauce
1 cup sugar    1 teaspoon sugar
Nutmeg to taste    ½ teaspoon cinnamon
1 15-ounce can evaporated milk

Melt margarine in 9x13-inch baking pan in 350-degree oven. Peel and cut apples into thin slices; set aside. Combine flour, 1 cup sugar and nutmeg in bowl. Add evaporated milk and egg; beat until smooth. Pour batter evenly into melted margarine in baking pan. Spoon applesauce evenly over batter. Arrange sliced apples in decorative pattern over top. Sprinkle with mixture of 1 teaspoon sugar and cinnamon. Bake at 350 degrees for 30 to 35 minutes or until toothpick inserted in center comes out clean. Serve hot or cold with ice cream or plain. May substitute 2 cans prepared apple pie filling, canned sliced apples or homemade applesauce for chunky applesauce. Increase amount of apples if desired or substitute 1½ cups milk for evaporated milk. Yield: 12 servings.

**Approx Per Serving:** Cal 267; Prot 4 g; Carbo 39 g; Fiber 2 g;
    T Fat 11 g; Chol 28 mg; Sod 247 mg.

*Annette Athanas, WEIU Friend*

**1924-25** *The following subjects were investigated through the Department of Research: Old-Age Provision for Working Women, Part-Time Gainful Occupations of Boston Women, and Part-Time Paid Work Done by Women Students in Colleges of Boston. The Research Fellows (all women) came from Oxford University, the University of Wisconsin, and the London School of Economics.*

# Baked Fruit

1  29-ounce can peach halves
2  16-ounce cans pitted apricot
   halves
1  16-ounce can pitted Bing
   cherries
1 lemon, thinly sliced

Sections and juice of 1
   grapefruit
1 orange, thinly sliced
Juice of 1 orange
1/2 cup packed dark brown sugar

Drain peaches and apricots, reserving juices. Drain Bing cherries, reserving 1/2 the juice. Combine reserved juices, lemon, grapefruit, orange, orange juice and brown sugar in saucepan; mix well. Simmer for 5 minutes, stirring frequently. Combine peaches, apricots, and cherries in large baking dish. Pour hot juice mixture over top. Bake at 350 degrees for 1 hour. Serve hot or cold. Garnish with sour cream. *This was my mother's recipe which I hated as a child but love as an adult. The sliced lemon and orange add a zip to the dish which makes it a refreshing finish for a rich meal.* Yield: 12 servings.

**Approx Per Serving:** Cal 195; Prot 1 g; Carbo 51 g; Fiber 3 g;
   T Fat <1 g; Chol 0 mg; Sod 12 mg.

*Jean R. Haffenreffer, WEIU Friend*

# Baklava

2 teaspoons cinnamon
1 1/2 pounds chopped walnuts
1/4 cup sugar
1 pound frozen phyllo dough,
   thawed
1 1/2 cups melted butter

3 cups sugar
1/3 cup honey
1 1/2 cups water
5 cloves
1 cinnamon stick

Mix cinnamon, walnuts and 1/4 cup sugar in bowl. Layer half the phyllo dough in greased 12x18-inch baking dish, brushing every 2 sheets with butter. Sprinkle with walnut mixture. Top with remaining phyllo dough, brushing every 2 sheets with butter. Slice vertically and then diagonally with sharp knife to make small diamonds. Bake at 325 degrees for 1 hour. Combine remaining 3 cups sugar, honey, water, cloves and cinnamon stick in saucepan. Cook for 5 minutes, stirring frequently. Discard cloves and cinnamon stick. Pour hot syrup over baklava. Let stand overnight. Yield: 100 servings.

**Approx Per Serving:** Cal 109; Prot 1 g; Carbo 12 g; Fiber 1 g;
   T Fat 7 g; Chol 7 mg; Sod 40 mg.

*Laura B. Schlesinger, WEIU Friend*

## DUMP CAKE DESSERT

1   29-ounce can crushed
    pineapple
1   2-layer package yellow cake
    mix

½ cup butter
1 cup chopped pecans

Dump pineapple into greased 9x12-inch baking dish. Sprinkle with cake mix. Slice butter; layer over cake mix. Sprinkle with pecans. Bake at 350 degrees for 35 to 40 minutes or until cake tests done. Garnish with whipped topping or ice cream. Yield: 20 servings.

**Approx Per Serving:** Cal 141; Prot 1 g; Carbo 30 g; Fiber <1 g;
        T Fat 2 g; Chol 0 mg; Sod 158 mg.

*Jacqueline J. Sheehan, WEIU Friend*

## QUINTESSENTIAL ICEBOX CAKE DESSERT

6 tablespoons butter, chilled
¾ cup flour
¼ cup chopped walnuts
¾ cup confectioners' sugar,
    sifted

8 ounces cream cheese, softened
1 cup whipped topping
2   3-ounce packages lemon
    instant pudding mix
3 cups milk

Cut butter into flour in bowl until crumbly. Stir in walnuts. Press into ungreased 8x8-inch baking dish. Bake at 350 degrees for 15 to 20 minutes or until brown. Cool to room temperature. Combine confectioners' sugar and cream cheese in bowl; mix well. Fold in whipped topping. Spread over cooled crust. Prepare instant pudding with 3 cups milk using package directions. Pour over cream cheese layer. Chill until set. Garnish with additional whipped topping. May substitute chocolate pudding mix for lemon. Yield: 9 servings.

**Approx Per Serving:** Cal 393; Prot 6 g; Carbo 41 g; Fiber 1 g;
        T Fat 24 g; Chol 59 mg; Sod 302 mg.

*Adam Kibel and Charlotte Dang, WEIU Friends*

1926   *The Director of the Handwork Shop organized a Craftsmen-at-Work exhibit, held in Horticultural Hall. It included such native American crafts as weaving, lace making, bookbinding, candle dipping, and pottery making.*

## AUNTY CLARA'S ICE CREAM

2 tablespoons cornstarch
1 quart milk
1½ cups sugar

2 cups half and half
1½ teaspoons vanilla extract

Mix cornstarch into a small amount of milk in bowl. Pour remaining milk into saucepan. Heat almost to boiling point, stirring occasionally. Stir in cornstarch mixture and sugar. Bring to a rolling boil that cannot be stirred down. Remove from heat. Let cool at room temperature for 1 hour. Add half and half and vanilla; mix well. Pour into two 8x8-inch pans. Freeze until almost firm. Spoon into mixer bowl. Beat until creamy. Return to pans. Freeze until firm. This will stay creamy and is delicious. *Great Aunt Clara was a contemporary of the founders of the Union. This recipe would be turn of the century.* Yield: 10 servings.

**Approx Per Serving:** Cal 323; Prot 4 g; Carbo 37 g; Fiber <1 g; T Fat 18 g; Chol 66 mg; Sod 58 mg.

*Joyce Mannis, WEIU Friend*

## MYSTERY TORTE

16 butter crackers, crushed
⅔ cup chopped pecans
3 egg whites
1 cup sugar
½ teaspoon baking powder

1 teaspoon vanilla extract
1 cup whipping cream
Sugar to taste
1  2-ounce bittersweet chocolate
   candy bar

Mix cracker crumbs and pecans in bowl; set aside. Beat egg whites in mixer bowl until stiff peaks form. Add mixture of 1 cup sugar and baking powder gradually, beating constantly until very stiff. Fold in cracker crumbs and pecans all at once. Fold in vanilla. Pour into greased 8-inch pie plate. Bake at 350 degrees for 30 minutes. Let stand until cool. Beat whipping cream in mixer bowl until soft peaks form. Sweeten to taste. Spread over cooled meringue layer. Shave chocolate bar; sprinkle chocolate shavings over whipped cream. Chill for 3 hours to overnight. Yield: 8 servings.

**Approx Per Serving:** Cal 338; Prot 4 g; Carbo 36 g; Fiber 1 g; T Fat 22 g; Chol 41 mg; Sod 112 mg.

*Marianne B. Abrams, WEIU Trustee*

1927  *The Appointment Bureau, in conjunction with the Wheelock School, the Ruggles Street Nursery, and others, organized a conference with educators from Columbia University to discuss the education of the pre-school child.*

# PEARS ISABELLA

| | |
|---|---|
| 8 Bartlett or Bosc pears | 1/4 cup cassis |
| Juice of 1 lemon | 1/2 teaspoon thyme |
| 1/4 cup sugar | 1 cinnamon stick |
| 1/2 cup honey | 1/4 cup chopped pecans |
| 1 1/2 cups dry red wine | 1/4 cup raisins |
| 1/2 teaspoon vanilla extract | 4 medium oranges |
| 2 whole cloves | |

Peel and core pears from bottom, leaving stems attached. Place in saucepan just large enough to hold pears upright. Combine lemon juice, sugar, honey, wine, vanilla, cloves, cassis and thyme in bowl; mix well. Pour into saucepan. Add cinnamon stick. Simmer, covered, for 30 minutes. Lift pears carefully. Strain wine sauce over pears. Cool at room temperature. Mix pecans and raisins in bowl. Fill cavities of pears. Remove orange rind from oranges in 1 continuous strip. Cut into halves. Wrap around pears in spiral. Serve with ice cream and wine sauce. *Because I portray Isabella Stewart Gardner on the stage, my friends have dubbed this "Pears Isabella" and it seems the sort of elegant dish one would associate with her.* Yield: 8 servings.

**Approx Per Serving:** Cal 290; Prot 2 g; Carbo 63 g; Fiber 7 g;
   T Fat 3 g; Chol 0 mg; Sod 5 mg.

*Robin Lane, WEIU Performer*

# SPICY APPLE BREAD PUDDING

| | |
|---|---|
| 3 cups milk, scalded | 4 apples, peeled, sliced |
| 3 eggs, beaten | 2 tablespoons sugar |
| 1/4 cup sugar | 1 teaspoon cinnamon |
| 4 slices white bread, torn into pieces | |

Combine milk, eggs and sugar in mixer bowl; beat well. Pour over bread in medium casserole. Top with apple slices. Sprinkle with mixture of 2 tablespoons sugar and cinnamon. Bake at 325 degrees for 1 hour. Yield: 6 servings.

**Approx Per Serving:** Cal 266; Prot 9 g; Carbo 42 g; Fiber 3 g;
   T Fat 8 g; Chol 123 mg; Sod 182 mg.

*Wendy Larson, WEIU Friend*

1928   *The School Lunch Program served nearly 19,000 children at 28 different schools in Boston.*

# BREAD PUDDING WITH WHISKEY SAUCE

1 loaf stale French bread
4 cups milk
3 eggs
1¼ cups sugar
2 teaspoons vanilla extract

1 teaspoon cinnamon
½ cup raisins
½ cup chopped pecans
1 recipe Whiskey Sauce

Crumble bread into bowl. Pour in milk. Let stand for 30 minutes. Beat eggs, sugar, vanilla and cinnamon in mixer bowl. Stir in bread. Add raisins and pecans; mix well. Pour into greased 9x13-inch baking dish. Bake at 350 degrees for 1 hour or until pudding tests done. Cut into squares. Serve with Whiskey Sauce. Yield: 12 servings.

**Approx Per Serving:** Cal 560; Prot 11 g; Carbo 70 g; Fiber 2 g;
T Fat 26 g; Chol 144 mg; Sod 345 mg.
Nutritional analysis includes Whiskey Sauce.

*Jeanne V. Adelson, WEIU Member*

# WHISKEY SAUCE

1 cup sugar
1 cup evaporated milk
3 egg yolks
½ cup butter

1 cup chopped pecans
¼ cup whiskey
1 teaspoon vanilla extract

Combine sugar and ¼ cup evaporated milk in saucepan; mix well. Add egg yolks 1 at a time beating well after each addition. Add remaining evaporated milk and butter. Cook over medium heat until thickened, stirring constantly. Remove from heat. Add pecans, whiskey and vanilla; mix well. Serve over Bread Pudding. Yield: 12 servings.

**Approx Per Serving:** Cal 203; Prot 2 g; Carbo 16 g; Fiber <1 g;
T Fat 14 g; Chol 64 mg; Sod 71 mg.

*Jeanne V. Adelson, WEIU Member*

**1928** *Printing became an integral part of the Union with a multigraph and multi-color press. This department also made personal stationery and did outside announcements and leaflets.*

# CHOCOLATE BREAD PUDDING

12 ounces bittersweet or
  semisweet chocolate
12 egg yolks
1¹/₃ cups sugar
1¹/₃ cups milk

4 cups whipping cream
1 loaf Chocolate Hazelnut
  Brioche
1 recipe Chocolate Hazelnut
  Sauce (page 169)

Melt chocolate in double boiler. Beat egg yolks with sugar in mixer bowl. Combine milk and cream in saucepan. Heat just to the simmering point; remove from heat. Add ¹/₂ the hot mixture to egg yolks, mixing well. Add remaining hot mixture; mix well. Add to chocolate; mix well. Pour through sieve into bowl. Trim crust from Chocolate Hazelnut Brioche; cut into cubes. Spread in 9x9-inch baking dish. Add warm pudding, filling almost to top of dish and pushing bread down into pudding to moisten. Cover baking dish with foil. Place in larger baking pan with water to depth of 1¹/₂ inches. Bake at 350 degrees for 1 hour and 15 minutes to 1 hour and 45 minutes or until set in middle. Serve warm or cold with Chocolate Hazelnut Sauce. Garnish with hazelnuts. This recipe may be time consuming at first glance but every creamy chocolate bite is worth it. Yield: 12 servings.

**Approx Per Serving:** Cal 1362; Prot 15 g; Carbo 108 g; Fiber 3 g;
  T Fat 100 g; Chol 497 mg; Sod 382 mg.
  Nutritional analysis includes Chocolate Hazelnut Brioche and
  Chocolate Hazelnut Sauce.

*Beverly Kypfer, Michela's Restaurant*

# CHOCOLATE HAZELNUT BRIOCHE

¹/₄ cup milk
1¹/₂ envelopes dry yeast
2 tablespoons sugar
4 cups flour
¹/₃ cup sifted baking cocoa
1¹/₂ teaspoons salt

1¹/₄ cups butter, softened
5 eggs
1 tablespoon vanilla extract
³/₄ cup chopped hazelnuts,
  toasted

Heat milk to 100 to 115 degrees in saucepan. Add yeast and sugar; mix well. Sprinkle surface with thin layer of flour. Let stand until flour starts to crack. Combine remaining flour, cocoa, salt and butter in mixer bowl; beat well. Beat in eggs 1 at a time. Stir in vanilla, hazelnuts and yeast mixture. Knead on floured surface, adding additional flour if necessary to form smooth dough. Place in greased bowl, turning to coat surface. Let rise, covered, in warm place until doubled in bulk. Punch down. Shape into 2 loaves. Place in 2 buttered 4x8-inch loaf pans. Let rise until doubled in bulk. Bake at 350 degrees for 30 to 40 minutes or until bread tests done. Remove to wire rack to cool. May substitute almonds or walnuts for hazelnuts. Yield: 2 loaves or 24 servings.

**Approx Per Serving:** Cal 211; Prot 4 g; Carbo 19 g; Fiber 1 g;
  T Fat 14 g; Chol 71 mg; Sod 230 mg.

*Beverly Kypfer, Michela's Restaurant*

## CHOCOLATE HAZELNUT SAUCE

3 cups whipping cream
1⅓ cups packed brown sugar
14 ounces bittersweet chocolate
½ cup butter
½ cup hazelnut liqueur

Combine whipping cream and brown sugar in saucepan; mix well. Add chocolate and butter. Heat until melted. Add hazelnut liqueur. Serve warm over Chocolate Bread Pudding. May substitute dark rum, orange liqueur or peppermint schnapps for hazelnut liqueur. Yield: 12 servings.

**Approx Per Serving:** Cal 569; Prot 4 g; Carbo 48 g; Fiber 1 g;
T Fat 41 g; Chol 102 mg; Sod 100 mg.

*Beverly Kypfer, Michela's Restaurant*

## MOM'S DENVER CHOCOLATE PUDDING

¾ cup sugar
1 cup flour
2 teaspoons baking powder
⅛ teaspoon salt
1 ounce unsweetened baking
  chocolate
2 tablespoons butter
½ cup milk
½ teaspoon vanilla extract
½ cup sugar
½ cup packed light brown sugar
¼ cup baking cocoa
1 cup cold water

Sift ¾ cup sugar, flour, baking powder and salt into bowl. Melt baking chocolate with butter in small saucepan over low heat. Add to flour mixture. Add milk and vanilla; mix well. Pour into greased 9x9-inch baking dish. Combine ½ cup sugar, brown sugar and baking cocoa in small bowl; mix well. Sprinkle over batter. Drizzle cold water over top. Bake at 325 degrees for 40 minutes. Serve with whipped cream or vanilla ice cream. Yield: 8 servings.

**Approx Per Serving:** Cal 290; Prot 3 g; Carbo 60 g; Fiber 2 g;
T Fat 6 g; Chol 10 mg; Sod 154 mg.

*Beth Andrews, Former WEIU Employee*

1928   *The Bookshop for Boys and Girls prepared "Realms of Gold," a book dealing with literature for children of all ages and published by Doubleday.*

# CRÈME BRULÉE

2 cups whipping cream
6 tablespoons superfine sugar
6 egg yolks

2 teaspoons vanilla extract
½ cup packed light brown sugar

Heat whipping cream in double boiler over boiling water. Add sugar gradually, stirring until dissolved. Beat egg yolks in bowl until light. Add hot cream gradually, whisking vigorously. Stir in vanilla. Strain into baking dish or individual ceramic molds. Place in baking dish; add 1 inch hot water. Bake at 300 degrees for 35 minutes or until silver knife inserted in center comes out clean; do not overbake. Chill thoroughly. Cover surface with brown sugar. Place on bed of crushed ice in baking pan. Broil until brown sugar melts; watch carefully. Chill in refrigerator. Serve chilled or at room temperature. This recipe does not curdle as some recipes do. Yield: 6 servings.

**Approx Per Serving:** Cal 458; Prot 4 g; Carbo 33 g; Fiber 0 g;
    T Fat 35 g; Chol 322 mg; Sod 46 mg.

*Markie Phillips, WEIU Trustee*


# PUMPKIN CRÈME BRULÉE WITH MAPLE WALNUT SAUCE

4 ounces chopped walnuts
1 cup maple syrup, warmed
2 cups whipping cream
⅓ cup sugar
4 egg yolks
½ teaspoon vanilla extract
1 cup pumpkin purée

2 tablespoons sugar
⅛ teaspoon cinnamon
⅛ teaspoon ginger
⅛ teaspoon nutmeg
⅛ teaspoon mace
6 tablespoons light brown sugar
¼ cup sugar

Spread walnuts on cookie sheet. Bake at 425 degrees for 45 minutes or until lightly toasted. Add to warm syrup immediately. Cool to room temperature. Combine cream, ⅓ cup sugar, egg yolks and vanilla in mixer bowl; beat well. Pour through sieve; set aside. Combine pumpkin, 2 tablespoons sugar, cinnamon, ginger, nutmeg and mace in bowl; mix well. Spread brulée in five 1x5-inch brulée molds. Add cream mixture. Place molds on baking sheet, add water to depth of ¼ inch. Bake at 300 degrees for 1 hour or until custard starts to set. Cool to room temperature. Mix brown sugar and ¼ cup sugar in small bowl. Sprinkle over custard. Broil until sugar is melted. Warm slightly in oven. Serve with maple walnut sauce. Yield: 5 servings.

**Approx Per Serving:** Cal 822; Prot 8 g; Carbo 83 g; Fiber 2 g;
    T Fat 54 g; Chol 301 mg; Sod 55 mg.

*Daniel T. Bruce, Boston Harbor Hotel Restaurant*

## COLD LEMON SOUFFLÉ WITH RASPBERRY SAUCE

1 pint whipping cream
4 egg yolks
1½ cups confectioners' sugar
¾ tablespoon unflavored gelatin
½ cup lemon juice
Grated rind of 1 small lemon
¼ cup white wine

¼ cup kirsch
2 tablespoons vanilla extract
¼ cup water
4 egg whites
¾ cup sugar
1 recipe Raspberry Sauce

Attach 5¼-inch collar of foil to 3-cup soufflé dish. Whip cream in bowl until soft peaks form. Chill in refrigerator. Combine egg yolks, confectioners' sugar, gelatin, lemon juice, lemon rind, white wine, kirsch, vanilla and water in stainless steel double boiler. Cook over hot water until mixture reaches 130 degrees and begins to thicken, beating constantly. Remove double boiler to bowl of ice water. Beat constantly just until mixture is cool to touch; do not overchill. Remove from ice water. Beat egg whites in mixer bowl until soft peaks form. Add sugar gradually, beating well after each addition until stiff peaks form. Fold egg whites into custard. Fold in whipped cream. Fill prepared soufflé dish to top of foil collar, leveling with spatula. Chill in refrigerator overnight. Garnish top of soufflé with confectioners' sugar. Remove foil collar. Serve with Raspberry Sauce. Yield: 12 servings.

**Approx Per Serving:** Cal 341; Prot 3 g; Carbo 43 g; Fiber <1 g;
T Fat 17 g; Chol 125 mg; Sod 36 mg.
Nutritional analysis includes Raspberry Sauce.

*Dennis Michel, Somerset Club Restaurant*

## RASPBERRY SAUCE

3  12-ounce packages frozen
unsweetened raspberries,
thawed

1 cup confectioners' sugar
½ cup framboise
½ cup kirsch

Purée raspberries in blender container. Press through fine sieve into bowl. Add confectioners' sugar, framboise and kirsch; mix well. Chill overnight. Serve with Cold Lemon Soufflé. Yield: 12 servings.

**Approx Per Serving:** Cal 208; Prot <1 g; Carbo 41 g; Fiber 4 g;
T Fat <1 g; Chol 0 mg; Sod 2 mg.

*Dennis Michel, Somerset Club Restaurant*

# ORANGE SOUFFLÉ

5 egg whites
5 tablespoons sugar
1/4 cup orange marmalade
1 teaspoon butter
2 egg yolks

1 cup confectioners' sugar
2/3 cup whipping cream,
  whipped
Brandy to taste

Beat egg whites in bowl until soft peaks form. Add sugar gradually, beating until stiff. Add orange marmalade; beat well. Pour into double boiler buttered with 1 teaspoon butter. Cook, covered, over hot water for 1 hour or until set. Combine egg yolks and confectioners' sugar in bowl; beat until mixture is too stiff to beat. Fold in whipped cream just before serving. Flavor with brandy. Serve brandy sauce with soufflé. May adjust this recipe for any number by using 1 egg white for each person plus 1 for double boiler and 1 tablespoon sugar for each egg white. Use 1 less tablespoon orange marmalade than number of egg whites. May hold soufflé in double boiler over hot water; soufflé will not fall.
Yield: 4 servings.

**Approx Per Serving:** Cal 390; Prot 7 g; Carbo 51 g; Fiber <1 g;
  T Fat 16 g; Chol 162 mg; Sod 97 mg.

*Mrs. Richard Norton, WEIU Friend*

# SURPRISE BROWN SUGAR PUDDING

1 cup packed brown sugar
2 cups water
2 tablespoons butter
1/2 cup sugar
1 cup flour

2 teaspoons baking powder
1/2 teaspoon salt
1/2 cup water
1 cup black cherries

Combine brown sugar, water and butter in saucepan. Cook until brown sugar dissolves, stirring constantly. Pour into baking dish. Mix sugar, flour, baking powder and salt in bowl. Add water; mix well. Stir in black cherries. Drop by spoonfuls into syrup in baking dish. Bake at 350 degrees for 25 minutes. *When we were invited to dinner at my Aunt Clara's in the bend of the Caussawaga River, we hoped she would serve this dessert. The surprise would be the fruit. It might be pineapple with coconut, tangerines or cherries.* Yield: 6 servings.

**Approx Per Serving:** Cal 328; Prot 2 g; Carbo 72 g; Fiber 1 g;
  T Fat 4 g; Chol 10 mg; Sod 324 mg.

*Evelyn W. Farnum, WEIU Trustee*

# OLD ENGLISH TRIFLE

3  3-ounce packages lady fingers
1  2-ounce package slivered
   almonds
1  8-ounce jar strawberry
   preserves
1 recipe Custard Sauce

1 pound almond macaroons,
   crumbled
9 ounces sherry
1 cup whipping cream
1 ounce sherry

Alternate layers of lady fingers, almonds, strawberry preserves, Custard Sauce and macaroon crumbs in large crystal bowl. Pour 9 ounces sherry over layers. Chill, covered with plastic wrap, overnight. Whip cream in mixer bowl until soft peaks form. Add 1 ounce sherry. Spoon over trifle at serving time. *This recipe comes from my English great-grandmother and has been served for Christmas dessert as long as I can remember.* Yield: 16 servings.

**Approx Per Serving:** Cal 324; Prot 5 g; Carbo 38 g; Fiber 1 g;
    T Fat 16 g; Chol 70 mg; Sod 42 mg.
    Nutritional information includes Custard Sauce.

*Mrs. Ernest Henderson III, WEIU Member*

# CUSTARD SAUCE

¼ cup sugar
1 tablespoon cornstarch
1 egg
1 egg yolk

2 cups milk, heated
Salt to taste
½ teaspoon almond extract

Combine sugar, cornstarch, egg and egg yolk in double boiler; mix well. Add heated milk gradually, mixing well. Cook over hot water until thickened, stirring constantly. Cool to room temperature. Add salt and almond extract. Chill in refrigerator. Yield: 16 servings.

**Approx Per Serving:** Cal 42; Prot 2 g; Carbo 5 g; Fiber <1 g;
    T Fat 2 g; Chol 31 mg; Sod 18 mg.

*Mrs. Ernest Henderson III, WEIU Member*

**1929** *The Emergency Employment Bureau for Part-Time Workers came into existence.*

# MILE HIGH STRAWBERRY DESSERT

1¼ to 1½ cups graham cracker
crumbs
¼ cup sugar
⅓ cup melted margarine
1   10-ounce package frozen
strawberries, thawed

1 cup sugar
⅛ teaspoon salt
2 egg whites
1 tablespoon lemon juice
1 teaspoon vanilla extract
1 cup whipping cream, whipped

Combine graham cracker crumbs, sugar and melted margarine in bowl; mix well. Press into 9x13-inch baking dish. Bake at 350 degrees for 8 to 10 minutes or until light brown. Combine strawberries, sugar, salt, egg whites and lemon juice in mixer bowl; beat at medium high speed for 15 minutes or until stiff peaks form. Add vanilla. Fold in whipped cream. Spread in prepared dish. Freeze overnight. Place in refrigerator 1 hour before serving time. Cut into squares. Yield: 12 servings.

**Approx Per Serving:** Cal 270; Prot 2 g; Carbo 35 g; Fiber 1 g;
T Fat 14 g; Chol 27 mg; Sod 190 mg.

*Liane L. Pfetsch, WEIU Friend*

# APPLE NOBBY CAKE

1 cup sugar
3 tablespoons margarine,
softened
1 egg, beaten
3 cups finely chopped apples
¼ cup chopped pecans

1 teaspoon vanilla extract
½ teaspoon cinnamon
½ teaspoon nutmeg
½ teaspoon salt
1 teaspoon soda
1 cup sifted flour

Cream sugar and margarine in mixer bowl until light and fluffy. Add egg; mix well. Stir in apples, pecans and vanilla. Combine cinnamon, nutmeg, salt, soda and flour in bowl. Stir into batter; mixture will be thick. Spoon into greased and floured 8-inch cake pan. Bake at 350 degrees for 40 to 45 minutes or until cake tests done. Cool in pan for several minutes. Remove to wire rack to cool completely. Yield: 9 servings.

**Approx Per Serving:** Cal 213; Prot 2 g; Carbo 38 g; Fiber 1 g;
T Fat 6 g; Chol 0 mg; Sod 206 mg.

*Elizabeth Lynch, WEIU Member*

1936   *There were three employment bureaus at the Union—the
Appointment Bureau, which placed business and professional
women, the Emergency Employment for Part-Time Workers,
and the Bureau for Handicapped Women. These three
departments helped 20,383 women that year.*

# APPLE CREAM CHEESE TORTE

1/2 cup margarine, softened
1/3 cup sugar
1/4 teaspoon vanilla extract
1 cup flour
8 ounces cream cheese, softened
1/4 cup sugar

1 egg, beaten
1/2 teaspoon vanilla extract
1/3 cup sugar
1/2 teaspoon cinnamon
4 cups sliced peeled apples
1/2 cup sliced almonds

Cream margarine, 1/3 cup sugar and vanilla in mixer bowl until light and fluffy. Blend in flour. Press over bottom and side of greased 9-inch springform pan. Combine cream cheese, 1/4 cup sugar, egg and 1/2 teaspoon vanilla in bowl; mix well. Pour into pastry-lined pan. Combine remaining 1/3 cup sugar and cinnamon in bowl. Add apples; toss to coat. Spread over cream cheese layer. Sprinkle with almonds. Bake at 450 degrees for 10 minutes. Reduce oven temperature to 400 degrees. Bake for 25 minutes longer. Cool in pan. Place on serving plate; remove side of pan. Yield: 10 servings.

**Approx Per Serving:** Cal 338; Prot 5 g; Carbo 36 g; Fiber 2 g;
T Fat 20 g; Chol 46 mg; Sod 183 mg.

*Megan O'Block, WEIU Member*

# ANNA BANANA CAKE WITH BROWN SUGAR GLAZE

3 medium ripe bananas
3 eggs
2 1/4 cups sugar
1 cup plus 2 tablespoons
  unsalted margarine
6 tablespoons plain yogurt
1 tablespoon vanilla extract
1 tablespoon dark rum
1 1/2 teaspoons soda

2 cups plus 2 tablespoons cake
  flour
Salt to taste
1/4 cup butter
1/2 cup packed brown sugar
3 tablespoons milk
1/2 cup confectioners' sugar,
  sifted
1 teaspoon vanilla extract

Process bananas in food processor until almost smooth. Remove to bowl. Add eggs and sugar to food processor; blend until fluffy, scraping sides 1 time. Cut margarine into 10 pieces. Add margarine to food processor; mix for 1 minute. Add yogurt, 1 tablespoon vanilla and rum; blend for 5 seconds. Mix soda, flour and salt in large bowl. Fold in egg mixture and bananas. Spoon into greased and floured bundt pan. Bake for 38 minutes or until cake tests done. Cool in pan for 5 minutes. Invert onto wire rack to cool completely. Melt 1/4 cup butter in saucepan. Stir in brown sugar. Increase heat to medium-high. Cook for 2 minutes or until bubbly, stirring constantly. Stir in milk. Add confectioners' sugar and remaining 1 teaspoon vanilla; mix well. Drizzle over cake.
Yield: 12 servings.

**Approx Per Serving:** Cal 510; Prot 4 g; Carbo 74 g; Fiber 1 g;
T Fat 23 g; Chol 65 mg; Sod 103 mg.

*Meredith Hutter, WEIU Employee*

# CHOCOLATE ROLL

5 egg yolks, beaten
½ cup confectioners' sugar
2 tablespoons baking cocoa
13 egg whites, stiffly beaten
1 teaspoon vanilla extract
1 cup whipping cream, whipped

1 square unsweetened chocolate
1 cup sugar
1 tablespoon butter
1 tablespoon maple syrup
¼ cup whipping cream
1 teaspoon vanilla extract

Combine egg yolks, confectioners' sugar and cocoa in mixer bowl; beat for 10 minutes. Fold in stiffly beaten egg whites and 1 teaspoon vanilla. Spoon onto greased 10x15-inch jelly roll pan. Bake at 350 degrees for 15 to 20 minutes or until cake tests done. Remove to towel; roll up in towel from narrow side. Cool to room temperature. Unroll to fill. Spread with whipped cream; reroll. Chill until serving time. Combine chocolate, sugar, butter, maple syrup and cream in saucepan. Cook until thickened, stirring occasionally. Stir in 1 teaspoon vanilla. Drizzle over Chocolate Roll. Yield: 12 servings.

**Approx Per Serving:** Cal 134; Prot 5 g; Carbo 7 g; Fiber <1 g;
    T Fat 10 g; Chol 116 mg; Sod 65 mg.

*Victoria Whitney, WEIU Trustee*

# NO-CHOLESTEROL CHOCOLATE CAKE

1½ cups flour
1 cup sugar
3 tablespoons baking cocoa
1 teaspoon soda

5 tablespoons unsaturated oil
1 cup water
1 teaspoon vanilla extract
1 teaspoon vinegar

Combine flour, sugar, cocoa and soda in bowl; mix well. Add oil, water, vanilla and vinegar; mix until smooth. Pour into greased 8x8-inch cake pan. Bake at 350 degrees for 30 minutes or until toothpick inserted in center comes out clean. This very moist cake will be about 1½ inches high. It is delicious without icing but may be garnished with a light dusting of confectioners' sugar. *It is similar to the Fudge Cake that was so popular in the Union restaurants.* Yield: 8 servings.

**Approx Per Serving:** Cal 264; Prot 3 g; Carbo 44 g; Fiber 1 g;
    T Fat 9 g; Chol 0 mg; Sod 104 mg.

*Helen H. Hodgdon, Former WEIU Food Shop Director*

1941  *For four years during World War II, the Union Hospitality Committee offered free lunches or dinners to service people.*

# CHOCOLATE CHESTNUT CAKE

1 15-ounce can unsweetened
  chestnut purée
1/3 cup whipping cream
1/2 cup brandy
3/4 cup sugar
6 tablespoons melted unsalted
  butter
1 pound semisweet chocolate,
  melted

5 eggs, at room temperature
2 egg yolks, at room temperature
2 tablespoons cornstarch
4 ounces semisweet chocolate
2 tablespoons unsalted butter
1 tablespoon strong brewed
  coffee
1 tablespoon brandy

Combine chestnut purée, cream and brandy in bowl; whisk until smooth. Add sugar, 6 tablespoons butter and melted chocolate; mix well. Add eggs and egg yolks 1 at a time, whisking well after each addition. Sift cornstarch over batter; fold in. Pour batter into greased and floured 9-inch cake pan. Place in cold oven. Set oven temperature at 300 degrees. Bake for 1 hour or until cake tests done. Cool in pan for 15 minutes. Invert onto serving plate. Let stand at room temperature overnight. Melt remaining 4 ounces chocolate and 2 tablespoons butter in double boiler over hot water, stirring until smooth. Stir in coffee and brandy. Cool to room temperature. Spread over top and side of cake. Garnish with whipped cream. This traditional Christmas favorite is very dense and rich.
Yield: 10 servings.

**Approx Per Serving:** Cal 542; Prot 6 g; Carbo 54 g; Fiber 2 g;
  T Fat 36 g; Chol 185 mg; Sod 49 mg.
  Nutritional information does not include chestnut purée.

*Marie Crocetti, WEIU Member*

# CHOCOLATE TRUFFLE CAKE

8 ounces semisweet chocolate
1 cup butter, softened
1 1/2 cups sugar

5 eggs, beaten
12 ounces semisweet chocolate
1 cup whipping cream

Butter 8-inch cake pan; line with parchment. Melt 8 ounces chocolate in saucepan, stirring until smooth. Cool for 1 to 2 minutes. Add butter a small amount at a time, beating with wire whisk until smooth. Add sugar; beat for 1 minute with whisk. Add eggs; beat until well mixed. Pour batter into prepared pan. Set pan in slightly larger pan with 1 inch hot water. Bake at 350 degrees for 1 1/2 hours. Cool at room temperature for 1 hour. Cake will fall. Chill in refrigerator for 2 hours or until set. Boil remaining 12 ounces chocolate and cream together until thickened. Chill until of spreading consistency. Invert onto serving plate. Spread over top and side of cake. This was taken from the Junior League Cookbook of Kansas City, Missouri. It looks beautiful with a fresh flower in the middle.
Yield: 16 servings.

**Approx Per Serving:** Cal 429; Prot 4 g; Carbo 40 g; Fiber 1 g;
  T Fat 32 g; Chol 118 mg; Sod 129 mg.

*Mary Gast Thaler, Former WEIU Food Shop Director*

# LEMON CAKE

1 2-layer package lemon cake
  mix
1 3-ounce package lemon
  gelatin
1 teaspoon lemon extract
4 eggs

1 cup water
1/2 cup oil
1 4-ounce package lemon
  instant pudding mix
1½ cups skim milk

Grease and flour 8-inch cake pan. Chill until ready to use. Combine cake mix, gelatin, lemon extract, eggs, water and oil in mixer bowl. Beat at high speed for 3 to 4 minutes. Pour into chilled cake pan; smooth batter evenly in pan. Bake at 350 degrees for 35 to 40 minutes or until cake tests done. Cool on wire rack. Prepare pudding mix with 1½ cups skim milk using package directions. Pour over cake. Chill until serving time. Garnish with lemon slices and sprigs of lemon balm. Yield: 8 servings.

**Approx Per Serving:** Cal 542; Prot 8 g; Carbo 79 g; Fiber <1 g;
  T Fat 22 g; Chol 107 mg; Sod 580 mg.

*Anthony M. Sammarco, WEIU Lecturer*

# ALL-BUTTER POUND CAKE

2/3 cup butter, softened
1½ cups sugar
2 eggs
2 cups flour

3/4 teaspoon baking powder
3/4 teaspoon salt
2/3 cup milk
1 teaspoon vanilla extract

Cream butter and sugar in mixer bowl until light and fluffy. Add eggs 1 at a time, beating well after each addition. Sift flour 3 times. Measure 2 cups; mix with baking powder and salt. Add to batter alternately with milk, beating just until blended; do not overmix. Add vanilla. Pour into greased and floured 5x9-inch loaf pan. Bake at 325 degrees for 1 hour to 1¼ hours or until cake tests done. Cool in pan for several minutes. Invert onto wire rack to cool completely. Yield: 12 servings.

**Approx Per Serving:** Cal 284; Prot 4 g; Carbo 42 g; Fiber 1 g;
  T Fat 12 g; Chol 65 mg; Sod 257 mg.

*Claire Labbe, WEIU Friend*

1942  *The shortage of all forms of shortening was so acute that doughnuts, patty shells, and all puff pastry items were dropped from the restaurant's menu.*

# MOCHA POUND CAKE

2/3 cup shortening
1¹/₄ cups sugar
2 cups sifted cake flour
1 tablespoon instant coffee
1 teaspoon salt
¹/₂ teaspoon cream of tartar
¹/₄ teaspoon soda

¹/₂ cup water
1 teaspoon vanilla extract
3 eggs
2  1-ounce squares
   unsweetened baking
   chocolate, melted

Cream shortening and sugar in mixer bowl until light and fluffy. Mix flour, instant coffee, salt, cream of tartar and soda together. Add to creamed mixture. Add water and vanilla; beat for 2 minutes. Add eggs and melted chocolate; beat for 1 minute longer. Pour into paper-lined 5x9-inch loaf pan. Bake at 325 degrees for 50 to 60 minutes or until cake tests done. Cool in pan for 10 minutes. Invert onto wire rack to cool completely. Garnish with sifted confectioners' sugar. My Mom once won a baking contest with this recipe. Yield: 12 servings.

**Approx Per Serving:** Cal 293; Prot 3 g; Carbo 38 g; Fiber 1 g;
    T Fat 15 g; Chol 53 mg; Sod 196 mg.

*Beth Andrews, Former WEIU Employee*

# MOLASSES SUGAR CAKES

1 cup molasses
1 cup boiling water
1 teaspoon soda
4 cups flour

1 cup sugar
1 cup butter
2 unbaked pie shells

Combine molasses, boiling water and soda in bowl; mix well. Mix flour and sugar in bowl. Cut in butter until crumbly. Layer crumbs and molasses mixture in pie shells. Bake at 375 degrees for 45 minutes. This was often served at breakfast by my grandparents at their summer cottage at Kennebunk Beach, Maine. Yield: 14 servings.

**Approx Per Serving:** Cal 350; Prot 4 g; Carbo 54 g; Fiber 1 g;
    T Fat 14 g; Chol 36 mg; Sod 192 mg.

*Sister Jane Margaret, WEIU Friend*

1946  *The Boston Herald on June 7 had the following headline for an article: "Full Pre-Cooked Frozen Dinners Complete on Plate Coming Soon." There was a conference at Simmons College on frozen dinners in which the Union participated.*

# ORANGE CAKE

| | |
|---|---|
| 2 large navel oranges | Salt to taste |
| 6 eggs | 1 teaspoon baking powder |
| 1½ cups ground almonds | 1 to 2 tablespoons Grand |
| 1 cup sugar | Marnier |

Boil oranges in water to cover in saucepan for 30 minutes; drain. Cool. Cut into eighths; remove seed. Process in blender container until finely chopped. Beat eggs in mixer bowl until thick. Stir in almonds, sugar, salt, baking powder and oranges. Stir in Grand Marnier. Pour into buttered and floured cake pan. Bake at 400 degrees for 1 hour or until cake is firm and pulls from side of pan; cake will rise slightly. Cool in pan for several minutes. Invert onto wire rack to cool completely. Garnish with confectioners' sugar and cinnamon. This cake is unusual in two respects. It has no flour and includes the oranges, rind and all. *I serve the cake with sliced fresh strawberries. James Beard introduced this cake to the east in a Boston Globe column on 28 April 1976.* Yield: 12 servings.

**Approx Per Serving:** Cal 211; Prot 7 g; Carbo 23 g; Fiber 2 g;
T Fat 11 g; Chol 106 mg; Sod 87 mg.

*Margo Miller, The Boston Globe*

# AMAZIN' RAISIN CAKE

| | |
|---|---|
| 2 cups sugar | ½ teaspoon nutmeg |
| 1 cup mayonnaise | ½ teaspoon salt |
| ⅓ cup milk | ½ teaspoon ground cloves |
| 2 eggs | 3 cups chopped peeled apples |
| 3 cups flour | 1 cup seedless raisins |
| 2 teaspoons soda | ½ cup coarsely chopped walnuts |
| 1½ teaspoons cinnamon | |

Combine first 4 ingredients in mixer bowl; beat well. Mix flour, soda, cinnamon, nutmeg, salt and cloves together. Add to batter, mixing well. Stir in apples, raisins and walnuts. Pour into 2 greased and floured 9-inch cake pans. Bake at 350 degrees for 45 minutes. Cool in pans for 10 minutes. Remove to wire rack to cool completely. Yield: 12 servings.

**Approx Per Serving:** Cal 481; Prot 6 g; Carbo 74 g; Fiber 3 g;
T Fat 19 g; Chol 47 mg; Sod 177 mg.

*Joan A. Cante, WEIU Employee*

**1955** *The Union won a competition for design for the needlepoint covers of the altar kneelers and stall cushions for St. Mary's Chapel in the Washington National Cathedral. The designs were by Caroline Bradley, Director of the Needlework Department.*

# Rum Cake

1 2-layer package yellow cake
  mix
3/4 cup apricot nectar
3/4 cup oil

4 eggs
1/2 cup rum
3/4 cup sugar
10 tablespoons margarine

Combine cake mix, apricot nectar, oil and eggs in mixer bowl. Beat for 4 to 5 minutes. Pour into greased bundt pan. Bake at 350 degrees for 50 minutes. Combine rum, sugar and margarine in saucepan. Heat until sugar dissolves, stirring constantly. Loosen cake from side of pan. Pour hot syrup over hot cake. Cool on wire rack for 1 hour. Invert onto cake plate. Yield: 12 servings.

**Approx Per Serving:** Cal 492; Prot 4 g; Carbo 51 g; Fiber <1 g;
  T Fat 29 g; Chol 71 mg; Sod 397 mg.

*Dorothy Almeida, WEIU Friend*

# Sauerkraut Cake

1/2 cup butter, softened
1 1/2 cups sugar
3 eggs
1 teaspoon vanilla extract
2 cups flour
1 teaspoon soda
1/4 teaspoon salt
1/2 cup baking cocoa
1 cup water

1 8-ounce can sauerkraut
6 ounces semisweet chocolate,
  melted
1/4 cup melted butter
1/2 cup sour cream
1/2 teaspoon vanilla extract
1/4 teaspoon salt
2 1/2 to 2 3/4 cups confectioners'
  sugar

Cream 1/2 cup butter and sugar in mixer bowl until light and fluffy. Add eggs and vanilla; beat well. Mix flour, soda, salt and cocoa together. Add to batter alternately with water, mixing well after each addition. Rinse and drain sauerkraut. Chop into fine pieces. Stir into batter. Pour into greased and floured 9x13-inch cake pan. Bake at 350 degrees for 35 to 40 minutes or until cake tests done. Cool to room temperature. Mix melted chocolate and 1/4 cup butter in bowl. Add sour cream, vanilla and salt. Stir in confectioners' sugar until of spreading consistency. Spread over cooled cake. Yield: 18 servings.

**Approx Per Serving:** Cal 338; Prot 4 g; Carbo 53 g; Fiber 2 g;
  T Fat 14 g; Chol 59 mg; Sod 243 mg.

*Priscilla J. Ruegg, WEIU Member*

## SLON'S CHRISTMAS FUDGE

½ cup butter
1 15-ounce can evaporated milk
4½ cups sugar
8 ounces marshmallows
2 cups semisweet chocolate
chips

3 4-ounce packages German's
sweet baking chocolate
2 ounces unsweetened chocolate
1 tablespoon vanilla extract
2 cups chopped pecans

Combine butter, evaporated milk and sugar in heavy saucepan. Cook over medium heat until sugar dissolves, stirring constantly. Bring to a boil; cover. Cook for 5 minutes; remove from heat. Stir in marshmallows and chocolate until melted. Add vanilla and pecans. Pour into buttered 10x15-inch pan. Let stand until firm. Cut into squares. *Close friends Katie and Bill Slon have made this special treat every Christmas for 22 years.* Yield: 24 servings.

**Approx Per Serving:** Cal 455; Prot 5 g; Carbo 61 g; Fiber 4 g;
T Fat 26 g; Chol 15 mg; Sod 62 mg.

*Alexis N. Voulgaris, WEIU Friend*

## TOFFEE CHOCOLATE BARS

36 2x2-inch crackers
1 cup butter
1 cup packed dark brown sugar

2 cups chocolate chips
½ cup chopped walnuts

Arrange single layer of crackers in 10x15-inch pan lined with buttered foil. Combine butter and brown sugar in small saucepan. Cook over medium-high heat until well blended, stirring constantly. Bring to a boil. Cook for 4 minutes. Pour evenly over crackers. Bake at 375 degrees for 5 minutes. Sprinkle with chocolate chips; let stand until softened. Spread evenly over top. Sprinkle with walnuts. Chill in refrigerator. Break into pieces. Store in airtight container in refrigerator. Yield: 48 servings.

**Approx Per Serving:** Cal 103; Prot 1 g; Carbo 10 g; Fiber <1 g;
T Fat 7 g; Chol 11 mg; Sod 61 mg.

*Barbara Evans, WEIU Friend*

**1955** *A summer Christmas Shop in Harwichport opened for ten weeks.*

# MARZIPAN

| | |
|---|---|
| 1 cup Almond Paste | ¼ cup water |
| 3 cups confectioners' sugar | ¼ cup corn syrup |
| ½ teaspoon vanilla extract | Vegetable food coloring |
| ¼ cup sugar | |

Combine almond paste, confectioners' sugar, vanilla and enough water to mix to desired consistency. Shape a small amount at a time as desired. Combine sugar, water and corn syrup in small saucepan. Bring to a full rolling boil. Tint small amounts of syrup in small dishes with drops of vegetable food coloring to brush on marzipan shapes. Suggestions: cucumbers, bananas, limes, lemons, eggplant, walnuts, red, green or yellow apples tinted with basic color and blushed with contrasting color, acorns with shredded chocolate on top for cap, snowmen, peas in a pod, strawberries pricked with fork for texture, peaches, plums, oranges, ears of corn, grape clusters, bird on nest, green holly leaves with red berries, potatoes lightly dusted with cocoa powder. Add cloves for stems where appropriate. *This is a very sentimental recipe. When my boys were little, we made tons of these every Christmas. Our fruit was only about 1 inch high, including the clove stem. We packaged it in candy cups in tins. They took these to their teachers with a note—"made with clean hands." Marzipan is "play dough" at its best!* Yield: 50 servings.

## Almond Paste

| | |
|---|---|
| 1½ cups finely ground almonds | ¼ cup water |
| ¾ cup sugar | Several drops of almond extract |
| ½ teaspoon salt | |

Combine ground almonds, sugar and salt in double boiler over hot water. Stir in water. Cook, covered, for 20 minutes, stirring frequently. Add almond extract; mix well. Pack into refrigerator containers. Store, tightly covered, for 24 hours or longer. I usually double this recipe.

**Approx Per Serving:** Cal 71; Prot 1 g; Carbo 13 g; Fiber <1 g;
T Fat 2 g; Chol 0 mg; Sod 23 mg.

*Evelyn W. Farnum, WEIU Trustee*

1956 *Fourteen college students came for internships in restaurant management and food production.*

## ANGELS OF KILIMANJARO

8 slices angel food cake                1 cup granulated brown sugar
1/2 cup melted butter

Dip pieces of cake quickly into melted butter. Coat with brown sugar. Place on baking sheet. Bake at 400 degrees for 5 minutes. Serve with coffee ice cream. We were first served this easy but elegant dessert at a Sunday night supper at the Cambridge Boat Club. To serve 40, use 5 cakes, 1½ pounds butter and 1 pound brown sugar. Yield: 8 servings.

**Approx Per Serving:** Cal 325; Prot 3 g; Carbo 53 g; Fiber <1 g;
   T Fat 12 g; Chol 11 mg; Sod 269 mg.

*Evelyn W. Farnum, WEIU Trustee*

## APRICOT TRIANGLES

1/3 cup butter, softened            1/3 cup butter
1/2 cup sugar                       1/2 cup sugar
1 egg                               2 tablespoons water
1 teaspoon vanilla extract          3/4 cup finely chopped almonds
1 1/4 cups flour                    1/3 cup coconut
1/2 teaspoon baking powder          2 ounces semisweet chocolate,
1   8-ounce jar apricot jam            melted

Cream 1/3 cup butter and 1/2 cup sugar in mixer bowl until light and fluffy. Beat in egg and vanilla. Add mixture of flour and baking powder; mix well. Press into greased 9x13-inch baking dish. Spread with jam. Melt 1/3 cup butter in saucepan. Stir in 1/2 cup sugar, water and almonds. Spread carefully over jam. Sprinkle with coconut. Bake at 350 degrees for 25 to 30 minutes or until golden brown. Cool for 15 to 20 minutes. Cut into 20 squares while still warm; remove to wire rack to cool completely. Cut into triangles. Drizzle with chocolate or dip 2 points of each triangle into chocolate. Let stand until firm. Yield: 40 servings.

**Approx Per Serving:** Cal 104; Prot 1 g; Carbo 14 g; Fiber 1 g;
   T Fat 5 g; Chol 14 mg; Sod 33 mg.

*Mary Maynard, WEIU Member*

1959  *In December, 2,500 dozen homemade cookies were sold.*

# BRANDY WAFERS

1 cup (scant) flour
2/3 cup sugar
1 teaspoon ginger

1/2 cup molasses
1/2 cup butter

Sift flour with sugar and ginger. Heat molasses to the boiling point in saucepan; remove from heat. Add butter; mix well. Add flour mixture gradually, mixing well. Drop by teaspoonfuls 2 inches apart onto the bottom of inverted baking pan. Bake at 300 degrees for 15 minutes. Cool slightly. Roll warm cookies around handle of wooden spoon. Let stand until cool. May fill with ice cream. *These cookies were sold in The Bakery at the WEIU.* Yield: 60 servings.

**Approx Per Serving:** Cal 35; Prot <1 g; Carbo 5 g; Fiber <1 g; T Fat 2 g; Chol 4 mg; Sod 16 mg.

*Susan G. Loring, WEIU Volunteer*

# BROWN SUGAR BROWNIES

10 tablespoons plus 2 teaspoons
  margarine, softened
2 cups packed light brown sugar
2 eggs
1 teaspoon vanilla extract

1 1/2 cups flour
2 teaspoons baking powder
1/2 teaspoon (or less) salt
3/4 cup broken walnuts

Cream margarine and brown sugar in mixer bowl until light and fluffy. Beat in eggs and vanilla. Add flour, baking powder and salt; mix well. Stir in walnuts. Spoon into 9x13-inch baking pan lined with baking parchment. Bake at 350 degrees for 20 to 30 minutes or until brownies test done. Cool in pan for 10 minutes. Invert onto work surface; remove baking parchment. Cut into squares. Garnish with confectioners' sugar. Yield: 24 servings.

**Approx Per Serving:** Cal 183; Prot 2 g; Carbo 27 g; Fiber <1 g; T Fat 8 g; Chol 18 mg; Sod 145 mg.

*Mary Mae Tanimoto, WEIU Volunteer*

**1962** *The first guide to nursing and rest homes in Massachusetts was first published under the name If You Need a Nursing Home.*

## PEPPERMINT CHOCOLATE BROWNIES

4 squares unsweetened baking
  chocolate
3/4 cup margarine
2 cups sugar

3 eggs
1 teaspoon peppermint extract
1 cup flour

Heat chocolate in saucepan over low heat until partially melted. Add margarine. Heat until melted, stirring to mix well. Stir into sugar in bowl. Add eggs and peppermint; mix well. Stir in flour. Spoon into greased 8x8-inch baking pan. Bake at 350 degrees for 30 to 35 minutes or until knife inserted in center comes out clean. Cool in pan. Cut into squares. We serve these with 2 big scoops of peppermint stick ice cream and a spoonful of hot fudge sauce. Yield: 12 servings.

**Approx Per Serving:** Cal 336; Prot 4 g; Carbo 44 g; Fiber 2 g;
  T Fat 18 g; Chol 53 mg; Sod 152 mg.

*Lily Faulhaber, WEIU Friend*

## TURTLE BROWNIES

1  14-ounce package caramels
1/3 cup evaporated milk
1  2-layer package dark
  chocolate cake mix
1/3 cup evaporated milk

3/4 cup margarine, softened
1 cup chopped pecans
2 cups semisweet chocolate
  chips

Combine caramels and 1/3 cup evaporated milk in double boiler. Heat until caramels melt, stirring to mix well; set aside. Combine cake mix, 1/3 cup evaporated milk and margarine in bowl; mix well. Stir in pecans. Press half the mixture into greased 9x13-inch baking pan. Bake at 350 degrees for 6 minutes. Sprinkle with chocolate chips. Spread caramel mixture evenly over chocolate. Top with remaining cake batter. Bake for 15 to 18 minutes or until brownies test done but are still moist. Cool completely. Cut into squares. Yield: 24 servings.

**Approx Per Serving:** Cal 323; Prot 3 g; Carbo 40 g; Fiber 1 g;
  T Fat 18 g; Chol 3 mg; Sod 244 mg.

*Mary Peters Hanson, Former WEIU Employee*

**1962** *In this year, 22,692 muffins were made and sold, along with 9,041 Parker House rolls and 3,599 fish cakes.*

## ELNA SOLVANG'S WHITE BROWNIES

2 eggs
1 cup sugar
1/2 cup melted butter
1 cup flour

2 teaspoons almond extract
Salt to taste
2 tablespoons sugar
1/2 cup chopped pecans

Combine eggs, 1 cup sugar, butter, flour, almond extract and salt in mixer bowl; mix well. Spoon into greased 9x9-inch baking pan. Sprinkle with 2 tablespoons sugar and pecans. Bake at 325 degrees for 30 minutes or until brownies test done; do not overbake. Cool on wire rack. Cut into squares. Yield: 16 servings.

**Approx Per Serving:** Cal 162; Prot 2 g; Carbo 22 g; Fiber <1 g;
    T Fat 8 g; Chol 42 mg; Sod 74 mg.

*Beth Andrews, Former WEIU Employee*

## BUTTERCUP SQUARES

1  2-pastry package pie crust
   mix
1 cup sugar
1/4 cup light corn syrup
3 eggs
1/2 cup margarine, softened
1/2 cup fine cracker crumbs

1 teaspoon almond extract
1/2 teaspoon salt
10 to 12 cherries, chopped
1/2 cup coconut
2 tablespoons confectioners'
   sugar

Prepare pie crust mix using package directions. Line 8x10-inch baking pan with half the pastry. Combine sugar, corn syrup, eggs, margarine, cracker crumbs, almond extract, salt, cherries and coconut in bowl; mix well. Spoon into prepared pan. Top with remaining pastry; seal edges and cut vents. Bake at 375 degrees for 20 to 25 minutes or until golden brown. Sprinkle with confectioners' sugar. Cut into squares. Yield: 20 servings.

**Approx Per Serving:** Cal 168; Prot 2 g; Carbo 20 g; Fiber 1 g;
    T Fat 9 g; Chol 33 mg; Sod 202 mg.

*Judith Buckjune, WEIU Friend*

**1965**  *The Union trained 200 neighborhood and teacher aides for the first Head Start program in Boston.*

## CHOCOLATE COOKIES

| | |
|---|---|
| 1 cup butter, softened | 1½ cups flour |
| 2 cups sugar | 1 teaspoon vanilla extract |
| 3 eggs, beaten | 1 cup chopped walnuts |
| 3 squares chocolate, melted | |

Cream butter in mixer bowl until light. Add sugar, beating until fluffy. Beat in eggs and chocolate. Add flour gradually, mixing well. Stir in vanilla and walnuts. Drop by spoonfuls onto buttered cookie sheet; flatten with spoon. Bake at 350 degrees for 8 to 10 minutes or until set. Remove to wire rack to cool. This recipe came from Thomas Perdue who worked for my parents; it dates to the 1930s. Yield: 48 servings.

**Approx Per Serving:** Cal 110; Prot 1 g; Carbo 12 g; Fiber 1 g;
    T Fat 7 g; Chol 24 mg; Sod 37 mg.

*Ruth LaCroix Darling, WEIU Member*

## ALMOND CHOCOLATE CHIP COOKIES

| | |
|---|---|
| 1¾ cups sifted flour | 1 egg |
| ½ teaspoon soda | 1 teaspoon vanilla extract |
| ¼ teaspoon salt | 1 cup toasted chopped almonds |
| ¾ cup butter, softened | 1½ cups semisweet chocolate |
| ½ cup sugar | chips |
| ¼ cup packed light brown sugar | |

Sift flour, soda and salt together. Cream butter, sugar and brown sugar in mixer bowl until light and fluffy. Beat in egg and vanilla. Stir in flour mixture, almonds and 1 cup chocolate chips. Drop by rounded teaspoonfuls onto greased cookie sheet. Bake at 350 degrees for 8 to 10 minutes or until golden brown. Remove to wire rack to cool. Melt remaining ½ cup chocolate chips in double boiler. Dip bottom half of each cookie in chocolate. Let stand on waxed paper until firm. Yield: 48 servings.

**Approx Per Serving:** Cal 126; Prot 2 g; Carbo 13 g; Fiber 1 g;
    T Fat 8 g; Chol 12 mg; Sod 43 mg.

*Lisa Rein-Woisin, WEIU Employee*

**1965** *The Partnership Teaching Program was started, providing two teachers in the same classroom, each teaching half the time.*

# CHOCOLATE CHIP COOKIES

2¼ cups flour
¼ teaspoon baking powder
½ teaspoon soda
½ teaspoon salt
1 cup shortening
½ cup sugar

½ cup packed brown sugar
2 eggs
1 tablespoon cold water
1 teaspoon vanilla extract
2 cups chocolate chips

Sift flour, baking powder, soda and salt together. Cream shortening, sugar and brown sugar in mixer bowl until light and fluffy. Beat in eggs, water and vanilla. Add flour mixture; mix well. Stir in chocolate chips. Drop by heaping teaspoonfuls onto greased cookie sheet. Bake at 375 degrees for 10 to 12 minutes or until golden brown. Serve warm with a tall glass of milk. Yield: 36 servings.

**Approx Per Serving:** Cal 153; Prot 2 g; Carbo 17 g; Fiber 1 g;
T Fat 9 g; Chol 12 mg; Sod 50 mg.

*Norma L. Burchard, WEIU Employee*

# CHRISTMAS KISSES

½ cup butter, softened
1 cup packed brown sugar
4 eggs
3 tablespoons milk
1 teaspoon vanilla extract
3 cups flour
1 teaspoon each cinnamon,
nutmeg and salt
8 ounces red candied cherries,
chopped

8 ounces green candied cherries,
chopped
1 pound candied pineapple,
chopped
8 ounces dates, chopped
1 pound golden raisins
5 cups chopped pecans
½ cup orange juice

Cream butter and brown sugar in mixer bowl until light and fluffy. Beat in eggs 1 at a time. Add milk and vanilla; mix well. Sift flour, cinnamon, nutmeg and salt together. Toss 1 cup dry ingredients with cherries, pineapple, dates, raisins and pecans in large bowl, coating well. Add remaining dry ingredients, creamed mixture and orange juice, mixing well. Drop by teaspoonfuls onto cookie sheet. Bake at 325 degrees for 15 minutes. Remove to wire rack to cool. Yield: 100 servings.

**Approx Per Serving:** Cal 131; Prot 1 g; Carbo 19 g; Fiber 1 g;
T Fat 6 g; Chol 11 mg; Sod 34 mg.

*Eleanor Goldthwait, WEIU Trustee*

# CINNAMON STRIPS

1 cup sugar
1 cup butter, softened
1 egg yolk
2 cups flour

1/2 teaspoon cinnamon
1 egg white
1 tablespoon water
3/4 cup finely chopped walnuts

Combine sugar, butter and egg yolk in mixer bowl; beat until smooth. Stir in flour and cinnamon. Press into lightly greased 10x15-inch baking pan. Beat egg white with water in small bowl until foamy. Brush over dough; sprinkle with walnuts. Bake at 350 degrees for 20 to 25 minutes or until light golden brown. Cut into 1x3-inch strips immediately. Remove to wire rack to cool. These Dutch cookies are also known as Jan Hagel. They are good with morning coffee or afternoon tea. Yield: 42 servings.

**Approx Per Serving:** Cal 94; Prot 1 g; Carbo 10 g; Fiber <1 g;
    T Fat 6 g; Chol 17 mg; Sod 39 mg.

*Mary Maynard, WEIU Member*

# ITALIAN COOKIES

1/3 cup sugar
1 2/3 cups flour
1 tablespoon baking powder
1/4 cup oil
1/3 cup milk

2 eggs, beaten
1 teaspoon anise extract
1  1-pound package
    confectioners' sugar
1 teaspoon anise extract

Mix sugar, flour and baking powder in bowl; make well in center. Add oil, milk, eggs and 1 teaspoon anise extract to well; mix well. Shape into 1-inch balls; place on lightly greased cookie sheet. Bake at 400 degrees for 10 to 12 minutes or just until light brown on top and brown on bottom. Remove to wire rack. Combine confectioners' sugar and 1 teaspoon anise extract with enough warm water in bowl to make a thin frosting. Spoon onto cookies. Let stand until cookies are cool and frosting is firm. May sprinkle with colored sugar. Yield: 36 servings.

**Approx Per Serving:** Cal 106; Prot 1 g; Carbo 21 g; Fiber <1 g;
    T Fat 2 g; Chol 12 mg; Sod 33 mg.

*Linda Carbone, WEIU Employee*

**1965** *The Homemaker Assistant Program, funded by the Boston Community Development, Inc., trained women in homemaking, planning and serving meals, and taking care of children.*

# KOULOURÁKIA

1 cup butter, softened
1 cup sugar
3 eggs
¼ cup milk
1 teaspoon vanilla extract

5 cups flour
1 tablespoon baking powder
Salt to taste
1 egg yolk, beaten

Cream butter in mixer bowl until light. Add sugar gradually, beating until fluffy. Beat in eggs 1 at a time. Add milk and vanilla gradually, beating until smooth. Sift in flour, baking powder and salt; mix well to form a stiff dough. Knead on floured surface for 5 to 10 minutes or until smooth and elastic. Shape by tablespoonfuls into wreaths, figure 8's or S curves. Place on buttered cookie sheet; brush with egg yolk. Bake at 350 degrees for 25 minutes or until golden brown. Remove to wire rack to cool.
Yield: 72 servings.

**Approx Per Serving:** Cal 70; Prot 1 g; Carbo 10 g; Fiber <1 g;
    T Fat 3 g; Chol 19 mg; Sod 43 mg.

*Alexis Xenakis, WEIU Friend*

# LACE OATMEAL COOKIES

1 cup oats
1½ teaspoons flour
1 cup sugar
¼ teaspoon salt

½ cup butter
1 egg
½ teaspoon (or more) vanilla
    extract

Mix oats, flour, sugar and salt in bowl. Heat butter in saucepan until bubbly. Add to dry ingredients; mix well. Add mixture of egg and vanilla; mix well. Drop very small amounts at widely spaced intervals onto foil-lined cookie sheet. Bake at 325 degrees for 10 to 15 minutes or until golden brown. Cool on cookie sheet. *These cookies were sold in the bakery at the WEIU.* Yield: 72 servings.

**Approx Per Serving:** Cal 28; Prot <1 g; Carbo 4 g; Fiber <1 g;
    T Fat 1 g; Chol 6 mg; Sod 19 mg.

*Susan G. Loring, WEIU Volunteer*

1966 *The New Directions Conference involved educators from Radcliffe and Columbia speaking on opportunities for women, as well as equal pay for equal work.*

# LEMON BARS

1 cup margarine, softened
2 cups confectioners' sugar
2 cups flour
4 teaspoons lemon juice
Grated rind of 2 lemons

4 eggs, beaten
2 cups sugar
1 teaspoon baking powder
1/4 cup flour
1 cup shredded coconut

Combine margarine, confectioners' sugar and 2 cups flour in bowl; mix well. Press into 10x15-inch baking pan. Bake at 350 degrees for 15 minutes or until light brown. Cool to room temperature. Combine lemon juice, lemon rind, eggs, sugar, baking powder, 1/4 cup flour and coconut in bowl; mix well. Spoon over crust. Bake for 25 minutes longer. Cool on wire rack. Cut into bars. *This is a Bush family favorite.* Yield: 48 servings.

**Approx Per Serving:** Cal 121; Prot 1 g; Carbo 19 g; Fiber <1 g;
    T Fat 5 g; Chol 18 mg; Sod 58 mg.

*First Lady Barbara Bush, WEIU Friend*

# LEMON WALNUT WAFERS

1/2 cup shortening
1 cup sugar
1 egg
1 tablespoon lemon juice
1 tablespoon grated lemon rind

2 cups flour, softened
1 teaspoon baking powder
1/8 teaspoon salt
1 cup chopped walnuts

Cream shortening and sugar in mixer bowl until light and fluffy. Beat in egg, lemon juice and lemon rind. Add mixture of flour, baking powder and salt; mix well. Stir in walnuts. Shape into rolls. Chill, wrapped in waxed paper. Cut into thin slices; place on greased cookie sheet. Bake at 350 degrees for 12 minutes. Remove to wire rack to cool. Yield: 48 servings.

**Approx Per Serving:** Cal 70; Prot 1 g; Carbo 8 g; Fiber <1 g;
    T Fat 4 g; Chol 4 mg; Sod 14 mg.

*Jennifer A. Thorp, WEIU Member*

1967 *Companions Unlimited, the Union's grocery shopping and medical transportation service for the elderly and disabled, was started.*

# MRS. SHAUGHNESSY'S MACAROON COOKIES

1 cup melted butter
1 cup packed brown sugar
1 cup sugar
2 eggs
2 cups flour
1½ teaspoons soda

½ teaspoon baking powder
½ teaspoon salt
½ teaspoon vanilla extract
2 cups coconut
2 cups cornflakes

Combine butter, brown sugar, sugar annd eggs in bowl; mix well. Add flour, soda, baking powder, salt and vanilla; mix well. Stir in coconut and cornflakes. Drop by teaspoonfuls onto greased cookie sheet. Bake at 375 degrees for 9 minutes. Cool on cookie sheet for 1 minute. Remove to wire rack to cool completely. Yield: 60 servings.

**Approx Per Serving:** Cal 86; Prot 1 g; Carbo 12 g; Fiber <1 g;
    T Fat 4 g; Chol 15 mg; Sod 81 mg.

*Lydia L. Hale, WEIU Friend*

# VERMONT MOLASSES COOKIES

½ cup molasses
½ cup melted shortening
½ cup sugar
1 egg, beaten
1 cup flour

1½ teaspoons baking powder
1 cup oats
½ teaspoon salt
½ teaspoon ginger

Combine molasses, shortening, sugar and egg in bowl; mix well. Add flour, baking powder, oats, salt and ginger; mix well. Drop by ½ teaspoonfuls onto well-greased cookie sheet. Bake at 350 degrees for 6 to 8 minutes or until golden brown. Remove from cookie sheet to wire rack immediately. Yield: 36 servings.

**Approx Per Serving:** Cal 69; Prot 1 g; Carbo 9 g; Fiber <1 g;
    T Fat 3 g; Chol 6 mg; Sod 50 mg.

*Persis Blanchard, WEIU Employee*

1969   *Construction begins on the John Hancock Tower, New England's tallest building.*

# OLD-FASHIONED RAISIN BARS

1 cup seedless raisins
1 cup water
1/2 cup shortening
1 cup sugar
1 egg, slightly beaten
1 3/4 cups sifted flour
1 teaspoon soda

1 teaspoon each cinnamon,
   nutmeg and allspice
1/2 teaspoon cloves
1/4 teaspoon salt
1/2 cup chopped pecans
1/2 cup confectioners' sugar

Bring raisins and water to a boil in saucepan. Remove from heat and cool. Stir in shortening, sugar and egg. Sift flour, soda, cinnamon, nutmeg, allspice, cloves and salt together. Add to batter; mix well. Stir in pecans. Spoon into greased 9x13-inch baking pan. Bake at 375 degrees for 20 minutes or until layer tests done. Cool on wire rack. Cut into bars. Sprinkle with confectioners' sugar. May use dark or golden raisins. Yield: 24 servings.

**Approx Per Serving:** Cal 143; Prot 2 g; Carbo 21 g; Fiber 1 g;
   T Fat 7 g; Chol 9 mg; Sod 61 mg.

*Mary F. Lynch, WEIU Member*

# BARBARA'S SHORTBREAD COOKIES

1/2 cup butter, softened
1/4 cup sugar

1 cup flour
1/4 cup sugar

Cream butter and 1/4 cup sugar by hand until light. Add flour, mixing until smooth. Shape into 15-inch log on waxed paper. Chill, wrapped in waxed paper, for 2 hours or until needed. Cut into 1/8-inch slices; place on greased cookie sheet. Bake at 350 degrees for 12 to 15 minutes or until light brown. Sprinkle with 1/4 cup sugar. Remove to wire rack to cool. May add 1/4 cup ground almonds, omit chilling step, shape into crescents and bake as above; garnish with confectioners' sugar. Yield: 50 servings.

**Approx Per Serving:** Cal 46; Prot <1 g; Carbo 3 g; Fiber <1 g;
   T Fat 4 g; Chol 10 mg; Sod 31 mg.

*Mrs. G. Leonhard Boveroux, WEIU Member*

1976 *The Union moved to its current location—356 Boylston Street.*

## SHORTBREAD CHOCOLATE CHIP COOKIES

1 cup butter, softened
1/2 cup sugar
2 1/2 cups sifted flour

1   6-ounce package miniature
semisweet chocolate chips

Cream butter and sugar in mixer bowl until light and fluffy. Add flour, mix well. Mix in chocolate chips. Divide into 3 portions. Roll each portion into 5-inch circle on cookie sheet; score each circle into 8 wedges. Bake at 325 degrees for 25 minutes or until golden brown. Remove to wire rack to cool. Yield: 24 servings.

**Approx Per Serving:** Cal 163; Prot 2 g; Carbo 17 g; Fiber 1 g;
    T Fat 10 g; Chol 21 mg; Sod 66 mg.

*Lisa Rein-Woisin, WEIU Employee*

## SPICY GINGER BALLS

3/4 cup shortening
1 cup sugar
1 egg
4 teaspoons molasses
2 cups flour

2 teaspoons soda
1 teaspoon cinnamon
1 teaspoon ginger
1/4 teaspoon cloves
1 cup (about) sugar

Cream shortening and 1 cup sugar in bowl. Beat in egg and molasses. Sift flour, soda, cinnamon, ginger and cloves together. Add to creamed mixture; mix well. Shape into 1-inch balls; roll in remaining sugar. Place 2 inches apart on lightly greased cookie sheet. Bake at 350 degrees for 12 to 15 minutes or until golden brown. Cool on cookie sheet for 1 minute. Remove to wire rack to cool completely. Yield: 24 servings.

**Approx Per Serving:** Cal 164; Prot 1 g; Carbo 25 g; Fiber <1 g;
    T Fat 7 g; Chol 9 mg; Sod 73 mg.

*Victoria Whitney, WEIU Trustee*

**1976**  *The Family Day Care Program trained and then licensed women
to take care of children in their own home.*

# SPRITZ COOKIES

2½ cups flour
¼ teaspoon salt
1 cup butter, softened
1¼ cups sifted confectioners'
  sugar

2 egg yolks
1½ teaspoons almond or vanilla
  extract

Sift flour and salt together. Cream butter in large mixer bowl until light. Sift in confectioners' sugar, beating until fluffy. Beat in egg yolks and almond extract. Add flour mixture; mix well. Spoon into cookie press. Press onto ungreased cookie sheet. Bake at 375 degrees for 10 to 12 minutes; do not brown. Remove to wire rack to cool. Store in airtight container. This recipe was handed down from my Swedish great-grandmother. Yield: 60 servings.

**Approx Per Serving:** Cal 55; Prot 1 g; Carbo 6 g; Fiber <1 g;
  T Fat 3 g; Chol 15 mg; Sod 35 mg.

*Beverly Butterworth, WEIU Friend*

# MRS. PERRY'S STRAWBERRY CAROUSEL COOKIES

1 cup butter, softened
¼ cup sugar
1 teaspoon vanilla extract
2 cups flour

½ teaspoon salt
1 cup (or more) strawberry
  preserves

Cream butter and sugar in bowl until light and fluffy. Mix in vanilla. Add flour and salt; mix well. Shape by rounded tablespoonfuls into balls. Place 2 inches apart on ungreased cookie sheet. Make indentation in center with thumb or finger. Spoon preserves into indentation. Bake at 400 degrees for 10 to 12 minutes or until light brown. Remove cookies to wire rack to cool. Yield: 24 servings.

**Approx Per Serving:** Cal 150; Prot 1 g; Carbo 19 g; Fiber <1 g;
  T Fat 8 g; Chol 21 mg; Sod 111 mg.

*Beth Andrews, Former WEIU Employee*

1980  *The Union began the tradition of the Amelia Earhart Award,*
      *which recognizes a woman in the Greater Boston area who has*
      *made a significant contribution to the community.*

# BUTTERSCOTCH TARTS

2 cups milk
2 cups whipping cream
1/2 vanilla bean
3/4 cup packed brown sugar
5 egg yolks
1 egg

Salt to taste
1/4 cup butter
2/3 cup packed brown sugar
2 tablespoons milk
4 ounces puff pastry

Bring 2 cups milk, cream and vanilla bean almost to a boil in saucepan; remove from heat. Let stand for 30 minutes; remove vanilla bean. Whisk in 3/4 cup brown sugar. Beat egg yolks and egg in bowl. Beat in milk mixture and salt gradually; strain and set aside. Melt butter in saucepan. Blend in 2/3 cup brown sugar and 2 tablespoons milk. Spoon into 6 ramekins; cool. Add strained mixture. Place in baking pan with hot water 2/3 up sides of ramekins. Cover pan with foil. Bake at 275 degrees until barely set. Let stand in water until cooled to room temperature. Chill in refrigerator. Roll pastry 1/8 inch thick. Chill in refrigerator. Roll very thin on lightly sugared surface; cut into 5-inch squares. Shape over inverted ramekins covered with baking parchment. Bake at 350 degrees until brown. Cool and peel off parchment. Loosen custards from baking ramekins; slip custards into puff pastry shells. Yield: 6 servings.

**Approx Per Serving:** Cal 490; Prot 6 g; Carbo 42 g; Fiber 0 g;
T Fat 34 g; Chol 266 mg; Sod 162 mg.
Nutritional information does not include puff pastry.

*Rick Katz, WEIU Friend*

# MOCK CHERRY PIE

2/3 cup shortening
2 cups flour
1 teaspoon salt
1/4 cup cold water
1 cup sugar

2 to 3 tablespoons flour
2 cups cranberries, chopped
1 cup raisins, chopped
2 to 3 tablespoons butter

Cut shortening into flour and salt in bowl until crumbly. Add water, stirring until mixture forms a ball. Chill in refrigerator. Roll out half the dough on floured surface to fit 9-inch pie pan. Line pie pan. Mix sugar and 2 to 3 tablespoons flour in bowl. Stir in cranberries and raisins until coated. Pour into pie crust; dot with butter. Roll remaining dough on floured surface. Fit over pie, sealing edge and cutting vents. Bake at 425 degrees for 15 minutes. Reduce oven temperature to 350 degrees. Bake for 35 to 45 minutes or until brown. Yield: 8 servings.

**Approx Per Serving:** Cal 482; Prot 4 g; Carbo 70 g; Fiber 3 g;
T Fat 22 g; Chol 12 mg; Sod 307 mg.

*Linda F. MacGregor, WEIU Friend*

# CHOCOLATE MOUSSE PIES

1  12-ounce package chocolate
   chip cookie dough
2 cups chocolate chips
4 egg yolks

2 teaspoons orange liqueur
2 cups half and half
1 cup whipping cream, whipped

Slice cookie dough into thin slices. Press over bottoms and around sides of 2 lightly greased pie plates. Bake using package directions for 11 minutes or until puffed and light brown. Cool to room temperature. Process chocolate chips, egg yolks and orange liqueur in blender container until mixed. Heat half and half almost to the boiling point. Pour into blender container. Process on High for 60 seconds or until well mixed and uniform in color. Pour into cooled pie shells. Chill until set. Top with whipped cream. Yield: 16 servings.

**Approx Per Serving:** Cal 371; Prot 3 g; Carbo 26 g; Fiber 1 g;
    T Fat 31 g; Chol 107 mg; Sod 24 mg.

*Adair M. Burlingham, WEIU Friend*

# CRANBERRY AND BANANA PIE

1  16-ounce can whole berry
   cranberry sauce
1¹/₃ cups mashed bananas

1¹/₂ envelopes unflavored gelatin
¹/₃ cup cold water
1 baked 9-inch pie shell

Combine cranberry sauce and bananas in mixer bowl; beat until well mixed. Soften gelatin in cold water in saucepan. Heat for 2 to 3 minutes until gelatin is dissolved, stirring constantly. Pour into fruit mixture; mix well. Spoon into baked pie shell. Garnish with banana slices. Chill for 2 hours before serving. *This recipe is from my mother, Mrs. Marjory Hurd. My great-grandfather owned and managed cranberry bogs and this recipe is derived from fresh cranberries.* Yield: 8 servings.

**Approx Per Serving:** Cal 195; Prot 2 g; Carbo 31 g; Fiber 2 g;
    T Fat 8 g; Chol 0 mg; Sod 146 mg.

*Susan R. Playfair, WEIU Friend*

1985  *Horizons Transitional Housing Program, the first transitional housing program for women and children in New England, was started by the Union.*

## CRANBERRY PAKE (PIE/CAKE)

| | |
|---|---|
| 1 recipe 1-crust pie pastry | ³⁄4 cup margarine, softened |
| 2 cups cranberries | 1 cup sugar |
| ¹⁄2 cup sugar | 2 eggs, beaten |
| ¹⁄2 cup chopped pecans | 1 cup flour |

Line 10-inch pie plate with pie pastry. Add cranberries. Sprinkle with ¹⁄2 cup sugar and pecans. Cream margarine and 1 cup sugar in bowl until light and fluffy. Add eggs; beat until well mixed. Add flour; mix well. Pour over cranberries. Bake at 350 degrees for 55 to 60 minutes or until golden brown. *My husband, Geoffrey, loves the Cape—the marshes, the topography, the lore. He went to the National Seashore Cranberry Bog one afternoon and came home with this recipe. It is easy to make, turns out well each time and the pie/cake aspect makes good conversation.* Yield: 8 servings.

**Approx Per Serving:** Cal 547; Prot 5 g; Carbo 64 g; Fiber 2 g;
  T Fat 31 g; Chol 53 mg; Sod 357 mg.

*Evelyn W. Farnum, WEIU Trustee*

## EGGNOG CHIFFON PIE

| | |
|---|---|
| 1  8-inch graham cracker crumb crust | 1¹⁄2 teaspoons vanilla extract |
| 1 tablespoon unflavored gelatin | 3 egg whites |
| 2 tablespoons cold water | ¹⁄4 cup sugar |
| 3 egg yolks | ¹⁄2 cup whipping cream |
| ¹⁄4 cup sugar | 2 tablespoons confectioners' |
| ¹⁄4 teaspoon nutmeg | sugar |
| ²⁄3 cup whipping cream, scalded | 2 tablespoons rum |
| 2 tablespoons dark rum | 2 tablespoons grated chocolate |

Bake graham cracker crumb crust at 350 degrees for 8 minutes. Cool to room temperature. Soften gelatin in cold water for 5 minutes. Beat egg yolks in mixer bowl. Add ¹⁄4 cup sugar and nutmeg; mix well. Stir a small amount of hot cream into egg mixture; stir eggs into hot cream. Stir in softened gelatin until dissolved. Add rum and vanilla. Chill for 3 hours. Beat egg whites until soft peaks form. Add ¹⁄4 cup sugar, beating until stiff peaks form. Fold into cold mixture. Spread cold mixture in cooled crust. Freeze for 8 hours. Move to refrigerator 2 hours before serving time. Beat whipping cream in mixer bowl until soft peaks form. Add confectioners' sugar and 2 tablespoons rum; beat well. Spread over pie. Garnish with grated chocolate. Yield: 10 servings.

**Approx Per Serving:** Cal 322; Prot 4 g; Carbo 33 g; Fiber 1 g;
  T Fat 19 g; Chol 97 mg; Sod 221 mg.

*Diane Spencer, WEIU Member*

# MILE HIGH LEMON PIE

1 stick pie crust mix
1 envelope unflavored gelatin
1/2 cup cold water
8 egg yolks, beaten
1 cup sugar
1 tablespoon grated lemon rind

1/2 cup lemon juice
1/4 teaspoon salt
8 egg whites
1/4 teaspoon cream of tartar
1 cup sugar

Prepare and bake 9-inch pie shell using package directions. Cool to room temperature. Soften gelatin in cold water. Combine egg yolks, 1 cup sugar, softened gelatin, lemon rind, lemon juice and salt in saucepan; mix well. Cook over medium heat just until mixture comes to a boil, stirring constantly. Chill in refrigerator until partially set, stirring occasionally until mixture mounds when dropped from spoon. Beat egg whites and cream of tartar in mixer bowl until foamy. Add 1 cup sugar, 1 tablespoon at a time, beating until stiff and glossy. Fold in partially congealed lemon mixture. Spoon into baked pie shell. Chill for several hours or until set. Yield: 8 servings.

**Approx Per Serving:** Cal 388; Prot 8 g; Carbo 62 g; Fiber 1 g;
T Fat 13 g; Chol 213 mg; Sod 263 mg.

*Amanda Jackson, WEIU Employee*

# PEACH CREAM PIE

3/4 cup flour
1 teaspoon baking powder
1/2 teaspoon salt
1   4-ounce package vanilla
    instant pudding mix
3 tablespoon margarine,
    softened

1 egg
1/2 cup milk
1   20-ounce can sliced peaches
1/2 cup sugar
8 ounces cream cheese, softened
1 tablespoon sugar
1 tablespoon cinnamon

Combine flour, baking powder, salt and pudding mix in mixer bowl. Add margarine, egg and milk. Beat for 2 minutes. Pour into greased 10-inch pie plate. Drain peaches, reserving 3 tablespoons juice. Arrange peach slices over batter. Combine 1/2 cup sugar, cream cheese and reserved peach juice in small mixer bowl. Beat for 2 minutes. Pour over peaches, leaving 1 inch border around edge. Sprinkle with mixture of 1 tablespoon sugar and cinnamon. Bake at 350 degrees for 30 to 35 minutes or until set. Yield: 8 servings.

**Approx Per Serving:** Cal 359; Prot 5 g; Carbo 52 g; Fiber 1 g;
T Fat 16 g; Chol 60 mg; Sod 423 mg.

*Jack Hutter, WEIU Friend*

# PEANUT SCOTCH PIE

½ cup sugar
¾ cup packed brown sugar
¼ cup sifted flour
½ teaspoon salt
½ cup cold milk
3 egg yolks
1 tablespoon butter, softened

1½ cups milk, heated
3 tablespoons peanut butter
3 egg whites
6 tablespoons sugar
1 baked 9-inch pie shell
¼ cup finely chopped peanuts

Combine ½ cup sugar, brown sugar, flour, salt, cold milk, egg yolks and butter in double boiler; mix well. Stir in hot milk. Cook over boiling water until thickened, stirring occasionally. Remove from heat. Add peanut butter; mix well. Cool to room temperature. Beat egg whites until soft peaks form. Add 6 tablespoons sugar, beating until stiff peaks form. Pour filling into pie shell. Top with meringue, sealing to edge of crust. Sprinkle with peanuts. Bake at 350 degrees for 12 to 15 minutes or until brown. Cool before serving. Yield: 8 servings.

**Approx Per Serving:** Cal 428; Prot 9 g; Carbo 59 g; Fiber 1 g;
T Fat 18 g; Chol 92 mg; Sod 365 mg.

*Jerome Rubin, WEIU Friend*

# SHOOFLY PIE

1¼ cups flour
½ cup packed brown sugar
¼ cup margarine
1 unbaked 9-inch pie shell

1 teaspoon soda
1 cup boiling water
¼ cup molasses
½ cup dark corn syrup

Combine flour and brown sugar in bowl; mix well. Cut in margarine until crumbly. Reserve ½ cup crumbs. Flute edge of pie shell. Spread remaining crumbs in pie shell. Combine soda and boiling water in deep bowl, stirring to dissolve soda. Stir in molasses and corn syrup. Pour over crumbs in pie shell. Bake at 350 degrees for 40 to 45 minutes or until crust is brown and filling puffed. Sprinkle with reserved crumbs. Yield: 8 servings.

**Approx Per Serving:** Cal 366; Prot 3 g; Carbo 59 g; Fiber 1 g;
T Fat 13 g; Chol 0 mg; Sod 337 mg.

*Eleanor Hutter, WEIU Friend*

**1989**  *The Parent Aide Program for Teenage Mothers, which matches former teenage mothers who are students at the University of Massachusetts/Boston to first-time teenage mothers, was founded.*

# MEMORY RECIPE INDEX

# RECIPE INDEX

# BOSTON AND UNION INDEX

# EPILOGUE

*Lives of all good cooks remind us*
*We can be good cooks ourselves.*
*So that all our friends shall find us*
*With well-laden pantry shelves.*

*Cooking that shall make each mother*
*Think she has not taught in vain.*
*Over father, brother, lover,*
*Like a queen good housewives reign.*

C. I. D.
*from* **The Kirmess Cookbook**, *1887*

# Notes

# Notes

# Notes

# Notes

# Notes

# Notes

# ORDER FORM

To order additional copies of *Boston Cooks*
Please return this form to:

**Women's Educational and Industrial Union**
**356 Boylston Street**
**Boston, MA 02116**
**Attn: Administrative Office**

Please send _____ copies of *Boston Cooks* at $15.95 per copy plus $2.00 for shipping and handling (Massachusetts residents, please include sales tax). Enclosed is my check or money order, payable to the WEIU, for $_____.

Name: _____

Address: _____

City, State, Zip: _____


For information on ordering the Swan Boat or other Boston needlepoint canvases, please call our Needlework Department at 617/536-5651.


For information on becoming a member of the Women's Educational and Industrial Union, please call the Membership Department at 617/536-5651.

Please send the following friends information about the
Women's Educational Union and *Boston Cooks*:

Name: _____
Address: _____
City, State, Zip: _____

Name: _____
Address: _____
City, State, Zip: _____

Name: _____
Address: _____
City, State, Zip: _____

Name: _____
Address: _____
City, State, Zip: _____

Name: _____
Address: _____
City, State, Zip: _____

Name: _____
Address: _____
City, State, Zip: _____

Name: _____
Address: _____
City, State, Zip: _____

Name: _____
Address: _____
City, State, Zip: _____